Werewolves!

OTHER BOOKS BY THOMAS MCNULTY

NON-FICTION

Errol Flynn : The Life and Career

FICTION

Trail of the Burned Man
Wind Rider
Death Rides a Palomino
Showdown at Snakebite Creek

Werewolves!
A Study of Lycanthropes in Film, Folklore and Literature

by Thomas McNulty

BearManor Media
2011

Werewolves! A Study of Lycanthropes in Film, Folklore and Literature

© 2011 Thomas McNulty

All rights reserved.

For information, address:

BearManor Media
P. O. Box 71426
Albany, GA 31708

bearmanormedia.com

Typesetting and layout by John Teehan

Published in the USA by BearManor Media

ISBN— 1-59393-675-3
978-1-59393-675-4

Table of Contents

Acknowledgments vii

Introduction 1

Historical Survey of the Werewolf Legend 3

The Werewolf in Literature 25

Lon Chaney, Jr. and The Wolf Man 59

Paul Naschy and the Werewolf 99

A Survey of Werewolf Films 127

Selected Werewolf Filmography 175

Notes 191

Bibliography 195

Index 205

*This Halloween treat is dedicated
to my wife Jan and daughter Brenna
with love.*

Acknowledgments

I am indebted to my wife Jan and my daughter Brenna for their love and encouragement. My friend Nick Ciccotosto, Ph.D., provided crucial bibliographic data on several occasions for which I remain grateful. Universal Studios film collector and aficionado Steve Campbell, known to his friends as "Universal Steve," generously shared his opinion on the Lon Chaney films. Film director and screenwriter Fred Olen Ray took time out from his busy schedule to answer my questions regarding *Tomb of the Werewolf*. Screenwriter and film director Steve Latshaw generously wrote an affectionate remembrance for the chapter on Paul Naschy. I am grateful for the participation of these fine people. Writing is a lonely craft and without the understanding of family and friends I would have faltered many times. My friend Trudy McVicker has always encouraged me to keep at it no matter what obstacles lie in my path. My parents, Tom and Pat McNulty, and my sister, Jan, have always encouraged my writing career. Taylor Kuhlman enthusiastically embraced the werewolf legend and created several outstanding illustrations for this book. A special note of thanks to Jack Marino, David DeWitt, Louis Kraft and Karl Holmberg for their friendship and kind words about my writing career—thank you chums! Interested readers are encouraged to peruse the bibliography for additional works relating to lycanthropy as many of them were vital resources as I plunged headlong into the dark and mysterious world of lycanthropes.

A note on the photographs: The photographs used in this book are believed to be in the public domain unless otherwise listed. Every effort has been made to determine ownership of the photographs appearing in this book for the purpose of giving appropriate credit. We regret any unintentional error concerning the attribution given to the photographs and will be pleased to make appropriate acknowledgments in any future printings.

With the moonlight there came a fierce sigh of the storm,
which appeared to resume its course with a long,
low howl, as of many dogs or wolves.

– Bram Stoker, *Dracula's Guest*

The encircling wolves advance with ghastly pace,
Hunger and murder in each gleaming face.

– H. P. Lovecraft, *Psychopompos*

Even a man who is pure in heart,
and says his prayers by night,
may become a wolf when the wolfbane blooms
and the autumn moon is bright.

– Curt Siodmak, *The Wolf Man* screenplay

Introduction

A SILVER MOON HANGS IN THE DARK, forbidding sky. The night is cold and there are few travelers on the road. The thickets are ripe with shadows and the woods are alive with unholy sounds. Something stirs in the darkness and pads along the moonlit path. If we venture too far into these woods we are risking our lives because this is the territory of the werewolf.

There are many creatures of the night to fear, but the werewolf is the most ferocious. He is possessed of a bloodlust that cannot be satiated. The werewolf hungers for flesh and fears nothing. The werewolf is to be feared because he is a man cursed by a transformation that buries his humanity deep within the shell of his body. He haunts the night seeking prey. The werewolf, some believe, is that part of humanity that remains bestial, driven by the need to kill.

This book is intended as an introduction and survey of werewolves in folklore, fiction and film. I have long been fascinated by the folklore and myths surrounding the lycanthrope (or one who, in folklore, possesses the magical ability to assume the form and characteristics of a wolf). My interest began in my youth when I saw Lon Chaney, Jr. in *The Wolf Man* on television. A great deal of the modern perception regarding werewolves stems from films and I have attempted to separate fact from fiction.

Because the films play such an important role I have chosen to cover a wide range of werewolf films. My purpose was to survey and examine key films and so I have ventured deeply into the lycanthrope's territory. I have intentionally included the relatively recent phenomenon of direct-to-DVD movies and various exploitation films that comprise a multi-million dollar part of the film industry. As a general rule, direct-to-DVD exploitation movies are scorned by film critics and often adored by fans. The critics will cite the poor quality of filmmaking as reason enough for their contempt, and most of the time I found they were correct. But not always: and those exceptions made my exploration into this part of the industry all the more fascinating.

Similarly, technological changes have nurtured the new industry of print-on-demand publishing, a venue that has quickly become a multi-million dollar industry of its own. Writers of genre fiction have embraced these publishers and I wanted to discover if any of the new werewolf stories were worth reading. You will find the answer to that question in the following pages, in addition to a survey of the key literary tales of lycanthropy.

While werewolves and shapeshifters have been a part of folklore for centuries, this book favors the premise that modern interest in lycanthropy begins with three key people: screenwriter Curt Siodmak, actor Lon Chaney, Jr. and make-up artist Jack Pierce. Everything we know, fear and appreciate about werewolves begins with them. They set the standard for everything to follow and writers and filmmakers since owe them a debt of gratitude.

I have also chosen to explore the Spanish horror films of Jacinto Molina (better known to American audiences as Paul Naschy) whose contribution to the lycanthrope's legacy cannot be ignored. Naschy was the heir apparent to Lon Chaney and his erstwhile efforts have left an indelible mark on the horror genre.

This book follows a comprehensive cycle of werewolf lore, from folktales and pulp novels through decades of films. The moonlit path beckoned, and I plunged headlong into a labyrinthine tale that was both fascinating and horrifying. Lon Chaney's spirit was never far away; snarling through Jack Pierce's make-up and stalking me from the pages of Curt Siodmak's original story.

Hollywood's continued interest in werewolf films as evidenced by the success of *Underworld*, *Van Helsing* and the 2010 *The Wolf Man* remake confirmed my conclusion. The werewolf is alive and well. I trust this book will provide answers to those investigating lycanthropy for the first time and encourage a deeper appreciation for the work of Lon Chaney, Jr., Jack Pierce, Curt Siodmak and Paul Naschy.

– Thomas McNulty
Crystal Lake, Illinois

Historical Survey of the Werewolf Legend

WITH ITS BODY LENGTH STRETCHING to over six feet, the wolf is an imposing animal. Powerful and agile, the wolf's body weight can exceed one hundred and seventy five pounds. Capable of adapting to diverse landscapes, the wolf can be found in forests, mountains or prairies. Primal, fierce, and intelligent, the wolf is a figure of power among many cultures.

There are two species of wolf: the gray wolf (often referred to as the timber wolf), and the red wolf. The wolf, *canis lupus*, is mammal in the *Carnivora* family. Once abundant over North America and Europe, centuries of encroaching civilization have diminished the wolf population. But the wolf still reigns, albeit in generally isolated, rugged country.

Wolves travel in packs, with alpha males and females capable of communicating via visual and scent signals. A wolf's famous howling is a signal for a gathering and an advertisement of its territorial claim.

The stories of people transforming into a wolf date back to the earliest recorded history. During the Middle Ages stories proliferated wherein certain persons were believed possessed. These people believed themselves to be wild animals and their mannerisms and habits mirrored that of the wolf they believed inhabited their bodies. Sometimes taking refuge in forests, they might let their hair and fingernails grow long, and often took to slaughtering small animals such as rabbits and birds and devouring them. Their savage habits might take an extreme turn and occasionally a child might be found murdered, partly eaten, the bloody trail leading authorities to the eccentric "Wolf Man" living in a nearby cave.

The word werewolf is Old English for "man-wolf." Tales of the werewolf are often based on fact and some carry on the oral tradition of storytelling, with embellishments, exaggerations, and conflicting circumstances depending upon the culture of origin. The word *lycanthropy* derives

4 • *Werewolves!*

With its body length stretching to over six feet, the wolf is an imposing animal. Powerful and agile, the wolf's body weight can exceed one hundred and seventy five pounds (original illustration by Taylor Kuhlman).

from two Latin words—*lykos* or "wolf" and *anthropos* or "man"—and is used to generally represent the condition of transforming from man into wolf. Historian Adam Douglas noted that "as early as the fifth century A.D. the condition was being described by doctors as one which resulted from disturbance of the melancholic humor."[1] Douglas went on to cite the account of Alexandrian physician Paulus Aegineta who described patients suffering from "melancholic lycanthopia." These patients were unable to produce tears or saliva and suffered wounds on their legs as a result of moving about wolf-like on all four limbs. They also suffered from a compulsion to wander into cemeteries at night and howl until dawn.

The image of the wolf has been linked with man from the time he first scratched his crude symbolism onto a cave wall. There are traces of werewolf lore in the *Epic of Gilgamesh* and in *The Odyssey*. Virgil's *Ecologue* depicts the first transformation of a werewolf. There is a werewolf story in *Satyricon* and in the *Metamorphosis* by Petronius. Each culture has its own version of the werewolf. For Scandinavians he is *volkodlak*; for the French he is *loup-garu*; the Scottish call him *warwulf*. He appears as half man, half wolf for some; for others he is a towering wolf figure, completely devoid of any human resemblance.

The elements of lycanthropy that we find most often are a hunger for blood and flesh, transformation into a wolf, nocturnal wanderings in search of prey, attacks upon people and animals in order to satiate the bloodlust, and finally a retransformation into a human. The rise of superstitions and public condemnation of witchcraft in the sixteenth century coincides with the growing folklore involving werewolves.

But for most of us the werewolf is Lon Chaney, Jr., crouched among the fog and the damp black trees, snarling and bestial.

This image of Chaney—and its ramifications—is explored in detail in the third section of this book. It is a starting point for most considerations of the werewolf in popular culture, but we are going to stall that introduction awhile and delve into the past for a clearer understanding of the Wolf Man in myth and legend.

Pierre Bourgot, the Werewolf of Poligny

In one of the earliest tales (1502), Pierre Bourgot of *Poligny* was tending to his flock of sheep when a terrific storm scattered them across the French countryside. After the storm abated Pierre set out in search of his flock and shortly came upon three horsemen all dressed in black (in some versions, the men have dark complexions in addition to their dark clothing, an obvious metaphor for evil). Telling the horsemen his tale of woe, Bourgot was promised assistance in exchange for his services in the future. Bourgot agreed and within a few days he located his sheep. To bind his bargain with the horseman he met one of them later and learned they were servants of the Devil. To keep his part of the bargain, Bourgot denied Christianity and swore fealty by kissing the horseman's left hand. Renouncing Christianity would prove his downfall. "I foreswore God and our lady and all saints and dwellers in paradise. I renounced Christianity, kissed his left hand, which was black and ice cold as that of a corpse. Then I fell to my knees and gave my allegiance to Satan."[2] Some time passed and Bourgot was encouraged to attend a Sabbat where he believed he would receive satanic gold. Here he was met by Michel Verdung whose purpose was to stop Bourgot from drifting back to Christianity. Bourgot was stripped naked and Verdung applied a salve to his body. The magic salve turned Bourgot into a wolf. "Michel persuaded me to move with the greatest celerity, and in order to do this, after I had stripped myself, he smeared me with a salve, and I believed myself then to be transformed into a wolf. I was at first somewhat horrified at my four wolf's feet, and the fur with which I was covered all at once, but I found that I could now travel with the speed of the wind."[3] There is more than an obvious hint in the story of the homo-eroticism that both repulsed and captivated audiences.

Bourgot, who was later captured and tortured, confessed that during his time as a wolf he committed several atrocities. He attacked and wounded a seven year old boy, murdered and ate a four year old girl whose flesh he admitted tasted delicious, and he also tracked and killed a nine-year-old girl by breaking her neck. Similar confessions were wrought from the three dark horsemen after their capture. All the men confessed to having sex with real wolves and admitted that "they had as much pleasure in the act as if they had copulated with their wives."[4] Bourgot and the three horsemen came to their end by being burned at the stake.

Burning at the stake was common in Europe during this period, a practice that stemmed in part from the theology of Augustine who held that "…not only every pagan, but every heretic…will go to the eternal fire, which is prepared for the Devil and his angels, unless before the end of his life he be reconciled with and restored to the Catholic Church…"[5]

The burning of witches and werewolves followed a pre-ordained set of rules. If the culprit cooperated with authorities, the accused had their hands tied behind their back and they were strangled, which was deemed charitable prior to burning the body. However, if the accused witch, warlock or werewolf were aggressive or impenitent, they were left alive at the stake. In order to prolong their agony, such criminals were often tortured beforehand and when the burning commenced the fire was begun under a fair sampling of greenwood in order to prolong their demise.

Gilles Garnier, the Werewolf of Dole

In 1573, the French village of Dole experienced attacks on young children that had reached epidemic proportions. The sudden violent and mysterious deaths of children so horrified the community that the local parliament issued a proclamation that read in part:

> According to the advertisement made to the sovereign court of parliament at Dole…(in) the neighboring villages, has often been seen and met, for some time past, a werewolf, who it is said has already seized and carried off several little children, so that they have not been seen since. And since he has attacked and done injury in the country to some horsemen, who kept him off only with great difficulty and danger to their persons, the said court, desiring to prevent any greater danger, has permitted, and does permit, those who are abiding or dwelling in the said places and others, notwithstanding all edicts concerning the chase, to assemble with pikes, halberds, arquebuses, and sticks, to chase and to pursue the said werewolf in every place where they may find or seize him; to tie and to kill, without incurring any pains or penalties…[6]

The perpetrator of these attacks was discovered to be Gilles Garnier, formerly from Lyon where he was known as "the hermit of St. Bonnot." Garnier lived in a hovel near Armanges with his wife, Appoline. They were considered to be nothing more than two sullen and impoverished recluses.

Within a few months of the proclamation authorizing the local residency to take matters into their own hands, some peasants came across a small injured girl in a field. She suffered bites from a huge wolf. Upon their approach the peasants spied a wolf fleeing into a nearby wood. Although it was dusk, they thought they recognized in the wolf's countenance the features of Gilles Garnier. A week later a fifteen year old boy was reported missing. Rumors spread like wildfire and soon Garnier and his wife were arrested. Apparently, Garnier offered no resistance and promptly confessed to his crimes. His confessions include revelations of cannibalism, a vice that is exclusive to the lycanthrope.

Garnier confessed that on August 24, 1573 he killed a twelve-year-old boy in a pear orchard near the village of Perrouze. Garnier stated that no matter that it was Friday, he eschewed Catholicism and decided to eat the boy's flesh. In this endeavor, however, he was halted by the appearance of some men and Garnier reverted to the form of a human in order to avoid detection.

On October 6 of that year, Garnier attacked a ten-year-old girl in a vineyard near the village of La Serre. Garnier killed her with his teeth and claws and then stripped her naked. He devoured much of her flesh and found the corpse so tasty that he took portions of the girl's flesh home to his wife. There is no record of Appoline's reaction.

In November, Garnier attacked another girl in a meadow but was forced to flee before killing her. Several travelers had seen him and gave pursuit but Garnier escaped. A week later he killed a ten-year-old boy outside of Dole by strangling him. Then, in a violent frenzy consistent with werewolf behavior, he tore off the boy's leg and ate the flesh of his thighs before disemboweling the corpse and eating most of the belly.

Unrepentant, Garnier was sentenced to death and executed in Dole on January 18, 1574. His crimes were so ghastly the court determined to forgo the mercy of strangulation and so Garnier was burned alive at the stake.

Peter Stub, the Werewolf of Bedbur
Bedbur, Germany, October 31, 1590.

History has not recorded if Peter Stub spoke near the end. We can only imagine what thoughts he harbored as he was lashed to a wagon wheel with heavy twine. Bound in this manner to a giant wooden circle, he resembled Michelangelo's sketch of a universal man, the geometry of his life a precise consideration in the crisp light of a fresh October day. First, they heated the long metal pinchers (a blacksmith's tool) until the fire turned the metal into a hot yellow spear, and then they applied the pinchers to his skin, pulling the flesh from his bones. The pinchers were applied ten times, removing a substantial portion of his flesh. With his sinew and epidermis scorched, he now resembled the crude anatomical sketch a medical student might render after dissecting a corpse. This was followed by the breaking of his legs and arms with an axe. Striking at his arms, then his legs with great force, the bones ruptured, leaving him twitching in agony upon the wheel. Only then, and after he had suffered a considerable amount of time, was his torture alleviated by taking the axe and striking his head from his body. Perhaps as an afterthought, his body was burned until all that remained of Peter Stub was a pile of ashes.

What had he done to deserve such a fate?

From the time he was a child, Peter Stub (some accounts vary in the spelling of his name: 'Peeter Stubbe' being the common spelling in Old English; 'Stump' and 'Stumpf' are additional variants) was described as a youth with an interest in witchcraft. They say he was evil from birth and prone to converse with demons and evil spirits. Early on he made a pact with the devil (a recurring theme in the literature of the supernatural) and Satan promised him anything he desired, presumably in exchange for his soul. Industrious from the beginning, Stub requested the ability to change into a beast so that he might promote his wicked desires without fear of discovery. The Devil provided him with a girdle to wear around his waste, upon donning the garment he was transformed into a wolf. But Stub was no average wolf. The description of him in his wolf guise is a virtual blueprint for the descriptions of werewolves to follow. The trial transcripts were translated into English in 1590 and reveal many details that later served as inspiration for scriptwriters in Hollywood. As we shall see, Satan gets blamed for many werewolf transformations: "The devil gave him a girdle which, being put around him, he was transformed into the likeness of a greedy, devouring wolf, strong and mighty, with eyes great and large, which in the night sparkled like brands of fire, a mouth great and wide, with most sharp and cruel teeth, a huge body and mighty paws."[7]

Stub proceeded to enjoy himself, taking his pick of victims. Sometimes, he encountered a traveler upon the road, he would don the girdle and rip out their throats and pull their limbs from their bodies. If by chance any townspeople offended him in some way, or appeared rude, he would exact revenge by stalking them. There were never any survivors of his malice, and the bodies were always horribly mutilated. It was said that often he ate the flesh of his victims. For years he played a duo role: that of the werewolf and that of the comely citizen happily greeting his neighbors as he strolled about the town. For 28 years he copulated with a succubus to satisfy his carnal desire, and tore out the throats of countless victims. But the succubus apparently wasn't quite enough for a werewolf with an appetite like Peter Stub's. Presently, he began ravishing maidens if they happened beyond the city limits. He waited for them in the countryside, appeased his sexual fever, and murdered them. In the space of a few years he had murdered 13 children and two pregnant women who had their unborn children torn from their wombs. Then, with their hearts still beating in his bloody paws, he would eat their aortic organ and the small palpitating hearts of the unborn children as well.

Sixteenth century woodcarving depicting the death of Peter Stub.

Prior to his pact with the Devil, Stub had fathered a daughter who became his concubine when she reached the age of fertility. When his daughter subsequently gave birth to another female, he raised the child in the same fashion, and copulated with her as well. With his two daughters as his slaves, and the surrounding community living in fear of his attacks, Stub had achieved the pinnacle of evil.

Stub's tale offers the traditional elements of the werewolf legend: the proper citizen by day and werewolf by night; and the intense violence of both the werewolf's attacks and his subsequent destruction. Stub's end is particularly gruesome, equal to that of the violence inflicted upon his victims.

Perhaps the best known of the early werewolf tales, owing no small part to its inherent gruesomeness, Stub was immortalized in verse by Samuel Rowlands in *Knave of Hearts* (1612):

> A German, called Peter Stump, by charm of an ancient girdle,
> Did much harm, transformed himself into a wolfish shape,
> And in a wood did many years escape
> The hand of justice, till the hangman met him,
> And from a wolf, did with a halter set him.

Jacques Roulet, the Werewolf of Angers

Jacques Roulet, a beggar dwelling near Angers in France, was discovered by some soldiers crouching in the bushes. His hands were smeared with blood. His hair was unkempt and Roulet was half-naked, but most disturbing was the fact that his fingernails were clotted with shreds of human flesh. The mutilated body of a young boy was soon discovered nearby. On August 8, 1598, Roulet confessed before Judge Pierre Herault. Although Roulet offered contradictory answers to the questions, there was no doubt of his guilt:

> Q: What is your name and what your estate?
> A: My name is Jacques Roulet, my age thirty-five. I am poor and a beggar.
>
> Q: What are you accused of having done?
> A: Of being a thief; of having offended God. My parents gave me an ointment; I do not know its composition.
>
> Q: When rubbed with this ointment do you become a wolf?
> A: No. But for all that, I killed and ate the child Cornier. I was a wolf.
>
> Q: Were you dressed as a wolf?
> A: I am dressed as I am now. I had my hands and face bloody because I had been eating the flesh of the said child.
>
> Q: Do your hands and feet become paws of a wolf?
> A: Yes, they do.
>
> Q: Does your head become like that of a wolf—your mouth become larger?
> A: I do not know how my head was at the time; I used my teeth. My head was as it is today. I have wounded and eaten many other little children. I have also been to the sabbat.[8]

Roulet was sentenced to death but in one of the rare instances of mercy, he appealed his sentence and was thus incarcerated in an insane asylum. Roulet's lycanthropy was deemed to be the result of an unspecified mental disease. His poverty and generally wretched lifestyle had contributed to his aberrant behavior and the court found him to be feeble-minded and epileptic. While incarcerated in the asylum, Roulet was given lessons in religion which apparently succeeded in curing his rampages. After two years, Roulet was released and it is presumed lived a relatively normal, if not obscure, life.

The Four Gandillon Werewolves of St. Claude

In addition to Pierre Bourgot and Gilles Garnier, the Jura region of France also harbored three werewolves from the Gandillon family: two sisters, a brother and his son.

Perrenette Gandillon has been described as a "poor demented creature"[9] whose life was cut short one day when sixteen-year-old Benoit Bidel climbed a tree to pick some fruit. While in the tree Benoit looked down to see a tailless wolf attacking his younger sister in the field. Benoit leaped from the tree and rushed to defend his sister. He began struggling with the wolf-creature and noticed its front paws resembled human hands. Benoit was unable to overpower the wolf's superior strength. Benoit attempted to kill the wolf with his knife but the wolf overpowered him, snatched his knife from his hand, and delivered a fatal wound to Benoit's neck. Before he died he related how the wolf had human hands. Shortly thereafter, Perrenette Gandillon was discovered in the vicinity and without the benefit of a trial, she was torn to pieces by the enraged peasants in a bloody frenzy that was equal to the ferocity of a werewolf's attack.

Perrenette's sister, Antoinette, would later admit to being a lycanthrope, to possess the ability to produce hail, attend the sabbat, and engage in sexual relations with the devil who she said appeared to her as a goat. Their brother, Pierre, also confessed to lycanthropy, producing hail, enticing children to the sabbat, and to killing and eating animals and men. He stated that he transformed into a wolf and ran through the wilderness on all fours and killed as his appetite dictated. Pierre's son Georges confessed to changing into a wolf after covering himself with a salve.

A judge, upon visiting the three in jail, reported: "Satan clothed them in a wolf's skin which completely covered them, and that they went on all fours, and ran about the country, chasing now a person and now an animal, according to the guidance of their appetite. They confessed also that they tired themselves by running."[10]

The three were convicted, taken to the town square and lashed to posts. Deciduous branches, trash, and other combustible material was heaped around them and then set afire. Having failed to demonstrate remorse, the burning followed tradition and the combustible material included a share of freshly cut green sapling branches in order to prolong their agony.

Jean Grenier, the Werewolf Boy of Gascony

Jean Grenier's tale originates in 1603 in the southwest of France. It is an often repeated tale of lycanthropy, and as we shall see, a classic example of the werewolf mythology.

The tale begins with several young girls tending sheep in the countryside. They were approached by a hirsute young boy who promptly announced that he was a werewolf. The eldest girl, Jeanne Gaboriant, questioned the boy regarding his statement. To this the boy is said to have replied, "A man gave me a wolf-skin cape; he wraps it round me, and every Monday, Friday and Sunday, and for about an hour at dusk every other day, I am a wolf, a werewolf. I have killed dogs and drunk their blood; but little girls taste better, and their flesh is tender and sweet, their blood rich and warm."[11]

Recently, several children had been murdered in the St. Sever district of Gascony and so Grenier's tale was believed. The district attorney, Roche Charles, brought Grenier before the local judge who was shocked by the allegations. Admissions of lycanthropy and the murders of several children seemingly shattered the tranquility of their lives. Roche Charles sent the case to a higher judge. Since Jean Grenier had accused others of lycanthropy as well, searches were conducted of their homes. Investigators were looking for magic potions or other artifacts of witchcraft that would somehow implicit these people as murderers, or worse, werewolves.

No such artifacts were uncovered, however. Still, fear had spread since Jean Grenier's tale of lycanthropy and murder had surfaced and his father and a neighbor, M. del Thillaire, were imprisoned. During the subsequent court hearing, the father, M. Grenier, convinced the judge that his son Jean was well known as an idiot who had also bragged of sleeping with every woman in the village. The judge, after deliberation, believed the father's statements and released him and their neighbor.

But there was still the matter of the children's murders to be solved. The judge dispatched several investigators to research and document all of the known facts of Jean Grenier's life, including any associations that might link him to the murdered children. These investigators spent considerable care in documenting the facts; retraced Jean Grenier's steps and interrogated anyone that knew him or had encountered him during the period of his alleged exploits.

Their investigation determined that Jean Grenier roamed the neighborhood and surrounding countryside freely, and did, in fact, possess acute knowledge of the activities and habits of the children that lived here. They also uncovered the fact that several children had witnessed the abduction of a child, allegedly seized by a wolf and dragged away. Grenier was linked to this murder by the witnesses, although it was never clear if Grenier himself seized the child or happened to be in the area when the killing occurred. No matter, Grenier had confessed to lycanthropy and to the drinking of the rich, warm blood of little girls. His fate was sealed, although not quite in the manner one would anticipate.

The court ordered Grenier hanged and his body burned to ashes. Concurrently, Grenier's father and neighbor were again taken into custody and tortured. During the torture session both men confessed to having sought out little girls, but not to murder them. Their interest in girls appears to have been strictly sexual.

The saga played out with the Parliament of Bordeaux ordering a complete review of the testimony. This phase of the investigation provided a detailed account from Jean Grenier:

> "When I was ten or eleven years old, my neighbor, del Thillaire, introduced me, in the depths of the forest, to Maitre de la Foret, a black man, who signed me with his nail, and then gave me and del Thillaire a salve and a wolf skin. From that time I have run about the country as a wolf."[12]

When questioned touching the children, Jean Grenier further deposed that he had killed and eaten as would a wolf, and further, that once during a period of roaming the countryside he came upon a house that was empty save for an infant in its cradle. Grenier then confessed to taking the baby from the cradle and carrying it into the garden where he feasted upon its flesh until his hunger was satiated. What remained of the baby's corpse was then fed to a wolf.

Astonishingly, Grenier's tale doesn't end here. He continued by confessing to the murder of a little girl in another parish. She was, he stated, tending to some sheep and was dressed all in black. Grenier killed her by tearing her to pieces with his hands and teeth. He then proceeded to eat her flesh. Finally, Grenier admitted that shortly before his capture he had encountered another child near a stone bridge. His taste for human flesh apparently knew no boundaries. Grenier freely confessed to roaming the countryside dressed in a wolf skin and that he often smeared himself with a magical salve.

The Parliament instructed several physicians to examine Grenier and they concluded that he suffered from "a malady called lycanthropy."[13] and that he was also possessed by an evil spirit that deceived men into believing such things. On September 3, 1603, the Parliament condemned Grenier to life in prison. There is no specific reason why his death sentence was so commuted, but Grenier's tale concludes with a Christian ending that may indicate the influence of Catholicism. The court records read in part:

> "The court, in conclusion, takes into account the young age and the imbecility of this boy, who is so stupid and idiotic that children of seven and eight years old normally show intelligence, who has been ill fed in every respect and who is so dwarfed that he is not tall as a ten year old…Here is a young lad abandoned and driven out by his father, who has a cruel stepmother instead of a real mother, who wanders the over the fields, without a counselor and without anyone to take interest in him, begging his bread, who has never had any religious training, whose real nature was corrupted by evil promptings, need, and despair, and whom the devil made his prey."[14]

Seven years later, Grenier was visited in prison by Pierre de Lancre who later published his account in Paris in 1612 (*Tableau de l'inconstance des mauvais anges et demons*). Lancre found Grenier still diminutive, shy, and unwilling or unable to look anyone directly in the eye. Grenier reaffirmed that he had been a werewolf and that he still harbored an interest in killing and eating children. In fact, Grenier pointed out that he would do so if an opportunity presented itself.

Grenier died in prison on November 10, 1610, apparently a reformed man, as records stated that he died a good Christian.

The Werewolves of the Harz Mountains

While France may boast of numerous werewolf stories they are certainly not alone in nurturing an active werewolf culture. Germany is vibrant with tales of lycanthropy, werewolves, and ghouls of all kinds. One of the better known werewolf stories involves the lycanthropes of the Harz Mountains, an area rife with werewolf folktales. The Harz Mountains' werewolf tale is rich with sexual connotations. These erotic elements have proven successful for pulp writers and filmmakers when dealing with werewolf lore.

The tale begins with two gentlemen, Herr Hellen and Herr Schiller, on a walking tour in the Harz Mountains in 1840. During their sojourn Schiller slipped and injured his ankle. Unable to continue Herr Hellen went searching for assistance. Presently he came upon another man, also injured, but with a broken wrist. The man explained that he had been collecting firewood and had just climbed a tree when the howl of a wolf startled him. He fell and shattered his wrist. Herr Hellen assisted the man, Wilfred Gaverstein, in bandaging the arm and together they set out for the Gaverstein's cottage.

A grateful Gaverstein informed Herr Hellen that he would be granted two wishes for assisting him. Initially, Hellen scoffed at the idea, but to keep peace he wishes for his wife to see how well he bandaged the man's wrist, and secondly, he wished that his three daughters could be here with him. While walking to Gaverstein's cottage they hear again the ominous howl of a wolf.

Upon reaching the cottage Hellen is astonished to find his wife and daughters waiting for him. None can explain their presence, except they had gone to sleep in Frankfurt only to wake up at this strange cottage. Gaverstein explained that all of this was nothing more than the fulfillment of Herr Hellen's wishes. Gaverstein's wife and daughter are also present, and while Hellen's wife and daughters are pleading to depart the dreadful forest, Gaverstein convinced him to spend the night.

Herr Hellen, as it turns out, is captivated by Gaverstein's daughter, Marguerite. "Hellen's first impression of her was that she was marvelously beautiful, but that there was something about her that he did not understand—a something he had never seen in anyone before, a something that in an ugly woman might have put him on his guard, but in this face of such surpassing beauty a something he seemed only to ready to ignore."[15]

Presently, Marguerite is instructed to accompany Herr Hellen to retrieve and return with the wounded Herr Schiller. Their journey to the place where Hellen had left Herr Schiller was uneventful, but upon reaching the location there was no sign of his friend. Herr Hellen called out and "the reverberation of his voice rang out loud and clear in the silence of the vast, moon kissed forest."[16] With Marguerite's assistance he searched the forest until he found Schiller's body. The man had been torn to pieces and portions of his body had been eaten.

Horrified by the discovery, Hellen and Marguerite begin the journey back to the cabin where both their families awaited. But his proximity to the lovely Marguerite was too much for the amorous Herr Hellen, and he finally clasped Marguerite to his body and began kissing her. Initially reluctant to consummate the romance, Marguerite informed Hellen that the forest was alive with supernatural forces and that a man should be careful what he desires. Herr Hellen, caught up in the rapturous moment, professed his love for Marguerite. She then proceeded to kiss him, "not once but many times."[17]

Much later, after reaching the cabin, Herr Hellen could hear the screams of his wife and daughter. Inside he discovered Wilfred Gaverstein squatting near their corpses. Herr Hellen's wife and daughter had gaping wounds in their throats. Marguerite then informed Herr Hellen that he could not harm them for they were phantasms. Marguerite, using a nail, scratched a mark on Hellen's forehead, and told him that when the mark healed she would come for him again because Herr Hellen belonged to Marguerite now and forever. He was then rendered unconscious.

Upon awaking he fled to a nearby village where he was told that Marguerite and her father were werewolves who periodically visited the forest and mountains. The mark on his forehead did not heal until shortly before his death many years later.

The story is emblematic of an element crucial in werewolf lore, namely the erotic content. Herr Hellen's tale is particularly explicit and his fate is determined by his adultery. As we shall see, the device of characters having sexual relations either out of wedlock or as adulterers and then meeting a grisly fate would become a staple among filmmakers.

The Devil, Possession and the Metamorphosis

The concept of a metamorphosis predates the Greek tale of Lycaon who, after sacrificing a child at the altar of Zeus, was transformed into a wolf. By the sixteen century, however, lycanthropy was indelibly linked with the devil. Witchcraft was, for all intents and purposes, viewed as op-

The stories of people transforming into a wolf date back to the earliest recorded history. (original illustration by Taylor Kuhlman).

position to Christianity. Such individuals as witches and werewolves were in agreement to work with the devil to deny and oppose the Christian hierarchy. Their purpose could not have been clearer to the fearful populace being that their efforts were designed to plunge the world into a bestial and wicked society where Satan ruled from his throne of madness. Such thinking was not uncommon.

Christian demonologists such as Thomas Cooper, writing in *The Mystery of Witchcraft* (1617), described the blasphemies of witches: "The witches abjure their baptism, the Christian faith, withdraw their obedience to God, and repudiate the protection of the blessed virgin…"[18]

Pacts with the devil are also recounted as a means to better one's life. But another aspect of lycanthropy is possession by the devil of a human body. In such cases the werewolf, being possessed by the devil, or in some fashion influenced by his emissary, can be viewed as a victim. However, victimization doesn't appear to have spared the individual from judgment, and often these victims appear to enjoy their new role as nocturnal hunters.

To a lesser degree, individuals stricken with lycanthropy are viewed as recipients of *maleficia*; generally, a misfortune or calamity to their person for which no logical explanation exists. The onset of lycanthropy may have no immediate explanation, such as in the tale of the Herr Hellen at the Harz Mountains, but after investigation there is usually evidence of lycanthropy initiated by the influence of the devil or his emissary.

In early folklore, such as the tales from France, the metamorphosis from man into wolf often involves the smearing of an ointment or salve upon the body. Vampires can change their shape into a bat, or sometimes a wolf. In fact, vampires are associated with werewolves in several legends, and later, the two were linked by pulp writers and filmmakers who eschewed practical history for fictionalized characteristics that often became accepted as fact.

But there are also noticeable differences between vampires and werewolves. A vampire is a dead person re-animated by supernatural forces. A werewolf is someone afflicted by the transformation, either by supernatural forces or by a complex psychological process resulting in that person's belief that they have become a wolf. In the earliest tales of lycanthropy, they were carnivorous and their victims remained dead. Much later, some tales included a lycanthrope's victim becoming a lycanthrope themselves. Such a fate is similar to a vampire's victim who will rise from the dead to join the ranks of the undead.

Shape Shifters and The Wolf in World Cultures

The metamorphosis from man into wolf is among the more common transformation in folklore, but the lore of witchcraft also includes other animals. Other transformations include aeluranthropy (transforming into a cat), boanthropy (transforming into a cow), cynanthropy (transforming into a dog), and lepanthropy (transforming into a hare). In a broader sense, zooanthropy was the widely held belief during the Middle Ages that persons possessed by devil spirits often believed themselves to be wild animals. They took refuge in forests or cases, let their hair grow long, and often attacked unsuspecting children and devoured them. Cats are commonly associated with witchcraft and play a vital role in many witchcraft tales. For example, in 1607, an accused witch named Isobel Grierson was burned at the stake for allegedly surreptitiously entering a home as a cat.

A belief in shape shifting wasn't uncommon in the fifteenth and sixteenth centuries, indeed, there are cultures thriving today where such beliefs remain a staple among factions of the population. During the Scottish witch trials of 1622, the accused witch Isobel Gowdie, confessed with a verse:

When we go in the shape of a hare, we say thrice over:

I shall go into a hare,
With sorrow and sigh and much care;
And I shall go in the Devil's name
Ay while I come home again.

And instantly we start in a hare.
And when we would be out of his shape, we will say:

Hare, hare, God send thee care.
I am in a hare's likeness just now,
But I shall be in a woman's likeness even now.

When we would go in the likeness of a cat, we say thrice over:

I shall go into a cat,
With sorrow and sigh and a black shot.
And I shall go in the Devil's name
Ay while I come home again.[19]

Animal possession also exists in Africa. Among certain tribes in South Africa the men are believed capable of transforming themselves into a were-lion. In his 1906 book, *British Central Africa*, author A. Werner cites a case of animal possession:

> A number of murders had taken place near Chiromo in 1891 or 1892, and were ultimately traced to an old man who had

The word werewolf is Old English for "man-wolf." The word *lycanthropy* derives from two Latin words—*lykos* or "wolf" and *anthropos* or "man"—and is used represent the condition of transforming from man into wolf. (original illustration by Taylor Kuhlman).

been in the habit of lurking in the long grass beside the path to the river, till some person passed by alone, when he would leap out and stab him, afterwards mutilating the body. He admitted these crimes himself.

He could not help it (he said, as he had a strong feeling at times that he had changed into a lion and was impelled as a lion to kill and to mutilate). As according to our view of the law he was not a sane person, he was sentenced to be detained "during the chief's pleasure," and this "were-lion" has been most usefully employed for years in perfect contentment keeping the roads of Chiromo in good repair.[20]

Other aspects of shape shifting include Africa's leopard men, Russia's bear-men, Bengal tiger-men and the Japanese were-cat. Norse legends tell us that warriors often dressed themselves in the skins of animals. As we have seen with the French tales, a wolf skin girdle or cloak often appears as a talisman that induced the lycanthropic state. A wolf skin garment evoked the animal's ferocity, and was thought to induce fear in a warrior's enemies.

Your Friendly Neighborhood Werewolf

But are lycanthropes real?

According to the medical community, yes, one type of lycanthrope has been identified. This is the pathological lycanthrope, spurred by a psychologically induced mania to howl and conduct oneself in the manner of a wolf. This type of lycanthrope was much more common in medieval Europe than it is today.

Psychological conditions relating to lycanthropy are uncommon, but do occur. Perhaps the most famous case was that of Sergei Pankejeff, a Russian aristocrat who became a subject of study under Sigmund Freud, a Viennese neurologist. Freud developed a theory of personality and a system of psychotherapy known as psychoanalysis. According to Freud, people are strongly influenced by unconscious forces, including innate sexual and aggressive drives. Pankejeff met Freud in 1910. Freud met with him numerous times through 1914 in his effort to understand Pankejeff's insomnia, nervousness and other restless characteristics. Freud referred to Pankejeff as the "Wolf Man" because of a dream Pankejeff had as a young child. In this dream Pankejeff was confronted by a pack of white wolves. Pankejeff believed the wolves wanted to eat him and he screamed and woke from his dream. But the images of the wolves had been so real that Pankejeff believed the incident to be real.

Freud conjectured that Pankejeff's dream symbolized a trauma and that, as a toddler, Pankejeff had witness his parents having intercourse. While Freud's ideas on psychoanalysis have been criticized, the Pankejeff case played a major role in Freud's development of psychosexual analysis.

In 1975, physicians reported the case of a twenty-year-old white male from Appalachia with a history of using senses-altering drugs such as psilocybin and LSD (lysergic acid diaethlmide). During one of his LSD experiences he found himself in a forest where he perceived fur growing from his hands and felt the sensation of hair growing from his face. He admitted to "a sudden uncontrollable urge to chase and devour live rabbits."[21] This experience convinced the young man that he was a werewolf. In a second case, another male from Appalachia demonstrated extraordinary behavior that included allowing his facial hair to grow long and then pretending it was fur. This young man also had the habit of sleeping in cemeteries and occasionally howling at the moon. These two aberrant individuals were diagnosed as schizophrenic with compounding mental and physical problems, though their cases are unique.

Modern physicians don't welcome a diagnosis of lycanthropy easily while the psychiatry industry seems baffled by it, and today the occurrence is quite rare, but they do occur. The case reported by two Canadian physicians, F. Surawicz and F. Banta, documented a case of a young man with a history of drug usage that included marijuana, amphetamines, psilocybin and LSD. Under these circumstances the individual believed that he had transformed into a wolf. Cases such as this are attributed to mental aberrations induced and accentuated by heavy drug use. The so called "mental werewolf" is at odds with the mythological werewolf that never seems to vanish completely. Werewolf sightings and modern folktales surface periodically to frighten, entertain and even entice us. Of more recent vintage is the highly celebrated case of the Wisconsin werewolf.

Commencing in 1991, journalist Linda Godfrey became aware of an alleged werewolf sighting on Bray Road near Elkhorn, Wisconsin. For the next several years she followed the story, interviewed witnesses, wrote reports for a local paper, and even employed her talents as a cartoonist to create sketches that accompanied some news reports. Her 2003 book, *The Beast of Bray Road*, is an entertaining review of the events that briefly became a media sensation in the Midwest.

Godfrey's amazing tale includes a call from a Hollywood producer who had read an article about the Bray Road werewolf and invited Godfrey to write a screenplay. Godfrey unabashedly reports that "after reading a dozen or so how-to books, I managed to crank out what I judge in hindsight to have been the worst stinker of a screenplay seen in Hollywood since the legendary horror-meister Ed Wood."[22]

The film effort was orchestrated by producer Jack Scanlan. After a re-write, Mick Fleetwood (from the musical group Fleetwood Mac) expressed some interest in the project. The film wasn't made, and while screenwriting might not be Godfrey's forte, her skill as a journalist is sharp as ever. Her book is a lively and fascinating look at the phenomena of lycanthropy. She wisely includes an historical overview of werewolves and recounts numerous plausible explanations for the still-unsolved sightings in Wisconsin.

Clearly, the fascination with werewolves isn't soon to fade. In *The Werewolf Complex: America's Fascination with Violence,* author Denis Dudos points out that "the horrifying nightmares which American fiction serves up ad nauseam are merely the symptoms of a worldwide ill."[23] And so the mythology that began with oral storytellers would eventually find its home in an impressive body of literature spanning several centuries. There is no end to the range of werewolf stories, although specific patterns and motifs are in vogue in different eras. The werewolf lurks omnisciently in the shadows awaiting those scribes who have burned the midnight oil while filling pages with tales of lycanthropes who roam the outer reaches of night when the moon is full.

The Werewolf in Literature

WEREWOLF STORIES ARE MORALITY PLAYS: allegories on mankind's temptation and sinning, his search for salvation, and his redemption in death. The literature of lycanthropy has its origins in folklore and was considered a sin against God. The image of a demonic lycanthrope will be repeated throughout the literature on werewolves, and the demonic image is certainly a recurring motif in the films.

In the first century A.D., Petronius, (sometimes referred to as Petronius Arbiter), a Roman writer believed to have written *Satyricon*, also wrote a novel *Cena Trimalchionis* (*Feast of Trimalchio*) that featured a strong lycanthropic element. Trimalchio, traveling to visit Trimalchio's mistress Melissa, encounters a man near a cemetery who strips, sets his clothes on the ground, and urinates in a circle around them. The man then transforms into a wolf. Astonished by what he has seen, Trimalchio rushes to Melissa who tells him that a wolf had been after their cattle. A hired hand repelled the wolf's attack by running a spear through his neck. Returning home the following day, Trimalchio revisits the place where the man had left his clothing and discovers a fresh patch of blood. It turns out the werewolf was an acquaintance and Trimalchio, horrified, could no longer share a meal with his friend.

The *Feast of Trimalchio* isn't the more graphic werewolf tale, but it featured the essential element of transformation, the spooky symbolism of a cemetery, the removal of clothing (which will later become a staple among exploitative filmmakers), and finally the regaining of human shape.

Little Red Riding Hood is one of the earliest tales involving wolves. Conceived by the Brothers Grimm, Jacob and Wilhelm, they first published their collection of fairy and folktales in 1812, with a subsequent expanded edition in 1814. In 1857, they published yet another edition featuring 212 stories. The Brothers Grimm were not the first to recount the tale of the red-hooded girl who encounters a wolf, but their version has become the accepted standard.

The tale is well-known to readers even today: a red hooded girl, traveling through a forest to visit her grandmother, encounters a wolf. The wolf is intent on eating the girl but is fearful of being caught. He suggests that the girl pick some flowers. While she is at her task the wolf visits the grandmother's house where he eats her. He then disguises himself as the grandmother and awaits Little Red Riding Hood's arrival. Upon her arrival Little Red Riding Hood is also eaten by the wolf. Soon a hunter traveling nearby comes to the rescue and slices open the wolf. Thus Little Red Riding Hood and her grandmother are spared as they tumble from the wolf's belly.

The tale connects several issues that will become a staple among stories of lycanthropes. In each instance, a female will be threatened by the lycanthrope, and the lycanthrope will possess a calculating and evil mind.

The first full-length werewolf novel appeared in book form in 1865. G. W. M. Reynold's *Wagner, the Wehr-Wolf*, was published just as the American Civil War was ending. George William MacArthur Reynolds was born in 1814 in England where he undoubtedly became familiar with the "Grimm's Fairy Tales" during his youth. He began publishing in the 1830s and became a prolific fiction writer. He enjoyed enormous popularity, and by today's standards he would be considered the equivalent of a Stephen King or a Dean Koontz. In fact, during his lifetime, Reynolds was more popular than Charles Dickens; while Dickens wrote novels with a universal appeal that have transcended time, while Reynolds is forgotten.

Reynolds wrote tempestuous novels featuring deformed villains, comely maidens, gravediggers and harlots. His characters acted out their parts in graveyards, jails, and brothels. He often published his tales in serialized form in "penny dreadfuls," the British equivalent of the American "dime novel." That is to say, these were tales rich on action, with wildly convoluted and unbelievable plots that entertained the masses. A hundred years later the American film industry would use these same story devices with their matinee adventure films and weekly serials such as Universal's twelve installments of *Flash Gordon* in 1936.

Wagner, the Wehr-Wolf made its debut in a penny dreadful titled *Reynold's Magazine of Romance, General Literature, Science and Art* on November 8, 1846. Thus, Reynolds is credited with the first significant use of the word "werewolf" in literature. Reynolds wrote with a ferocity matched by Edward George Earle Lytton (1803-1873), better known

Werewolf stories are morality plays; allegories on mankind's temptation and sinning, his search for salvation, and his redemption in death (original illustration by Taylor Kuhlman).

today as Bulwer (Baron) Lytton, and famous for writing prose that is considered the antithesis of a quality literary work; i.e., overly dramatic and embellished with anachronistic descriptions. The 1865 book version of *Wagner, the Wehr-Wolf* became an instant bestseller and a first edition remains highly sought-after by bibliophiles.

The opening lines of *Wagner, the Wehr-Wolf* make clear its appeal:

> "The night was dark and tempestuous;—the thunder growled around;—the lightning flashed at short intervals;—and the wind swept furiously along in sudden and fitful gusts.
> The streams of the great Black Forest of Germany bubbled in playful melody no more, but rushed on with deafening din, mingling their torrent-roar with the wild creaking of the huge oaks, the rustling of the firs, the howling of the affrighted wolves, and the hollow voices of the storm."[24]

In some sense, literature has not changed; while an editor today would remove the dashes, a good story requires prose that can be visualized in the reader's mind. Reynolds was an expert in creating memorable images. The book is dense with subplots and characters of all types: the Rosicrucians, the Turks, Italians, deserts islands, dungeons and demons all form a tapestry of intrigue, evil, and redemption.

Thus we have the first prolonged werewolf transformation in literature:

> Darkness seemed to dilate upon the sky like an image in the midst of a mirage, expanding into superhuman dimensions,—then rapidly losing its shapeliness, and covering the vault above densely and confusedly.
>
> But by degrees countless stars began to stud the colourless canopy of heaven, like gems of orient splendor; for the last—last flickering ray of twilight in the west had expired in the increasing obscurity.
>
> But, hark! What is that wild and fearful cry?
>
> In the midst of a wood of evergreens on the banks of the Arno, a man—young, handsome, and splendidly attired—has thrown himself upon the ground, where he writhes like a stricken serpent.
>
> He is the prey of a demonic excitement: an appalling consternation is on him;—madness is in his brain—his mind is on fire.
>
> Lightenings appear to gleam from his eyes—as if his soul were dismayed, and withering within his breast.
>
> "Oh! No –no!!" he cries, with a piercing shriek, as if wrestling madly—furiously—but vainly, against some unseen fiend that holds him in his grasp.
>
> And the wood echoes to that terrible wail: and the startled bird flies fluttering from its bough.
>
> But, Lo! What awful change is taking place in the form of that doomed being? His handsome countenance elongates into one of savage and brute-like shape;—the rich garment which he wears becomes rough, shaggy, and wiry skin;—his body loses its human contours—his arms and limbs take another form; and, with a frantic howl of misery, to which the woods give horribly faithful reverberations, and with a rush

like a hurling wind, the wretch starts wildly away—no longer a man, but a monstrous wolf![25]

The lush style and complicated structure was effective in presenting a vivid image to readers in 1865, and it is easy to see the comparison with Bulwer-Lytton. But *Wagner, the Wehr-Wolf* makes for difficult reading because of its labyrinthine plot. Reynolds packed his books with historical references and excessive character sketches, which, while acceptable at the time, are deemed cumbersome by today's readers. The character of Agnes has an elaborate history that takes up two full chapters. The plot is infused with elements of the adventure story, the torrid romance, the gothic mystery, and historical biography.

Yet Reynolds established a pattern for werewolf tales that persists to this day. His lycanthrope is a victim and tormented by supernatural powers. His transformation is horrific and his redemption can only be found in his death. Above all, there will be a woman involved and her role transcends that of a moral conscience; she is both a victim and sex object. The werewolf tale has deviated only slightly from those ideas in the decades since *Wagner, the Wehr-Wolf* became a literary sensation.

Robert Louis Stevenson's horror story *The Strange Case of Dr. Jekyll and Mr. Hyde* (1886), is perhaps the more famous transformation story in history. While not specifically referring to Mr. Hyde as a werewolf, Stevenson is tackling the idea that there is a monster within all of us, and that these repressed and primitive desires can be unleashed at a moment's notice. Dr. Jekyll is a seeker of forbidden knowledge who becomes victim to his own greed. In some ways Jekyll enjoys being the ape like creature and Mr. Hyde offers an outlet from the repressive Victorian society.

The extremes of good and evil represented by Hyde and Jekyll are identical to the werewolf folktales where the victim is often transformed from a model citizen into an evil lycanthrope. Thematically, *The Strange Case of Dr. Jekyll and Mr. Hyde* is too closely related to lycanthrope folktales to be dismissed. The two are inexorably linked thematically on the page, and the film industry would fuse these elements in several key cinematic outings.

Clemence Housman's *The Were-wolf* first appeared in the British magazine *Atalanta* in 1896. It appeared in book form later that year and has seldom been out of print since. Houseman was an author and illustrator and activist in the woman's suffrage movement. When *The Were-wolf* was published in book form, her brother, Laurence Houseman, provided the illustrations. *The Were-wolf* is set amongst the snow-laden landscape of Scandinavia and tells the story of White Fell, a female werewolf. Houseman's characterization of White Fell will differ noticeably from the traditional werewolf. She does not howl at the moon, and her transformation is never fully described. White Fell is, however, the embodiment of pure evil. That she revels in her bestiality lends the story a chilling tone.

The plot unfolds in a leisurely manner: one winter's evening the occupants of a farmhouse hear a voice pleading for sanctuary from the storm. The occupants allow admittance to a stunningly beautiful, fur-clad young woman, White Fell, who is instantly attacked by the family's dog, Tyr. White Fell demonstrates a lithe and athletic manner as she brandishes an axe from the confines of her garments and prepares to defend herself against the tempestuous hound. Among the occupants is Sweyn, a hunter, who prevents Tyr from injuring White Fell. Sweyn is immediately impressed with White Fell and bewitched by her beauty.

White Fell then informs Sweyn, "I fear neither man nor beast; some few fear me."[26] Enamored of White Fell, the child Rol is blessed with a kiss from the beautiful stranger. Rol eventually disappears and is believed to have been killed by a wolf. But Sweyn's brother, Christian, having arrived home later, has noticed wolf tracks leading to the cabin, but none retreating. Christian recognizes White Fell's true nature, that she is a werewolf, and warns Sweyn of the danger. But Sweyn is far too infatuated with White Fell to heed his brother's advice.

Christian decides to destroy White Fell before she can harm his brother. He informs White Fell that she may live until midnight, but White Fell flees across the snowy landscape. The subsequent chase is among the most exciting in horror fiction:

> "The edge of the teeth and the glitter of the eyes stayed a moment, and her right hand also slid down to the axe haft. Then, without a word, she swerved from him, and sprang out and away swiftly over the snow.
>
> And Christian sprang out and away, and followed her swiftly over the snow, keeping behind, but half a stride's length from her side.
>
> So they went running together, silent, toward the vast wastes of snow where no living thing but they two moved under the stars of night.
>
> Never before had Christian so rejoiced in his powers. The

gift of speed and the training of use and endurance were priceless to him now. Though midnight was hours away he was confident that go where that Fell Thing would hasten as she would, she could not outstrip him, nor escape from him. Then, when came the transformation, when the woman's form made no longer a shield against a man's hand, he could slay or be slain to save Sweyn."[27]

The prolonged chase spans several pages and Christian is obviously an allegorical Christ figure. He represents the religious side of humanity while the werewolf, "That Fell Thing," represents an unholy alliance with Satan. The Christian allegory is profoundly stated in the conclusion when Christian battles White Fell to the death:

Like lightning she snatched her axe, and struck him on the neck—deep—once—twice—his life blood gushed out, staining her feet.
The stars touched midnight.
The death scream he heard was not his, for his set teeth had hardly yet relaxed when it rang out. And the dreadful cry began with a woman's shriek, and changed and ended as a yell of a beast. And before the final blank overtook his dying eyes, he saw that She gave place to It; he saw more, that life gave place to Death—incomprehensibly.
For he did not dream that no holy water could be more holy, more potent to destroy an evil thing than the life-blood of a pure heart poured out for another in willing devotion.[28]

The transformation from human to werewolf in death is a reversal of the typical werewolf tale. Sweyn would discover his brother's body in a crucifixion pose "face forward in the snow, with his arms flung up and wide,"[29] and next to him the body of the she-wolf. The final paragraph, where Houseman states that Christian had died as Christ, has been routinely deleted from modern anthologies, perhaps because the blatant Christian motif was deemed unpalatable for a politically-correct audience.

While Bram Stoker is best remembered as the author of *Dracula* (1897), he was a skilled writer whose other novels earned him a reputation as a writer of suspense and terror. *Dracula*'s appeal has not diminished in the past century and remains one of the most often filmed novels in history.

Two illustrations by Laurence Houseman for his sister Clemence Housman's 1896 edition of *The Were-wolf*. The story has seldom been out of print and is widely regarded a landmark tale in the canon of lycanthopic literature.

The character of Dracula is as well known as Mary Shelley's Frankenstein monster. Well-known among aficionados of the vampire tale is the fact that Stoker excised the first chapter at his publisher's insistence. The publisher felt the book was overlong, although in retrospect trimming the first chapter, which is quite brief, appears illogical. Still, Stoker complied and cut the material. Shortly before his death, Stoker was compiling a collection of short stories and decided to include the excised first chapter from *Dracula*. His widow completed the task of preparing the manuscript and the first chapter made for the title story in *Dracula's Guest and Other Weird Stories* (1914).

With Stoker we are ushered into the modern era of lycanthropy which includes changes in literary styles. Bram Stoker's tales are far more accessible to readers today than the work of G. W. M. Reynold or Clemence Housman. It is difficult to imagine a library or bookstore today without a copy of *Dracula* on its shelves. Bram Stoker was the Stephen King of his time (albeit less prolific); i.e., he wrote highly popular suspense fiction, often with supernatural plots.

Although written as the first chapter for his novel, *Dracula's Guest* can stand on its own merits as a complete short story. The tales begins with Jonathan Harker wandering from his Munich hotel room on Walpurgis

Night (April 30) which in German folklore is believed to be the night Satan roams the earth and witches gather to celebrate the arrival of spring. Entering a valley during a storm he encounters a tomb. Stoker's descriptive powers are in evident in this passage:

> "...for suddenly the moonlight broke through the clouds, showing me that I was in a graveyard, and that the square object before me was a great massive tomb of marble, as white as the snow that lay on and all around it. With the moonlight there came a fierce sigh of the storm, which appeared to resume its course with a long, low howl, as of many dogs or wolves. I was awed and shocked, and felt the cold perceptibly grow upon me till it seemed to grip me by the heart. Then while the flood of moonlight still fell on the marble tomb, the storm gave further evidence of renewing, as though it was returning on its track."[30]

This is the tomb of Countess Dolingen who perished in 1801. Upon the tomb are carved the words "The dead travel fast." As the snowstorm increases in ferocity, Harker seeks refuge in the tomb's columned Doric entrance just as lightning begins crashing from the sky. In the next moment Harker witnesses a remarkable event:

> "In that instant, as I am a living man, I saw, as my eyes were turned into the darkness of the tomb, a beautiful woman, with rounded cheeks and red lips, seemingly sleeping on the bier. As the thunder broke overhead, I was grasped as by the hand of a giant and hurled out into the storm...At the same time I had a strange, dominating feeling that I was not alone. I looked towards the tomb. Just then there came another blinding flash, which seemed to strike the iron stake that surrounded the tomb and to pour through to the earth, blasting and crumbling the marble, as in a burst of flame. The dead woman rose for a moment of agony, while she was lapped in flame, and her bitter scream of pain was drowned in the thundercrash."[31]

Rendered unconscious, he awakes later to find himself in the company of a wolf which remains seated on his chest until the sound of a search party is heard advancing. The wolf had licked at Harker's neck "to keep his blood warm," and his rescuers refer to the creature as "A wolf—and yet not a wolf!" Harker learns that his rescuers had been contacted by his future host, Dracula, who encouraged the rescue party to find him as "there are often dangers from snow and wolves and night."[32]

While Stoker never specifically refers to the wolf as a werewolf, his intent was clear and the supernatural elements he described would become standard fare in werewolf tales to come. The elements of storms, graveyards, vampires and werewolves were forever linked in this one chilling tale.

The Undying Monster (1922) by Jesse Douglas Kerruish is a tepid affair that borders on the drawing room comedy, although it wasn't intended to be humorous. Set in an English country house, the convoluted plot concerns a centuries old curse on a family. Apparently the Hammand family is related to Sigmund the Volsung, a lycanthropic character. Oliver Hammand, worried about this affliction, enlists the aid of a psychic investigator named Luna Bartendale who seeks to cure Oliver through hypnosis. It turns out that the family is haunted by an apparition known as "The Undying Monster" and that family members die mysteriously after encountering the monster. There are intimations of a fifth dimension, vampires, Black Magic, and assorted plots.

The Undying Monster suffers from over-writing that borders on the ridiculous. A typical example can be found in this sentence: "Past the wall shewed copses and hangers like so many clumps of hearse-plumes; ground in the valley between all a soft mistiness of starlit frost-fog."[33]

The standards of quality literature, even melodramas, have changed very little since the 1922 publication of *The Undying Monster*. By any standard, this book is deserving of study by students of hackery intent on puzzling out the mysteries of effective fiction. In other words, *The Undying Monster* is so bad it's laughable. Characters that shout "Eureka!" and gasping participants investigate strange occurrences at every turn. Yet *The Undying Monster* is often cited in reference works on lycanthropy. This is unfortunate, as the lycanthropic element is minor. In fact, according to Brian J. Frost, writing in the superb *The Essential Guide to Werewolf Literature*, "one can well understand why the manuscript was initially rejected by every publisher to whom it was submitted."[34]

The Undying Monster remains an oddity in the canon of werewolf literature. It is more likely remembered only because of the 1942 film which turned out so much better than its source material. So we shall leave Kerruish's tale with an appropriate final quote that unwittingly sums up its contents: "Black butterflies ridden by blue Devils?" suggested Goddard, gaily. "We've had our fill of nastiness this morning"[35]

Guy Endore's *The Werewolf of Paris* was a sensation upon its publication in 1933. Based upon a true story, Endore's novel enjoys critical acceptance as a *bona fide* "literary" work because of its intelligent writing and comprehensive historical detail. One might argue that what constitutes "literary quality" for one might be another's pulp masterpiece. All the same, *The Werewolf of Paris* is an excellent book, although reading it may require effort. Dense with historical background, even labyrinthine footnotes, it requires diligence that's rewarded by some effective prose. The elaborate plot involves Bertrand Caillet, born on Christmas Eve and cursed with a canine appearance; he grows into manhood resisting the bestial urges that rage within.

But Bertrand's rages continue and he finally succumbs to sexually assaulting his mother:

> "She struggled against his youthful, muscular body, then she ceased and made no further resistance. A strange glow of satisfaction emanated from her sacrifice and caused her features to relax into an ecstatic smile. All the years of her life coalesced, Pitamont, Aymar, Bertrand. They were all one. They had melted into a single body, with many arms flailing about her, but with only one face.
>
> When Bertrand awoke several hours later, he noted with dismay his mother lying naked beside him, her limbs flung apart in complete relaxation."[36]

Bertrand becomes a sympathetic lycanthrope because the incest is desired by his mother while he finds it repugnant. He flees to a nearby forest where his desire to kill enflames him as he encounters a stranger on the road:

> "A wild desire to lay his hands on that man coursed through Bertrand's body and set his brain aflame. His eyes were so hot that he could not blink without a stab of pain. Every part of his body was sore and so sensitive that every stitch of clothing on his back pressed on his skin like the point of a needle. …as his clothes fell about him in a heap, he felt much better. But the sudden contact of his naked body with the cool wind,

called attention to a feeling of distention in his bladder. He relieved himself, making an arc of his water away from his clothes."[37]

Bertrand's transformation is never described as an actual emergence of man into wolf, but rather as a bestial transformation in attitude and perception. He is a wolf in mind and spirit. Fleeing to Paris he keeps body parts stolen from a cemetery in his room for nourishment. The writing in these sections is appropriately gruesome:

> "But by now the tongue was curling out of his mouth, was hanging over his teeth. Unable to resist any more, he sprang from his bed. He went to the corner of his room, muzzled under a piece of cloth and dragged forth an arm, a human arm. The last of the two arms he had taken from La belle Normande.
>
> He sank his teeth into it. His eyes glared around suspiciously. Low growls came from his throat. For awhile there was silence, then there were more noises; the slap of the hard, dead hand as it hit the floor, the crunching of a bone, and occasionally a sharp tick as a ring on one finger struck wood."[38]

Bertrand begins a relationship with Sophie de Blumenberg. Their lovemaking borders on masochism, but both rejoice in their relationship. Early on, Bertrand kisses her fingertips, nipping at her flesh with his teeth. Sophie enjoys the sensation and asks Bertrand to bite her fingers, and Bertrand "felt as he had once when as a little boy he had confessed to his mother of a pain in his groin and she had wanted to see."[39]

The conclusion debates the existence of the werewolf. A certain Dr. Dumas, who had treated Caillet in the asylum, believes that his affliction is psychological in nature. Bertrand's guardian, Aymar Galliez disagrees and argues that Bertrand's affliction was a truce case of lycanthropy. Readers are left to decide for themselves if Caillet was indeed a werewolf, although it matters little. Galliez argues that what appears unnatural or unscientific may be the greater reality: "Have you never seen water change to ice?" he argues, "And a worm change into a showy butterfly?"[40] Dr. Dumas may be unconvinced but readers had already made up their mind about the man known as the werewolf of Paris. "I have never seen the wolf, true enough." Aymar states, "But I have as many good proofs as I want."[41]

But finally, Bertrand's end comes by suicide after he is found guilty of murdering a soldier. Some years later, when the coffin is disinterred, it is found to contain the skeleton of a dog (*ne´* wolf) "with the fleshy parts and the furry hide…mingled in a fatty mass of indistinguishable composition."[42]

The frank sexuality, sadistic lovemaking and psychological depiction of a troubled soul reverberated with readers and critics alike.

The rise of the American pulp magazine market is the 1920s resulted in a new, popular literature that encompassed multiple genres including westerns, science fiction, romance and horror. Today, many of these writers (and their fictional creations) are considered among the more talented imaginative writers during the early twentieth century. Chief among these was Robert E. Howard, best known as the creator of Conan the barbarian.

In his short but brilliant career (Howard was born in 1906 and died in 1936 of a self-inflicted gunshot wound) he produced a vast array of short stories. He is widely considered the father of "sword and sorcery" fiction. Creatures that change shapes were fairly commonplace by the mid-thirties and these stories were greeted eagerly by fans of supernatural and hard-boiled fiction. Howard's two primary contributions to the lore of lycanthropy appeared in the pages of *Weird Tales* magazine, the legendary publication that published the works of H.P. Lovecraft, Robert Bloch, Henry Kuttner, Ray Bradbury and many other masters of the macabre.

Howard's "In the Forest of the Villefere" appeared in the August 1925 issue of *Weird Tales*. It's a brief tale, told in but a few scintillating pages. Basically a vignette, it recounts the tale of *Signor* de Montour who encounters Carolus de loup, a werewolf who attacks him while de Montour is fleeing a pack of wolves in a forest. The story reads like a fragment of something Howard had hoped to flesh out to novel length. It's but a tantalizing early tidbit.

Howard returns to *Signor* de Montour with "Wolfshead" published in the April, 1926 issue of *Weird Tales*. Here, a narrator recounts accepting an invitation to visit a friend, Dom Vincente da Lusto, and during his visit encounters another guest, de Montour. A series of ghastly attacks plague the festivities and de Montour encourages the narrator to bolt his door at night. De Montour explains that years before he'd met and battled a werewolf (a reference to Howard's "In the Forest of the Villefere") and slew it. But according to de Montour a true werewolf is not a man that takes the form of a wolf, but rather a wolf that takes the form of a man. This unique variation by Howard works well enough, although this story also hints at a larger tale that Howard never lived to write. Still, "Wolfshead" is a notable addition to werewolf literature because of Howard's mastery of language, pacing and tone. He was a superb writer, one of the best of the pulp writers, and it's often been said that teachers today would be thrilled to discover a student that could write as well as Robert E. Howard.

Seabury Quinn began publishing in *Weird Tales* magazine in 1923 and eventually published over 180 stories. That first year, his story "The Phantom Farmhouse" established him as a pre-eminent creator of dark fiction. Involving a family of werewolves, "The Phantom Farmhouse" is recounted by Mr. Weatherby, a clergyman recovering from an illness. Weatherby encounters this family while walking through the Maine countryside. "Strange fancies strike us in the moonlight, sometimes." Weatherby intones at one point. Although there is a strong religious undertone to "The Phantom Farmhouse" Quinn's writing is imagistic and fast-paced as was typical of the better pulp writers. His take on the werewolf legend echoes Clemence Housman but at a faster pace.

By comparison, Quinn's 1933 story "The Thing in the Fog" revisits the werewolf theme, but as a stylistic detective story. Here, French detective Jules de Grandin and his physician friend , Dr. Trowbridge, engage against a Greek werewolf who has enchanted a beautiful young woman. Grandin and Trowbridge are cut from the same cloth as Arthur Conan Doyle's Sherlock Holmes and Doctor Watson, although Quinn wisely avoids a direct pastiche.

H. Warner Munn's werewolf stories for *Weird Tales* magazine commenced with "Return of the Master" in 1927, followed by "The Werewolf's Daughter" in 1928. Each story involves a descendant of Wladislaw Brenryk and pre-dates the familial theme of werewolf clans that would become a routine device by the 1980s.

Brand of the Werewolf by Kenneth Robeson (pseudonym for Lester Dent) is overlooked by scholars and fans of lycanthropy and is rarely mentioned in any of the reference works. *Brand of the Werewolf* remains one of the best-selling werewolf titles of all time. Originally published in *Doc Savage Magazine* in January 1934, it was reprinted by Bantam in paperback in April 1965 and sold over 200,000 copies more than thirty years after it was first published. Although the famous Bantam edition is long out of print, it continues to sell on Internet sites such as eBay. *Brand of the Werewolf* refuses to go away. It is less a tale of lycanthropy than anything yet discussed, and its long life can be attributed to the immense popularity of its main character, Doc Savage.

In this archetypical adventure, Doc Savage and his assistants set out to find Doc's missing uncle and are quickly involved in a search for lost pirate treasure that sets them against the plans of El Rabanos and his cut-throat gang. During these adventures the sign of a wolf's head is found marked at various locations, a door or wall, an ominous warning to the adventurers that a werewolf was about. We soon learn that El Rabanos is seeking a small ivory cube two inches in diameter. The ivory cube holds the secret location to the pirate's treasure. Naturally, Doc and company discover a preserved Spanish galleon, occupied now by the skeletons of its crew, and still holding the desired the treasure. In the final battle, El Rabanos is defeated but escapes. Doc determines that the treasure will be used to create hospitals.

The werewolf here is limited to an ominous warning brand that appears on doors or walls. There is no physical appearance of a werewolf although the Bantam paperback depicted Doc Savage battling a ferocious werewolf that bears a strong resemblance to the Jack Pierce-Lon Chaney visage from the acclaimed film. Bantam Books had skillfully marketed the Doc Savage reprints with colorful, masculine covers, often by renowned artist James Bama. As with *Brand of the Werewolf,* the covers did not always match the text, but fans of Doc Savage hardly complained. Doc Savage is such an appealing, heroic character that his adventures remain popular today. *Brand of the Werewolf* sold briskly thanks to Doc Savage's popularity and perhaps to the spooky image on the Bantam cover. It remains an anomaly in werewolf literature: the only best-selling werewolf title without an actual werewolf in the story.

L. Ron Hubbard began publishing stories in pulp magazines in 1934 and quickly established himself as a master of all genres—mystery, science fiction, fantasy, westerns, thrillers, far-flung adventure, and tales from the Orient—which were published under his own name and 15 pen names. His 1934 story "Dead Men Kill" for *Thrilling Detective* magazine gives a twist to the transformation theme that had become a staple plot device for pulp writers. In this fast-paced tale detective Terry Lane finds himself investigating the murders of several respected citizens. Suspicion and fear runs high that the victims had been killed by zombies. The mystery deepens when Lane meets a beautiful nightclub singer who has information relevant to his case. Meanwhile, Lane has been threatened by a mysterious figure known as "Loup-garou." Hubbard never lets on that *Loup-garou* is the French term for werewolf and he uses the name here as pure symbolism. The fusion of a detective story with Haitian voodoo makes for a powerful and entertaining story, all of which was typical for L. Ron Hubbard. Everything that Hubbard wrote was fast-paced and entertaining. Zombie tales share the transformation from death into an ungodly creature motif with tales of lycanthropes, a fact that was clearly not lost on Hubbard who skillfully blends elements of both into what is essentially a crime story.

In "The Beast" from 1942, Hubbard again plays with the transformation idea but gives it a twist befitting the science fiction magazine where the story appeared. Here, the great white hunter Ginger Cranston finds himself at odds with a beast unlike anything he has encountered before: "A ruthless, pure animal."[43] In this short but powerful tale, Cranston finds his nerves shattered as he comes face to face finally with "The beast some unknown and probably unknowable crash of a small tramp spacer had made from a man."[44] "The Beast" is hardboiled pulp fiction at its finest. "Dead Men Kill" and "The Beast" were published at the onset of a remarkable career that endured fifty years. L. Ron Hubbard remains one of the respected and influential icons from the golden age of pulp fiction.

As we have seen, it wasn't unusual for pulp writers to take the basic idea of lycanthropy—the transformation from man to beast—and give it a twist as we have seen with L. Ron Hubbard's "The Beast." The 1930s was a significantly prolific decade for writers of imaginative fiction; however, by 1939, such luminaries as Jack London, H. P. Lovecraft, Robert E. Howard and Zane Grey were already dead. Their influence, and that of the pulp magazine market, would resonate for decades to come.

Jack Williamson's *Darker Than You Think* (1948) is a modern masterpiece that remains in print. What elevates the book above the mundane is its strong writing, unique premise, and believable characterization. Originally published in *Unknown* magazine in December 1940, the expanded 1948 book version has become the accepted masterpiece. Like so many of the pulp stories during this period, Williamson's prose is of the hard-boiled postwar variety, but rendered with greater skill than most. His prose fairly crackles on the page: "She looked as trimly cool and beautiful as a streamlined electric icebox."[45] Such lines are the envy of professional and amateur writers alike, and *Darker Than You Think* is loaded with strong descriptions.

Williamson's take on lycanthropy is much different than what we've seen in traditional folktales. *Darker Than You Think* proposes that earth was once populated by a species of shape shifters and witch folk. Their reign was subjugated by homo sapiens and their ability to negate the mental faculties of the witch population. The story is told through the eyes of a newspaperman, Will Barbee, who finds himself covering the findings of a group called The Human Research Foundation. The group's leader, Dr. Mondrick, and a friend of Barbee, is about to reveal a new view on the origin of human life. But a subculture of descendents of the shapeshifters want this information suppressed because it will reveal their presence and result in a literal witch hunt to exterminate them.

Barbee soon meets April Bell, a beautiful seductress and shapeshifter. Bell's intention is to murder all of The Human Research Foundation members that had participated in the expedition that uncovered their secret. Bell may be the most successful seductress in werewolf literature. "You can see why men must always hate us." Bell says, "Because we have inborn powers that are greater than are given men."[46] Barbee easily falls under her spell, and so do readers whose interest in this excellent book have helped to keep it in print for over fifty years. Through Bell, Barbee learns that he, too is a descendent of the witch folk and that shapeshifting is also within his capabilities. Bell's transformation falls along traditional lines as she morphs into a wolf: "Her urgent velvet voice was human, still. Her long, dark eyes were changed, with that same exotic hint of a slant. Her white wolf coat was evidently part of her now. For she had become a white were-wolf, sleek and wary and powerful."[47]

Throughout the book Barbee transforms into a wolf, a sabre-toothed tiger (with Bell astride him in the nude), a snake and finally into a winged saurian. Barbee's powers grow as he joins Bell in a murderous rampage against The Human Research Foundation group. Ultimately, he learns he has been bred as the Messiah—the Child of Night—for the witch-folk and he gives himself completely to April Bell's seductive influence.

Darker Than You Think offers a sampling of traditional lycanthropic imagery while reinventing the folklore surrounding werewolf legends. It is a science fiction pulp tale as well as a *noir* supernatural thriller, an action story, and a psychological examination of a disturbed mind. The premise that a subculture of shapeshifters and witch exist at all levels of modern culture was unique in 1948, and several decades would pass before this became a standard plot device in werewolf films and literature.

The 1960s brought extraordinary culture changes that included an apolitical counterculture that experimented with drugs and promoted a vigorous interest in rock and roll music. A new wave of science fiction writers and filmmakers created works that decried materialism and provided stringent social commentary. The proliferation of television that began a decade earlier resulted in a nostalgia craze for films and literature of the 1930s and 40s. This included a resurgence in popularity of Universal Studios' famed monster series and films and literature once again began emulating the style and elements of the Jack Pierce/Lon Chaney *Wolf Man* films (a full discussion of the Universal series is found in Chapter Three). Additionally, there was a tendency toward realism in the approach to horror literature that would see varying levels of success.

Leslie H. Whitten's *Moon of the Wolf* was available only in paperback in 1967 and enjoys awareness among bibliophiles and aficionados of werewolf literature. The Ace paperback cover depicted a man-wolf creature howling at the moon although there is little traditional lycanthropic elements in *Moon of the Wolf*. Primarily a suspense thriller, *Moon of the Wolf* is superbly written and author Leslie H. Whitten was even compared to William Faulkner by an enthusiastic reviewer for the *Greensboro Daily News*.

Set in the late thirties, the plot involves the murder of a black girl, initially believed to have been committed by a group of wild swamp dogs. Investigating the case is Deputy Aaron Whitaker who isn't convinced that a pack of wild dogs or wolves are responsible for the girl's death. Whitten's prose crackles with moody descriptions, although at times he appears to intentionally creating scenes that are the antithesis of werewolf tales: "The moon was as flat and uninteresting as a bowl of white cereal."[48]

What unfolds is more of a police procedural with commentary on modern psychology. The antagonist, Andrew Rodanthe, is surmised to be suffering from a psychological disorder that causes him to imagine he is a werewolf. But Whitten toys with the reader, setting up the idea that Rodanthe might actually be a werewolf:

> "Andrew's snarl of angry pain as he recoiled from the bed was unhuman. Even in the dimness, the white teeth broke from the dark face. The eyebrows, unruly and standing out from the head, were matched by the tangled locks on the top of his head and the erect clutch of hair at his temples. His two-day whiskers seemed to writhe on his tendoned face like the hair on a fighting dog's maw."[49]

But such traditional moments are scarce in this book. It isn't until the very conclusion that Whitten is willing to reveal a preference for an actual werewolf:

> "In the moonlight, Whitaker could see the features change. The distortion began at his mouth, which snapped downward in a vicious grimace. The lips whipped back from the white teeth. His eyes bulged, then glazed into fiery pits of hate. His brows crawled up his forehead like hairy bugs and the smooth hair sprang up ferally, giving his head a wild, leonine look. "[50]

He drives the point home, literally on the last page, in a climactic scene that leaves readers wishing for a less gimmicky tale: "The Wolf Man's grotesque features already were relaxing into the darkly handsome face of Andrew Rodanthe."[51]

The end result is unsatisfying for horror fans who waded through 180 pages of a suspense thriller before encountering the werewolf. Whitten would later write the screenplay for a television film based upon his book that capitalizes on the werewolf theme with an equally unsatisfying result.

Night of the Vampire (1969) by Raymond Giles is long out of print. It also plays fast and loose with references to lycanthropy as a psychological condition, and perhaps this is due the influence of the vastly superior *The Werewolf of Paris* by Guy Endore. *Night of the Vampire* has its gothic moments thanks to descriptive lines such as: "Somewhere under the high eaves a bat chittered, scarcely audible. Somewhere in the night an owl hooted."[52] The prose is a direct reflection of countless stock footage from horror films. Duffy Johnson, a psychiatrist who had belonged to a Satanic coven as a teenager, returns to Sanscouerville with his wife Roxanne who coincidentally happens to be the last of the Sanscouer family. The Sanscouer's had been suspected of being lycanthropes and Duffy has returned to her namesake town with the hope of curing her of her delusions. The action shifts back and forth between the coven's current activities and Roxanne's unsuccessful attempt to rid herself of her lycanthropic tendencies. Naturally she fails.

Unlike Leslie H. Whitten's *Moon of the Wolf,* the author immediately establishes supernatural elements into the story. The fusion of the vampire tale with lycanthropy had become a mainstay among the pulp writers of the 70's. Author Raymond Giles, however, can't seem to resist a clichéd approach to his descriptions. Chapter Two ends simply enough with "A bat flew across the moon."[53] *Night of the Vampire* is neither the best nor the worst of the paperback originals. It's brisk style and often cornball

Werewolf stories run the gamut of pulp action tales and serious intellectual studies.

approach to its subject matter place it solidly in the entertaining but unmemorable category and its unlikely that readers objected to parting with the sixty cents it cost them.

Nearly forgotten, *Vampire's Moon* (1970) by Peter Saxon enjoyed popularity in England and the United States upon its publication in paperback. It was reprinted a few times and then disappeared. It would be entirely forgotten today if not for a modest renewal of interest in the horror paperback novels of Peter Saxon.

Peter Saxon was a pseudonym created by W. Howard Baker who was an editor and writer for Amalgamated Press. The name Peter Saxon became a publishing house pseudonym for a variety of supernatural and horror titles. In addition to Baker, several other writers wrote under the Saxon *nom de guerre*, including Wilfred G. McNeilly and Martin Thomas. Peter Saxon's name was quickly associated with entertaining horror novels. In addition to *Vampire's Moon*, other popular titles included *The Torturer* (1966), *The Darkest Night* (1966), *Satan's Child* (1968), *The Curse of Rathlaw* (1968), *Black Honey* (1968) and *The Haunting of Alan Mais* (1969).

It is generally believed that Baker himself wrote *Vampire's Moon*, although this hasn't been verified. *Vampire's Moon* is an entertaining gothic tale in the tradition of Bram Stoker. Set in modern times (1970), the story takes place in Transylvania and Saxon sets the tone early: "Transylvania was the home of the vampire and the werewolf. No mere shadows from horror films, they were still feared in the manner of centuries."[54]

The vampire here is Count Zapolia, simply another version of the Dracula legend. Zapolia's intent is to lure a woman under his influence to create a vampire bride. "Tonight would be a step forward in a plan conceived by the brain of the undead human. His brain, poised between natural life and eternal death, needed a mate, as a man does." (p.27) Count Zapolia also possesses the power of transformation. He can become a werewolf or a bat, as he chooses. Zapolia's transformation follows the established routine:

> "The jaw thrust forward and the lips curled away from the teeth in a dreadful rictus. His eyebrows became bushier and grew together, as his hair became coarse and tufts of it sprouted from his smooth forehead. The mouth, in its shocking gape, widened and deepened. The gums thrust forward and the teeth extended into points.

> The two canine incisors grew out and curved below the others, as he changed into a creature with the face half of a man and half of a wolf.
> He seemed to tower above her. Her shrieks came automatically, she was not aware of them in the horror of the moment.
> She felt her body lifted and laid on the altar. Strong hands held her down. Zapolia ripped the white silk away from her neck and bosom but he had no eyes for her young, hard breasts.
> They were fixed on the hollow at the base of her throat, where the blood pulsed gently under the satin smoothness of her skin."[55]

There seems little doubt that such transformation scenes in pulp fiction owe a debt of gratitude to Universal Studio's *The Wolf Man* (1941). Saxon takes the transformation a step further by maintaining that Zapolia is both vampire and werewolf, a duality that Stoker hinted at in *Dracula's Guest*.

Vampire's Moon found itself on paperback racks during a period when small budget horror films were turning a profit in the drive-in movie market. Nudity had become a prominent feature of such films and Saxon's books bordered on the explicit. The strong sexual images, realistic dialogue, and supernatural plot made it a memorable pulp experience.

Gary Brander's *The Howling* (1977) is the most influential werewolf book since Guy Endore's *The Werewolf of Paris*. Brander set the standard for werewolf literature that crossed over into a profitable series of films. Brander follows medieval thinking that lycanthropes were associated with Satan: "The werewolf is a servant to the devil. No one becomes a werewolf by chance. It's like witchcraft. In return you pledge your everlasting soul."[56]

The plot follows Karyn Beatty and her husband Roy to the peaceful California village of Drago. They had come here after Karyn was brutally raped in her Los Angeles apartment, subsequently suffering a miscarriage. But Drago turns out to be far more than a peaceful rural setting. The town harbors a group of lycanthropes. Brander's concise prose elevates the traditional imagery:

> "It was a wolf, but bigger than any wolf should be. As the animal sat on its haunches, the big head came to nearly four feet above the ground. It did not move when the light came on,

but glared defiantly at the window. The reflected light of the bulb out in front made the eyes glow like jewels. The wolf's fur was a dull gray-brown color, shaggier around the neck. The chest was full, the large forepaws planted solidly on the ground. As Karyn watched, the thin black lips of the animal skinned back and she saw the teeth."[57]

Gary Brander's *The Howling* became an instant classic and a prototype for werewolf novels to follow. Its popularity was enhanced by an equally popular film (discussed in part three).

Brandner followed with *The Howling II* and *The Howling III*, both equally entertaining. He remains an active and fascinating writer of popular fiction.

The Wolfen (1979) by Whitley Streiber was equally as popular as Gary Brander's series and was also made into a profitable film. *The Wolfen* rivals Brander's *The Howling* as the best of the modern werewolf novels. It shares with *The Howling* and *Darker Than You Think* a textured plot that

Werewolf fiction includes books by traditional New York publishers, such as *The Wolfen* by Whitley Strieber, and print-on-demand titles such as *Werewolf Island* by Tony Gardner.

involves a subculture of lycanthropes living in secret amongst the general population. The idea that the earth was once populated by a superior race of lycanthropes has become commonplace. But Streiber's version is compelling. Two police detectives, George Wilson and Becky Neff, come to the conclusion that tow recently murdered police officers were slain by a pack of wolves. But as their investigation progresses they discover there was an underlying intelligence behind the murders. Eventually, they uncover a pack of Wolfen, lycanthropic mutant creatures that have remained hidden from mankind for centuries. Survival of the Wolfen is paramount: "Here was another human meddling in the affairs of the pack, further evidence that knowledge of the clan was spreading."[58] What ensues is a prolonged cat and mouse game with the Wolfen intent on destroying Wilson and Neff.

While there are similarities to Gary Brander's *The Howling*, Streiber manages to keep the action at a breakneck speed. The *Wolfen* is excellent, and Streiber continues to publish captivating and suspenseful novels of weird fiction.

Stephen King's *Cycle of the Werewolf* (1983) appeared in the first decade of his career. Stephen King is equally as famous as Edgar Allan Poe and H. P. Lovecraft, and far more prolific. His early novels, *Carrie* (1972), *Salem's Lot* (1975), *The Shining* (1977), and *Cujo* (1981) are among the best horror novels ever written. *Cycle of the Werewolf* is among his shorter novels, really no more than a short story, but published in book form with illustrations by acclaimed artist Bernie Wrightson. The book's 12 chapters recount an episode of a werewolf attack in the town of Tarker's Mills, Maine.

Stephen King's many talents lie in his brisk narratives, strong characterizations (often realized with a few, carefully chosen words), and his knack for pacing. He also appears to possess a wicked imagination that has thrilled and delighted readers for well over thirty years. *Cycle of the Werewolf* is typical, and gets right to the point: "Something inhuman has come to Tarker's Mills, as unseen as the full moon riding the night sky high above. It is the Werewolf, and there is no more reason for its coming now than there would be for the arrival of cancer, or a psychotic with murder on his mind, or a killer tornado."[59]

It may be difficult to argue with those who believe that Stephen King's best work can be found in his short story collections. Certainly, many of his novels are overlong and leave one with the impression of being self-indulgent. But of these novels, *IT* (1985) is probably his masterpiece.

Overlong though it may be, *IT* tells a compelling tale of boyhood terror that remains an influential work on horror writers everywhere.

IT is a massive book of 1,138 pages. Set in 1958 in the fictional town of Derry, Maine, King weaves a compelling about an evil creature that lives in the sewer drains beneath the city's streets. The creature manifests itself in various forms, including variations of famous movie monsters such as the Mummy and the Creature from the Black Lagoon. The creature's appearance as a werewolf is traditional:

> "The face of the werewolf suddenly swam out of the dark. Its forehead was low and prognathous, covered with scant hair. Its cheeks were hollow and furry. Its eyes were a dark brown, filled with horrible intelligence, horrible awareness. Its mouth dropped open and it began to snarl. White foam ran from the corners of its thick lower lip in twin streams that dripped from its chin."[60]

While the werewolf is but one of many guises of *IT*'s evil protagonist, it is a crucial element in an epic tale of good versus evil. King's masterful characterizations and dialogue, compounded by these horrific creatures, helped elevate *IT* to bestseller status. In his long, varied (and ongoing) career, Stephen King has justifiably become the pre-eminent voice in popular horror fiction.

Blood of the Wolf by Jeffrey Goddin (1987) is typical of the werewolf literature that followed the success of *The Howling* and *Wolfen*. Goddin's style is not far removed from Stephen King or Gary Brander, and one can argue this style has become accepted as the standard "house style" for many paperback publishers.

Goddin follows the example set by Gary Brander and Whitley Streiber by incorporating a subculture of lycanthropes into a modern setting. *Blood of the Wolf* is well written with strong characters, tight descriptions and realistic dialogue. It is among the better of 1980s era werewolf books although it had little impact, perhaps because at that time the market was flooded with horror novels. The werewolves here are almost superhuman: "…she went into the second form—the wolf that walked on two legs with the use of hands, and razor sharp fangs in a jaw so strong it could bend steel."[61]

This is the trend that continues today: stronger, ferocious werewolves that form a subculture unknown to the average person.

Roger Zelazny's *A Dark Traveling* (1987) is short novel for young readers, which uses lycanthropy as part of its backdrop for an alternate reality adventure story. "I'm a normal fourteen year old boy, my name is James Wiley, and I live in a large building in a southwestern state capital in the United States. My sister Becky is a witch, my older brother Dave lives in a castle, and our exchange student Barry is a trained assassin. I also have an Uncle George who is a werewolf. And my own palms do get itchy whenever there's a full moon."[62] Wiley enters into a cat and mouse game between realities as he searches for his missing father. The lycanthropic element doesn't manifest itself until late in the story. The transformation sticks to traditional formulae: "I halted, panting, and raised my hands to my face. I could feel the stubble again in the places I had shaved earlier. I was suddenly aware of cramps in my legs, beginning in my calves and spreading up into the muscles of my thigh shortly thereafter...I seemed cross-eyed, for my nose suddenly seemed longer and darker by moonlight."[63] Zelazny was among the best of the science fiction and speculative fiction writers that came into prominence during the 1970s and his novels all sparkle with insight. *A Dark Traveling* is considered among his lesser novels, although not without merit. Zelazny's fusion of the werewolf tale with teen angst and alternate realities makes for a brisk and entertaining romp, which is precisely what he intended.

Robert McCammon's *The Wolf's Hour* has demanded an audience since its initial publication in 1989. A cross-genre adventure tale with supernatural elements, the story of Michael Gallatin, who was raised by a pack of werewolves, includes his efforts to destroy Hitler's Third Reich during World War II. A fascinating combination of historical novel and werewolf thriller, *The Wolf's Hour* has been reprinted several times.

The Werewolf's Kiss (1992) by Cheri Scotch appeared with only modest promotion from its publisher. Billed as "Book One of the Voodoo Moon Trilogy" *The Werewolf's Kiss* is well known and coveted by admirers of werewolf fiction and horror novels in general. The series chronicles the history of a lusty clan of lycanthropes in Louisiana. This first volume follows the adventures of Sylvie Marley who is oblivious to her family's lycanthropic history. But when she begins staying out late and returning at sunrise with her clothes in tatters, her father begins to suspect that Sylvie hasn't escaped her family's proclivity to lycanthropy. Shortly, she meets a composer, Lucien Drago, and a *loup-garou*, the werewolf of the Louisana bayous. Lucien represents the werewolf culture and Sylvie is torn between two world views, that of the average human and that of the lycanthrope.

The Werewolf's Kiss is loaded with historical background, interesting characters and heavy doses of mood. The transformation is to the point: "one by one, the loups-garous began to moan as the transformation began. Each loup-garou changed in his own way, at his own speed; in some claws grew first, some sprouted hair immediately, for some the bones lengthened and hardened before anything else happened. But the thing that stayed the same was the look of pleasure, as in a prolonged earthshaking orgasm."[64]

The sexual connection is explicitly rendered, finally bluntly establishing the erotic symbolism that had been present in werewolf literature from the onset.

Scotch followed *The Werewolf's Kiss* with *The Werewolf's Touch* (1993). Equally absorbing, *The Werewolf's Touch* is a prequel. This second volume chronicles the history of a young Angelican priest named Andrew Marley who discovers that a werewolf curse has tormented his family for centuries when his grandfather rejected the amorous advances of a voodoo queen, La Reine Blanche. Spurned, she cursed his family line. Seeking a cure, Andrew solicits assistance from Zizi, the Queen of the Louisianan werewolves. Scotch isn't afraid to ladle up heaps of imagery and traditional pulp images: "So when the moon is finished with me for tonight and I stagger home, blinded by blood, I'll begin the story of the Marley werewolves, a nasty little tale of a good family gone bad."[65]

The final volume of the "Voodoo Moon Trilogy," *The Werewolf's Sin* (1994) satisfies the expectations created by the earlier books. Here, the story is set fifteen years after the events depicted in *The Werewolf's Kiss*. Sylvie Marley (née Drago) has transformed her brother, Walt, into a loup-garou, but their father has disowned them both. They are soon influenced by the sociopath Lycaon, Arcadia's ancient king who was cursed by Zeus and became the first werewolf. Sylvie and her husband Lucien find themselves at odds against Lycaon in a battle for survival.

Cheri Scotch's books remain popular. The rough sexuality, stark images, and gothic mood have made "Voodoo Moon Trilogy" mandatory reading for fans of werewolf tales.

Nancy A. Collins, perhaps best known for her superb Sonja Blue vampire books, turned in a modern classic werewolf tale with *Wild Blood* (1994). Freshman college student Skinner Cade discovers that he was adopted and soon dreams he is visited by his father's ghost who warns him that he is about to undertake a "dark and bloody" journey. (p. 20) Restless and bewildered, Skinner begins searching for his birth mother only to encounter a world of gruesome dreams and a growing discontentment. Collins' easy and often colloquial style is refreshing. Her writing is marked by its strong characters, tight plots and sometimes dark imagery. *Wild Blood* incorporates the lycanthrope's mythology alongside Native American folklore to good effect. Skinner Cade is a sympathetic character, a rarity in werewolf stories. The edition published by (appropriately enough) Two Wolf Press includes a sequel, "The Nonesuch Horror" featuring Skinner and the vampire Sonja Blue. Collins also featured werewolves and werecougars in *Right Hand Magic* (2010), the first of a series about witches in a section of New York known as Golgotham.

Annette Curtis Klause's *Blood and Chocolate* (1997) is another in the recent proliferation of quality werewolf novels. Again, the premise involves a subculture of werewolf families living in secret among the general population. Sixteen-year-old Vivian Gandillion is a typical angst-suffering teenager who also happens to be a werewolf. She enjoys the ferocity and sensuality of her werewolf life:

> "The flesh of her arms bubbled and her legs buckled to a new shape. She doubled over as the muscles of her abdomen went into a brief spasm, then grimaced as her teeth sharpened and her jaws extended. She felt the momentary pain of the spine's crunch and then the sweet release."[66]

Blood and Chocolate examines this hidden society of werewolves through Vivian's eyes as she falls in love with a human. Her loyalties are now divided as the werewolf pack struggles to remain anonymous in an increasingly hostile world. Intentional or not, there is a hint of Jack Williamson's influence with Klause's almost off-hand explanation for lycanthropy: "Those who preferred science to myth said they descended from something older—some early mammal that had absorbed protean matter brought to Earth by a meteorite."[67]

The werewolf's appeal sometimes crosses genres. It's not uncommon to find romance novels, and occasionally westerns, with a lycanthropic subplot. These page turners make for popular mass market books. In some instances, the mix of genres can be effective as in *The West Wolf* (2001) by Lance Howard, a pseudonym for Howard Hopkins, a prolific and entertaining writer whose canon includes both westerns and horror. Published in Great Britain as part of Robert Hale Publishers famed "Black Horse Western" series, *The West Wolf* is a masculine, taut thriller. Set in the town of Wolf's Bend where the inhabitants are plagued by a creature known as the West Wolf. When a gunman named Tom Hogan returns to this once peaceful town he's immediately swept into a mystery that jeopardizes the woman he loves. His quest will be to stop two murderous outlaw brothers while solving the mystery of the man-beast that terrorizes the town.

William Gagliani's *Wolf's Trap* (2003) is one of the few werewolf novels in recent years to receive major publicity. *Wolf's Trap* caught the eye of James Argendeli and was favorably reviewed on CNN's website shortly after its publication. Gagliani's book is among the best of the recent werewolf tales, a unique and exciting rendering of the lycanthrope's mythology. Set in Milwaukee, Wisconsin, *Wolf's Trap* concerns police detective Nick Lupo, himself a werewolf, who finds he is being stalked by a serial killer. Lupo has worked at controlling the beast within by isolating himself at a cabin in the north woods whenever the moon is full. Gagliani's werewolf is intelligent and calculating, but the fact that he's also a detective adds a welcome plot twist: "The first sign of the Change was an infusion of smells so great that it made his head spin. It was as if the nostrils had been securely blocked but now were thrown open like shutters."[68]

Lupo is conscious of his transformation and works to put his lycanthropic skills to use in his career as a police detective. "Besides, he wondered if the Creature under his control could help his police work. If not to catch criminals, then at least to track them. The Creature's heightened senses had helped him already, but once completely harnessed they could rewrite his approach to investigations."[69]

Wolf's Trap combines the horror genre with that of the modern police procedural. Basically, a detective story with a lycanthropic twist, the characters are cut from today's headlines, a rogues gallery of killers and slimeballs. Lupo then becomes the lycanthrope as hero against modern society's degenerates. The unflinching, descriptive prose and tightly woven plot all fuse into a fresh and spellbinding tale.

With the success of the Yard Dog Press publication, *Wolf's Trap* was eventually reprinted as a mass market paperback by Leisure books, but bibliophile's will tell you the Yard Dog Press edition with artist Brad Foster's snarling, colorful cover is the preferred edition.

Of the self-published, print-on-demand entries, Tony Gardner's *Werewolf Island* (2007) is an entertaining inclusion in the canon of werewolf literature. The first person narrative is simplistic and Gardner's preference for simple, declarative sentences keeps the narrative sliding along at a clipped, journalistic pace. There are no plush descriptions or elaborate details and the straightforward manner works well enough. *Werewolf Island* recounts the tale of Doc (the narrator) and his wife Janice who take a vacation on an island when something goes awry. Waking up in a hospital bed, they are told they had been in an accident, but Doc isn't convinced. He soon learns they were attacked by a werewolf who had raped Janice.

Gardner's werewolf follows traditional descriptions:

> "A few seconds later I saw something very odd was beginning to happen to him. Hair was starting to grow all over his face. His nose started to enlarge into what looked like a snout. His ears were growing longer and becoming pointed. I could see his hands and feet changing into what looked like claws. Then his hands and feet changed into paws. At that point, he/it dropped to the ground on all fours. He howled as if in a lot of pain. I could hear the sound of crunching bones as this incredible metamorphosis took place in front of me. I was frozen with shock. I could not believe what I was seeing."[70]

Heavy on action, *Werewolf Island* lacks the pretentious and intentional sleaze found in modern horror writing. There are the requisite bloody scenes, but the gore factor is moderate. Although *Werewolf Island* has an overall adult tone, there is also no explicit sex. The book's traditional plot is held together by Gardner's willingness to keep the story simple.

Dancing With Werewolves (2007) by Carole Nelson Douglas is the first in a series featuring Delilah Street, a paranormal investigator. Set in the not to distant future, Television reporter Delilah Street finds herself at odds with the werewolf mob that controls Las Vegas. In a world populated with werewolves and vampires, the passionate Delilah is among the more interesting protagonists in werewolf literature. Douglas keeps the characters fresh and interesting. In this first outing she meets the oldest living vampire in Vegas, CinSims (Cinema Simulacrums), Hector Nightwine, a producer and Ric Montoya, an F.B.I agent, and Cocaine, a wild albino rocker. The book is loaded with creepy but fun moments.

The premise of a world where humans, vampires and werewolves coexist has clearly become a staple plot device.

The book owes its title to Michael Blake's Western classic *Dances with Wolves* (1988) which formed the basis for Kevin Costner's triumphant 1990 film version. So does another book, also published in 2007, Niki Flynn's *Dances with Werewolves: Memoirs of a Spanking Model*. Aside from their titles these two books bear no similarities to Michael Blake's popular story.

In fact, Niki Flynn's *Dances with Werewolves: Memoirs of a Spanking Model* is non-fiction. The book is an account of her roles as an actress in adult films. Unable to achieve sexual satisfaction through traditional methods, Flynn became a spanking enthusiast and relocated to Europe where she starred in underground adult films, submitting herself to extreme sexual situations that involved spanking and caning. The werewolves here are a metaphor for the filmmakers and spanking enthusiasts who dare to explore the sometimes dark and taboo world of underground sexploitation films.

Lonely Werewolf Girl (2007) by Martin Millar was an instant success. At 558 pages it may be the longest werewolf tale in print. It involves the adventures of teenage werewolf girl Kalix MacRinnalch. The book reads like a parody of any popular teen angst story except here the world is populated by werewolves. As it turns out, Kalix is being pursued across London by werewolf hunters. Kalix has a sister, the Werewolf Enchantress, who creates designer clothing for the Fire Queen. Other members of the MacRinnalch werewolf clan, situated in the Scottish Highlands, are in turmoil after the death of the clan leader. Clan members are keen on soliciting Kalix's vote to ensure the proper clan leadership is put in place. But Kalix has no interest in her werewolf clan's political intrigue. She's far more interested in laudanum.

Lonely Werewolf Girl must surely have been written with Millar's tongue firmly planted in his cheek as he weaved this expansive and often ridiculous (albeit entertaining) coming of age story. The book's jacket copy aptly describes its contents: "…elegant werewolves, troubled teenage werewolves, friendly werewolves, homicidal werewolves, fashionista werewolves, warriors, punks, cross-dressers, musicians—an entire clan of werewolves getting in trouble…" There are more werewolves here than in any other book yet mentioned and Millar stack up his werewolves with a humorous touch.

Ray Garton's *Ravenous* (2008) is a pulp thrill ride that never lets up for any of its 342 pages. Garton, best known as the author the modern vampire classic *Live Girls*, has published over fifty books and rivals Stephen King as the Master of the horror genre. The premise is simple: a werewolf has come to the California town of Big Rock and a sheriff and his men set out to stop its deadly rampage. What follows quite naturally is a roller coaster ride of sex and violence as Garton swings around town like a voyeur. The book delivers what readers have come to expect, *i.e.*, a generous dose of tension and violence.

Werewolves also feature in numerous short stories, many of which have been anthologized. Editor Roger Elwood's *Vampires, Werewolves and Other Monsters* (1974) reprints Joseph Payne Brennan's classic pulp tale "Diary of a Werewolf" along with 11 other supernatural tales.

Bill Pronzini's *Werewolf! A Connoisseur's Collection of Werewolfiana* (1979) collects 12 chilling tales including Clemence Housman's "The Werewolf," "Dracula's Guest" by Bram Stoker, and other tales of recent vintage worth considering. Notable among these are "The Hound" by Fritz Leiber, "Lila the Werewolf" by Peter S. Beagle and "Full Sun" by Brian W. Aldiss.

The Ultimate Werewolf (1991) edited by Byron Preiss, was created specifically to celebrate the 50th anniversary of Universal's *The Wolf Man* (1941) with a collection of new and recent tales of lycanthropy. The line-up of writers contributing stories is breathtaking: Harlan Ellison (who also contributed the introduction), Philip Jose Farmer, Craig Shaw Gardner, Nancy A. Collins, Larry Niven, Robert J. Randisi, Stuart Kaminsky, Robert E. Weinberg, Kathe Koja, Nina Kiriki Hoffman, Kim Antieau, Jerome Charyn, Mel Gilden, Pat Murphy, Kevin J. Anderson, A. C. Crispin, Kathleen O'Malley, Brad Linaweaver, and Robert Silverberg turned in wholly original work of lasting value.

Among these, Harlan Ellison's story "Adrift Just off the Islet of Langerhans: Latitude 38° 54´ N Longitude 77° 00´ 13´ W" is now widely considered among the finest short stories in American letters. In fact, Harlan Ellison has made a career of producing the finest short fiction for over fifty years. "Adrift Just off the Islet of Langerhans" tackles Larry Talbot's (the main character from Universal's acclaimed 1941 film, *The Wolf Man*) odyssey in search for his soul. When Talbot eventually finds his soul it turns out to be an old Howdy Doody button. The cultural symbolism and its meaning has been debated hotly since the story first appeared in *The Magazine of Fantasy and Science Fiction* in 1974. The tale is a textbook example of provocative and entertaining speculative fiction.

Equally useful is Charlotte Otten's *The Literary Werewolf: An Anthology,* (2002) which collects 22 pieces, although there are duplications between this and the Preiss anthology. The short story is a popular medium for werewolf tales. "Boobs" by Suzy Mckee Charnas, a humorous look at female lycanthropy in a modern setting, was originally published in

Isaac Asimov's Science Fiction Magazine in 1989 and found itself reprinted in *The New Hugo Winners, Volume III*. Interest in werewolves peaked in 2009 and 2010 with Hollywood's remake of *The Wolf Man* and the popular television series *True Blood* which featured werewolves and shapeshifters. The *True Blood* program was based on and inspired by a series of books by Charlaine Harris. The co-joining of vampires and werewolves in fiction and films is now commonplace.

Twilight (2005) by Stephanie Meyer, and its follow-up, *New Moon* (2006) incorporates shape shifters as part of her gothic storyline. A love story about a young girl, Bella Swan, and a vampire youth, Edward, she follows established vampire and lycanthropic plot lines when she finds herself in danger from opposing vampire forces. Meyer, an incredibly gifted writer, intentionally chose to write a vampire love story lacking in graphic violence and sex. The *Twilight* series of books were critically acclaimed and found an enthusiastic audience. Commencing with *New Moon*, the lycanthropic element was introduced for a supporting character.

L. A. Banks (a pen name for Leslie Esdaile Banks) began her "Crimson Moon" werewolf series with *Bad Blood* in 2008. This was followed by *Bite the Bullet* (2008), *Undead on Arrival* (2009), *Cursed to Death* (2009), *Never Cry Werewolf* (2010) and *Left for Undead* (2010.) This excellent series features Sasha Trudeau, the leader of an elite "military paranormal elimination squad" intent on saving humanity from supernatural forces.

S.A Swann's 2009 novel *Wolfbreed* is one of the better werewolf novels. Swann, a pseudonym for Steven Swiniarski, relies on strong characters and realistic historical background to tell his story. Swann set *Wolfbreed* in the Middle Ages and blends romance with traditional thrills, religious intrigue and fast-pacing. He followed *Wolfbreed* with *Wolf's Cross* in 2010.

The 2010 werewolf anthology, *Curse of the Full Moon* edited by James Lowder, features 19 werewolf tales. The writers included Peter S. Beagle, Charles de Lint, Joe Lansdale, Ursula K. Le Guinn, Michael Moorcock, Gene Wolf and Neil Gaiman among others. Matt Venne's story "The Brown Bomber and the Nazi Werewolves of the S.S." is an original and refreshing alternate take as is Darrell Schweitzer's "The Werewolf of Camelot." *Curse of the Full Moon* is memorable for these unique tales, all which proves that in the hands of a capable writer the canon of werewolf fiction will continue to thrill readers for generations to come.

With such a wealth of material relating to lycanthropes available, interested readers are encouraged to consult Brian J. Frost's *The Essential*

Guide to Werewolf Literature (2003), a superlative reference work and first comprehensive survey of the werewolf in literature.

The werewolf is far from dead. A new generation of writers is discovering the lycanthrope. Laurell K. Hamilton, Kim Harrison, L. A. Banks, and Sherrilyn Kenyon are among the top women writers who often include vampires and lycanthropes in their popular novels. Harry Shannon, R. L. Stine and others keep the werewolf alive for readers of all ages.

With such a rich tapestry of folklore and literature to draw from, it was only natural for Hollywood filmmakers to engage audiences with tales of the werewolf. As we shall see, the influence of popular films would have a permanent and lasting effect on the long suffering lycanthrope and his victims.

Lon Chaney, Jr. and The Wolf Man

In 1931 Universal Studios introduced the film versions of Bram Stoker's *Dracula* starring Bela Lugosi and Mary Shelley's *Frankenstein* starring Boris Karloff. Both films were overnight sensations and Lugosi and Karloff were rendered forever typecast as "horror actors." The year before these gentleman graced the screen as the vampire and monster, Hollywood had lost Lon Chaney, Sr. who had become suddenly ill and died from a throat hemorrhage. Chaney, the undisputed "Man of a Thousand Faces" was internationally acclaimed for his roles in *The Hunchback of Notre Dame* (1923) and *The Phantom of the Opera* (1925) among others. Who could replace him in the gruesome roles and fright films that audiences craved?

Initially, it was Lugosi and Karloff, and they reigned supreme in a series of chilling films throughout the 1930s. A decade after the success of *Dracula* and *Frankenstein,* Universal Studios ventured to tackle a new version of the lycanthrope legend. Their previous outing, 1935's *The Werewolf of London* starring Henry Hull, was an excellent film (see Chapter Five) and executives felt they could capitalize on the werewolf legend with a second, wholly original story.

But who would play the werewolf? Karloff? Lugosi? By 1941 Karloff had portrayed Frankenstein's monster in three critical and commercial successes but felt that he was now too old to don the heavy make-up. He didn't have much interest in another role that required grueling hours in the make-up chair. The role as a werewolf had been suggested to Karloff as early as 1933. In fact, the early treatments intended for Karloff later formed the basis for the Henry Hull film.

Curt Siodmak, newly arrived in Hollywood, landed the choice assignment of penning a new werewolf script. With Karloff showing no interest the question remained—who would play the werewolf?

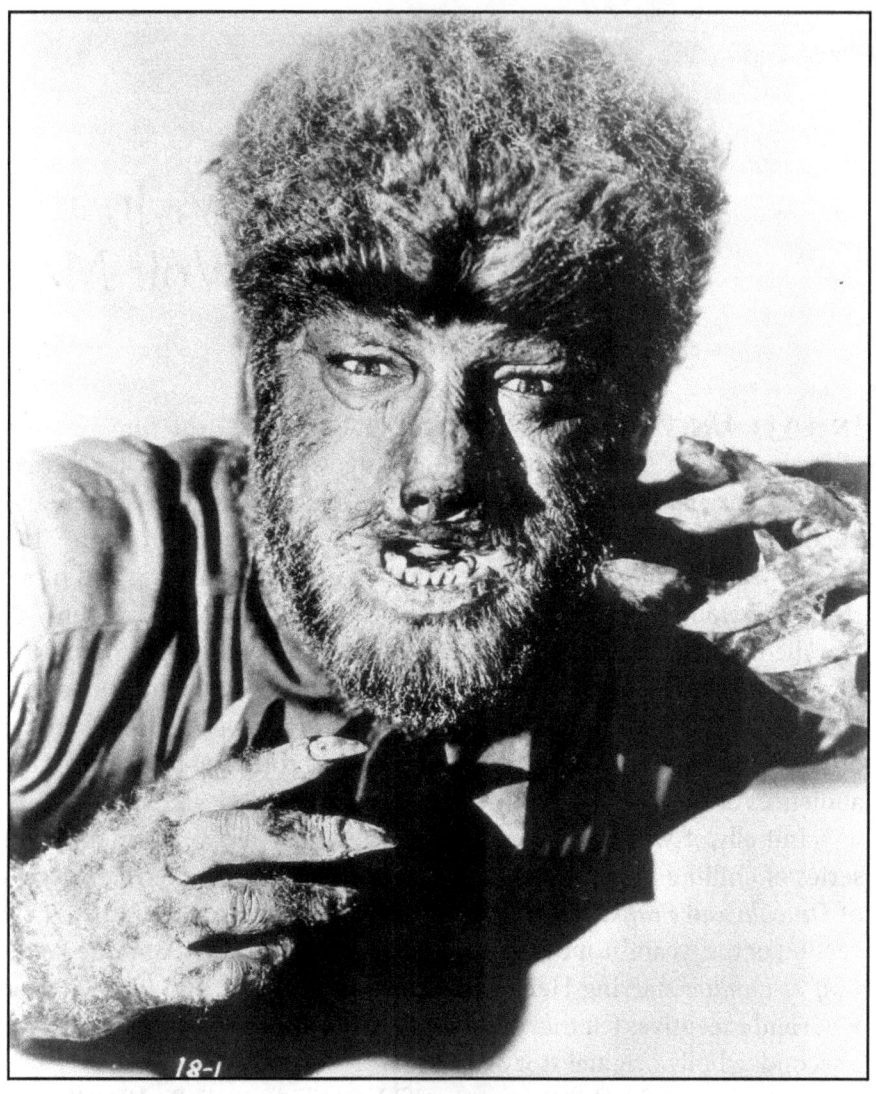

Lon Chaney, Jr. as The Wolf-Man, with make-up by Jack Pierce. Released in 1941 *The Wolf-Man* remains an iconic representation of the werewolf legend.

Lugosi was also disinterested. Henry Hull, who had deterred Jack Pierce, the make-up artist on *The Werewolf of London*, from entirely covering his face with yak hair, wasn't even a consideration.

Naturally, in retrospect it seems logical that Lon Chaney, Jr., should be cast as the werewolf. Born Creighton Tull Chaney on February 10, 1906 in Oklahoma City, Oklahoma, he was born prematurely at seven months and nearly perished. His mother, Cleva, had undergone a difficult pregnancy and after a difficult labor Creighton was born lifeless. His father Lon grabbed the infant, rushed outside, and submerged him in the icy waters of Belle Lake. The shock revived Creighton. These astonishing facts serve as the introduction to one of the most remarkable and talented actors to grace the silver screen.

His father Lon was a vaudevillian and Creighton made his debut at six months as a prop in one of his father's acts. Lon's relationship with his wife was strained and they divorced in 1914. Soon thereafter he married Hazel Hastings and Chaney began seeking working with the Los Angeles film studios. Times were difficult and money was scarce but Lon Chaney was a talented and capable man intent on caring for his family. Young Creighton would later recall sitting on a bench at the corner of Hollywood and Vine waiting for a trolley car with his father, and years later, after his father had become famous, Chaney would drive up to the same corner and offer a ride to an extras seeking work at the studio.

Creighton always spoke lovingly of his father and admired him. Sometime in 1916 Chaney sent Creighton to live with his deaf/mute grandparents and the experience is said to have instilled compassion and understanding for the handicapped in young Creighton. He attended Hollywood High School as his father was making history as an acclaimed actor in silent films. The elder Chaney had hopes that his son might take up a career far removed from the uncertain world of acting, but Creighton had an eye for the studios early on. But whatever acting ambitions Creighton harbored in his youth were delayed by his schooling and various summer jobs in a butcher shop or digging ditches and delivering ice. At over six feet tall, Creighton was a strong and imposing youth.

In 1930, at the height of his fame, Lon Chaney developed throat cancer and died from a hemorrhage. Creighton was 24, and within a year he was seeking work at the studios. When a casting director told him he ought to be in pictures, Creighton thought that sounded ideal. But it took several months—and several rebuffs—before he landed his first contract. But immediately RKO Pictures suggested he be billed as "Lon Chaney, Jr." to capitalize on his late father's name. Creighton refused.

He made his first screen appearance in RKO's *Bird of Paradise* (1932) directed by King Vidor. It was a small bit and numerous small parts followed. He had his first starring role in the Western serial *The Last Frontier* (1933). It was a difficult assignment for a rookie with so little experience, but Creighton was learning as he went.

Creighton Chaney made 58 films between 1932 and 1939 and starred with the top actors and actresses of the Golden 1930s: Joel McCrea, Fay Wray, Bruce Cabot, John Wayne, John Boles, Larry "Buster" Crabbe, Sylvia Sidney, Gene Autry, Brian Donlevy, Warner Baxter, Robert Taylor, Barbara Stanwyck, Tyrone Power, Don Ameche, Alice Fay, Ethel Merman, and Sidney Toler, among many others.

Perhaps relenting to the endless pressure or realizing the name change was a wise business decision, Creighton allowed himself to be billed as "Lon Chaney, Jr." with Republic's 1936 Gene Autry film, *The Singing Cowboy*. The name would stick although occasionally he would drop the "Jr."

In 1939, with his career stalling, Chaney auditioned for the stage version of John Steinbeck's *Of Mice and Men*. He won the role of Lennie, the dim-witted drifter on the lam with his pal George. The stage play was an immediate success and Chaney's performance was praised for its depth and sensitivity. He auditioned for the screen version and naturally landed the role. He co-starred with Burgess Meredith in the 1940 film version, proving to all that he was an actor of immense talent. Chaney's performance as Lennie remains one of the shining moments in his career and an indelible performance in screen history.

Chaney knew he had a winner. He said at the time: "As a matter of fact, I'd like to play heavies, if they're character parts or sympathetic. That's one of the reasons I was so happy to play Lennie on the screen. He's a heavy, but a sympathetic, understandable, human fellow, and I think, one of the grandest characters ever put on screen."[71]

His ability to elicit sympathy and make believable characters in a screen performance would turn out to be Chaney's defining quality as an actor.

By 1941 he'd left Republic Pictures for Universal studios and starred in *Man-Made Monster*, one of the best horror films of the period. Executives at Universal Studios recognized that the Chaney name had potential for box office gold because of the association with the elder Chaney's sterling performances in *London After Midnight*, *The Hunchback of Notre Dame* and *The Phantom of the Opera*. Karloff and Lugosi were still attracting audiences although Lugosi's star had waned somewhat in the decade since *Dracula* (Karloff would remain a staple player in horror films for the next twenty years). Chaney was an obvious choice for the increasingly popular horror film market.

The push for another success such as the one they'd experienced with *Dracula* and *Frankenstein* was very much on producer George Waggner's mind when he assigned the script duties to Curt Siodmak.

Born in Dresden, Germany in 1902, Siodmak was a highly intelligent writer who fled Germany for the United States in 1937 when Hitler increased his anti-Semitic propaganda. Siodmak was already established as a novelist and screenwriter in Europe and found the transition to English much easier than most. His uncanny intellect would serve him well in a long and productive career.

His 1942 novel, *Donovan's Brain*, remains a classic of science fiction. Other notable screenplays would include *Earth vs. the Flying Saucers*, *I Walked With a Zombie*, and *The Beast With Five Fingers*. But he's best remembered for his work on Universal's *The Wolf Man*.

Siodmak opted to ignore the existing scripts that had been tailored for Karloff and embarked on independent research. He read the existing texts on the werewolf legend and began drafting an original treatment. Siodmak envisioned a story that explored the timeless theme of good versus evil in a man's soul. For Siodmak, the lycanthrope was very much a Jekyll and Hyde character. But Siodmak also saw in the werewolf tale the elements of Greek tragedy. In the classic Greek plays it was the god's that would decide a man's fate from which he could not escape and Siodmak felt the same principal applied to the Wolf Man who was destined to transform and commit murder. He later wrote: "I had, by chance, constructed the film like a Greek tragedy, which seemed to have made that character a classic."[72]

Siodmak also included a short ryhme that would be spoken in the film by Maria Ouspenskaya:

> Even a man who is pure in heart
> And says his prayers by night
> May become a wolf when the wolfbane blooms
> And the autumn moon is bright.

The last line would be altered in subsequent sequels to read "when the moon is full and bright." So popular is this rhyme that today it is erroneously credited in various reference works as a folktale or an ancient gypsy rhyme when, in fact, Siodmak created the verse exclusively for *The Wolf Man*.

Rounding out this triumvirate of key players was Jack Pierce, the make-up artist who had transformed Henry Hull into a werewolf in *The Werewolf of London*. Pierce was born in Greece in 1889 and immigrated to the United States as a teenager. He began his film career as a stuntman and actor before focusing his talents on character make-up. His early, memorable success as the creator of Boris Karloff's make-up for the classic *Frankenstein* assured him a place in history.

Pierce originated a design for Frankenstein's monster that has become recognizable as the definitive interpretation of author Mary Shelley's creation. The scar across the forehead, and the famous neck bolts (electrodes which carried the electricity that revived the monster), and flat skull-cap are all elements synonymous with Frankenstein's monster thanks to Jack Pierce. Pierce also created Karloff's stunning make-up for *The Mummy* (1931).

His original concept for a werewolf for *The Werewolf of London* was rejected by actor Henry Hull because it covered too much of his features. With *The Wolf Man* Pierce was free to re-imagine his lycanthrope and the results would change film history, and the public perception of werewolves, forever.

Rounding out the cast were Claude Rains, Warren William, Ralph Bellamy, Patric Knowles, Bela Lugosi, Evelyn Ankers and Maria Ouspenskaya. Lugosi, of course, was best known for his portrayal of the vampire in

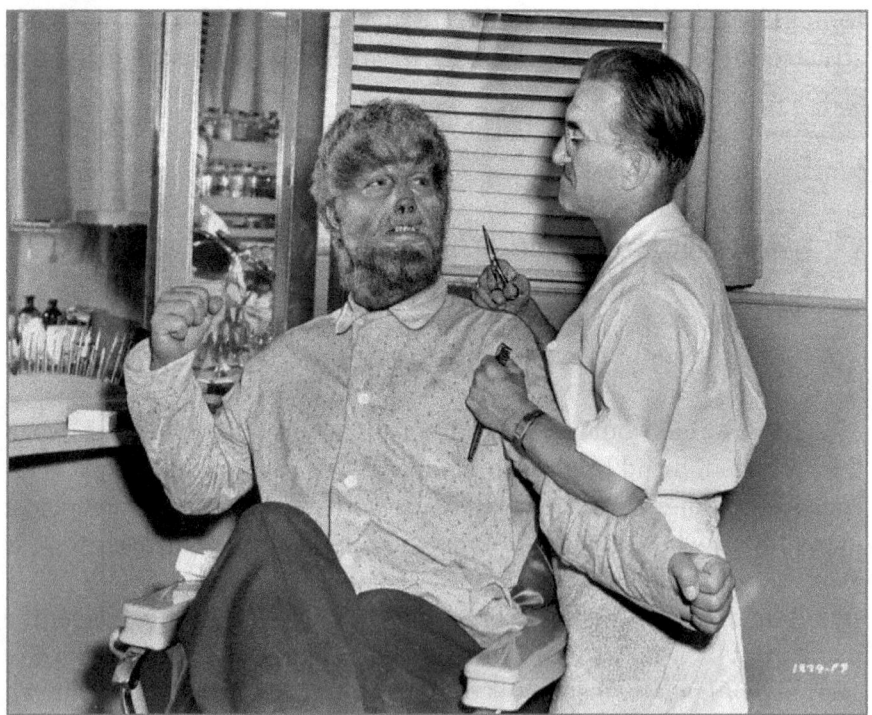

Lon Chaney, Jr. and Jack Pierce clowning around for a publicity photo.

Dracula. Born in Romania in 1882, he began his career on the European stage before transitioning to films. He immigrated to the United States and took various acting jobs, principally in stage productions. In 1927 he starred in the Broadway stage adaptation of Bram Stoker's *Dracula*, an acclaimed performance that led to his famous film role. Lugosi epitomized Dracula. He was fierce, suave, charming and ruthlessly calculating. His decline as an actor is generally attributed to his poor choice of roles after Dracula. He often took roles simply for a fast paycheck. He was so good at playing evil characters that most of the roles offered him were variations on his Dracula persona. However, some of these films are highly regarded today. Notable among them were *Murders in the Rue Morgue* (1932), *White Zombie* (1932), *Island of Lost Souls* (1932), and *The Black Cat* (1934). By the time he accepted the supporting role of "Bela" in The Wolf Man he longed for a role that would demonstrate his range.

Claude Rains was born in London in 1889, the son of stage actor Frederick Rains. He literally grew up on the English stage. He entered the New York theater community in 1913 with far more experience than many of those he would soon work with. He returned to England at the outbreak of World War I. After the war he remained in England and within a few years was recognized as one of the great stage actors of his time. He returned to New York in the late 1920s and within a few years had signed a contract with Universal Pictures. He played *The Invisible Man* (1933) where his rich baritone was used effectively to convey the madness that befell his character. By the late 1930s he was with Warner Brothers where he turned in some marvelously chilling roles opposite Errol Flynn in *The Prince and the Pauper* (1937) and *The Adventures of Robin Hood* (1938). Other great roles include *Anthony Adverse* (1936) and *Mr. Smith Goes to Washington* (1939). When he signed on to play Sir John Talbot in *The Wolf Man* he was widely viewed as the preeminent supporting actor in films.

Warren William was born in Minnesota in 1894 and took up acting after World War I. He established himself as a character actor adept at playing unscrupulous men in such films as *Skyscraper Souls* (1932), and *Employee's Entrance* (1933). In 1934 he played Julius Caesar apposite Claudette Colbert in director Ceil B. DeMille's classic *Cleopatra*. That same year he appeared as author Erle Stanley Gardner's quintessential attorney Perry Mason in *The Case of the Howling Dog*, a role he repeated the following year in *The Case of the Curious Bride*. He was working steadily as a supporting actor when he was cast in *The Wolf Man*.

Patric Knowles would outlive the entire cast and enjoy a remarkable career on stage and in films. Born in England in 1911 he fancied himself an actor at an early age and broke into films in the early 1930s. Tall, handsome and charming, he was a natural to play both leading roles and supporting parts. A few films in England led to a Hollywood contract and he was off to the United States. In 1936 he starred opposite Errol Flynn and Olivia de Havilland in the classic *The Charge of the Light Brigade* and his career galloped along at a brisk pace. Today he is well remembered as Will Scarlett (again opposite his friend Errol Flynn) in the 1938 classic *The Adventures of Robin Hood*. He became adept at supporting roles and while he never achieved the fame of Errol Flynn, he was well known by the public and highly regarded by his peers. He died in 1995.

Ralph Bellamy also enjoyed a long and fruitful career. Born in Chicago in 1904, his acting career began after he graduated from High School. He traveled the country with stock companies and performed in numerous of Shakespeare's plays. He made his Broadway debut in 1929 and began his long film career in 1931. His many character roles and stage roles earned him a Tony award, the Golden Globe award and an Oscar nomination. He was awarded an honorary Oscar statuette in 1987 for his outstanding contribution to the acting profession. His many notable screen roles included *The Awful Truth* (1937) opposite Irene Dunne and Cary Grant, *Dive Bomber* (1941) with Errol Flynn, the television mini-series *War and Remembrance* (1988) where he shined as President Roosevelt, and *Rosemary's Baby* (1968). Bellamy was also one of the founders of the Screen Actors Guild. He died in 1991.

Evelyn Ankers is among the first of filmland's "Scream Queens," an appellation that doesn't do her justice. But the label has stuck, perhaps because the Scream Queens have become a cottage industry in Hollywood. Frankly, Ankers was a better actress than most of the Scream Queens who have flourished for decades in low-budget horror films. She was born in Chile to English parents in 1918. She began her career in the English film industry before immigrating to the United States. At Universal studios she co-starred with Abbott and Costello in *Hold that Ghost* (1941) before being cast in *The Wolf Man*. She worked steadily in a variety of roles until her retirement in 1951. She died in 1985.

Maria Ouspenskaya was born in Russia in 1876. As a young woman she studied drama and singing in Moscow and became a participant in the Moscow Art Theatre. It was while a player with this group that she acme to America and worked on Broadway. After the Moscow Art Theatre's run

The Wolf-Man threatens Evelyn Ankers in the classic film. Sexual tension and bestiality became underling themes in Hollywood's take on the werewolf.

was completed she chose to remain in the United States and founded The School of Dramatic Art in New York. Her first Hollywood film was *Dodsworth* in 1936. Ouspenskaya was the more eccentric member of *The Wolf Man's* cast, but she her training and skill was the equal to that of the other cast members. She was small and weighed only about ninety pounds. She consulted with an astrologer almost daily and often refused to work unless her astrologer advised the time was appropriate for an on-camera performance. Still, she was brilliant and respected for her talent if not for her idiosyncrasies. She impressed critics, Hollywood producers and her fellow thespians with roles in *Love Affair* (1939), *Waterloo Bridge* (1940) and *The Mystery of Marie Roget* (1942) and a dozen other films. Ouspenskaya fell asleep while smoking a cigarette in November 1949 and suffered from third degree burns. She died three days later.

With the cast in place and a completed script by Siodmak, Universal secured cinematographer Joseph Valentine who had received an Academy Award® nomination for *Wings Over Honolulu* (1937). Valentine's photography, along with the production design by Robert Boyle would add the vital mood needed as the actors went through rehearsals and then filming.

Publicity still from *The Wolf-Man* signed by screenwriter Curt Siodmak (author's collection.) The Universal Studios series benefited from superb gothic sets and moody landscapes.

Director George Waggner and cast filmed *The Wolf Man* at Universal Studios from October 27 through November 25, 1941. The film was quickly edited and scored and premiered at New York's Rialto Theater on December 20, 1941.

Siodmak's original concept was to only show the fearsome face of the werewolf when he looked in a mirror and noticed his reflection in a pool of water. Siodmak later stated that George Waggner altered the storyline, and possibly for the better.

The film opens with a visual introduction of each actor, with their name and character's name in script on the screen's bottom as the music of Frank Skinner, Charles Previn and Hans Salter sets the tone. As the opening visuals end the camera pans across a fog shrouded moor, black trees twisted grotesquely, branches clawing at the fog. This moor, created on Universal's back-lot, was orchestrated by production designer Charles Boyle.

Under Boyle's supervision a forest was created on the backlot, but inside one of the larger buildings. Boyle and his crew took trees, stumps and branches from the vast area belonging to the studio, and painted all of the trees black. To give the forest its foreboding appearance they added a layer of glycerin that gave the trees a wet and shiny look.

The fog effect was created by a heavy chemical mist that clung to the ground. Because the forest was created inside, no wind would blow the mist away. This enabled the crew to shoot unhindered on the foggy moor.

As the film opens, Larry Talbot (Chaney) returns to his ancestral home at Talbot Castle, located in the Welsh village of Llanwelly. With a fresh American college diploma to his name, Larry is optimistic about his future.

Soon, while browsing through an antique store he meets a shopkeeper's daughter named Gwen Conliffe (Ankers). Talbot is immediately attracted to the blonde beauty and strikes up a conversation with her while examining a walking stick. The stick is capped by a silver wolf's head and a five pointed star, a pentagram. Gwen tells Larry that a werewolf is marked by the five pointed star because each lycanthrope will see that image in their next victim's hand.

It is here that Gwen recites the now famous "Even if a man is pure at heart..." poem that Siodmak had created specifically for his screenplay. Gwen informs Larry of the werewolf legends that still prevail in the area. In these early scenes Chaney demonstrates his personal charm and affable personality. As Talbot he is tall, beefy but handsome, charming, and good-natured. He would seldom have the opportunity to demonstrate these traits on screen, but when he did so he was superb. The smiling

Talbot would not be as well remembered as the moody, anguished victim of lycanthropy that Chaney was about to realize with his signature performance.

Larry purchases the cane and shows it to his father, Sir John Talbot (Rains). Larry tells his father of Gwen's superstitions but the elder Talbot refuses to dismiss the folktales. He warns his son that folktales often have a link to reality.

Later, Larry takes Gwen on date. Accompanying them is Gwen's girlfriend, Jenny. They walk to the nearby gypsy camp where Gwen is to have her fortune told. While Larry and Gwen are strolling through the camp Jenny enters the tent of Bela (Bela Lugosi, playing a character with his name), and looks at Jenny's hands and warns her to leave immediately. Bela had seen the five pointed star on Jenny's palm, a sign that she is soon to perish.

Frightened by Bela's nervousness, Jenny flees to the fog shrouded marsh. Unknown her to her, Larry and Gwen had strolled onto the marsh and stopped near a tree to talk. They hear a scream and Larry finds Jenny being mauled by a wolf. Using his silver-handled wolf's head cane, he beats the wolf to death but not before being bitten. He crumbles to the ground as Gwen races forward. The gypsy woman Maleva (Maria Ouspenskaya) helps Gwen take Larry home. They soon learn that Bela, the gypsy, had been bludgeoned to death and that Larry's wolf's head cane was found next to the body. Larry insists that he only saw a wolf and that he was bitten by it, but when he attempts to show Dr. Lloyd (Warren William) and Captain Paul Montford (Ralph Bellamy) his wound it's mysteriously healed.

The set-up of having Larry bitten by a werewolf is keeping within the traditional folktales. Audiences already knew that Larry Talbot was destined to become a werewolf himself. Although the plot offers no surprises, the superior production values, solid action, and tight script all served to elevate the suspense.

Dr. Lloyd and Captain Montford are immediately suspicious of Larry. It's here that the film's tone becomes darker. Chaney handles this transition expertly; his Talbot character is now a man conflicted with emotions. He becomes nervous, impatient, brooding. These are the traits that Chaney instills in Talbot with his body language, gestures, and expressions.

Disturbed by Jenny's death and Bela's unsolved murder, Larry ventures to the cemetery to observe Bela's coffin being interred in his crypt. Here he encounters Maleva speaking over her son's body. The dialogue, among the more well-known lines in horror films, is at once chilling and poetic: "The way you walked was thorny, through no fault of your own. But as the rain enters the soil, the river enters the sea, so tears run to a predestined end. Your suffering is over, Bela, my son, now you will find peace…"

Maleva departs, but overcome with emotion, Larry weeps over the coffin. Later, Larry confronts Maleva and she tells him that whoever is bitten by a werewolf is destined to become a wolf himself. Bela, she explains, was a werewolf. According to Maleva a werewolf can only be killed by a silver bullet, a silver knife, or a stick with a silver handle. Maleva gives Larry a pentagram necklace which claims can break the evil spell, but Larry refuses to believe the old gypsy's story. He departs and finds Gwen and offers her the necklace. Meanwhile, Maleva spreads the words among the gypsys that there's a werewolf in the vicinity and they break camp.

Confused and upset, Larry's mind is awash with images of Bela, the wolf, the pentagram, and Gwen. He returns to his room at Talbot Castle. Removing his shirt, he stares at himself in the mirror, relieved to see that he looks perfectly normal. In the screenplay, Siodmak had Talbot look upon the visage of the wolf, but instead they opted for a physical transformation. Talbot sits himself in a chair and looks at his feet which have transformed into hairy claws. Audiences don't see Talbot's face (and Pierce's makeup) until Larry flees the room and stalks through the fog shrouded moor. Here, we see the werewolf in profile until Larry approaches a tree in the foreground and turns to snarl into the camera.

Universal horror film collector and aficionado Steve Campbell points out the historical significance of Jack Pierce's make-up: "The Wolf Man had a different look for every film he was in. In the original 1941 film Jack Pierce used a make-up idea he was originally going to use in *The Werewolf of London*, but he didn't because Henry Hull did not want his face covered in make-up. So Pierce redesigned the make-up and shelved his first design. He felt *The Wolf Man* was the perfect film for his first creation. The make-up took a long time to apply to Lon Chaney, Jr., but I think the results were worth it. It was very convincing make-up."[73] Chaney's hirsute visage is now widely recognized as the preeminent werewolf characterization in film history.

The Wolf Man approaches a gravedigger and slays him, his unearthly howl awakening the nearby town. A search is conducted for the animal and the gravedigger's body is discovered. Captain Monford follows the wolf tracks to Talbot Castle but Larry has already reverted to his human form.

Larry involves himself in conversation with his father who expresses that lycanthropy is a form of schizophrenia. Larry has become a brooding tortured figure. His awareness of his actions, and his refusal to accept the truth, plague him. Years later Chaney spoke of Talbot's connection with sympathetic audiences: "All the best of the monsters played for sympathy. That goes for my father, Karloff, myself and all the others. They all won the audiences sympathy. The Wolf Man didn't want to do all those bad things. He was forced into them."[74]

Larry also questions Dr. Lloyd about lycanthropes. Dr. Lloyd believes a man can believe he's a wolf if he suffers from self-hypnotism, but privately Lloyd tells Sir John Talbot that Larry has suffered some type of psychic shock and that he believes he's seriously ill. With conflicting theories and suspicion of Larry growing throughout the town, wolf traps are set on the moor.

That night the Wolf Man once more stalks prey in the gloomy forest. With his leg caught in a wolf's trap, Talbot thrashes wildly in pain as hunters and their dogs close in. Falling unconscious, Larry is discovered by Maleva who helps Larry escape from the metal trap. Larry flees, once more in human form, and seeks out Gwen at the antique store. He confesses that he's a werewolf but Gwen doesn't believe him. When Larry sees the sign of the pentagram on Gwen's palm he realizes she's destined to become his next victim. Anguished, he returns to Talbot Castle and convinces his father to strap him a chair.

That night, with Larry locked in his room, the senior Talbot takes the silver wolf's head walking cane and joins police in their search for the wolf. A shooting platform has been constructed and Dr. Lloyd, Captain Monford, and Frank Andrews are all intent on killing the wolf. Desperate for news of Larry, Gwen enters the forest as the Wolf Man makes his final appearance.

Gwen is attacked by the Wolf Man but her screams bring John Talbot running to her aid. Swing the silver tipped cane he clubs the Wolf Man mercilessly, finally destroying the werewolf. As John looks down upon the dead creature Maleva approaches and speaks over the corpse and the werewolf slowly transforms into Larry Talbot. This scene is the first on-screen transformation of Talbot's face, seen in reverse from werewolf to man. Audiences would have to wait for the sequel to view the transformation from man to wolf. The film ends with Montford saying, "The wolf must have attacked her and Larry came to the rescue. I'm sorry Sir John." And John Talbot's face is a mask of grief as the credits roll.

The film's appeal has never waned since its release. Chaney would never quite escape the typecasting the role brought him, and reflecting on horror films in the late sixties he said: "The trouble with most of the monster pictures today is that they go after horror for horror's sake. There's no motivation for how the monsters behave. There's too much of that science fiction baloney."[75]

Certainly, Chaney's superb acting as the tortured Larry Talbot lends the film a depth that might otherwise have been lacking. The film was a box-office smash and left moviegoers eager for a sequel. Universal Pictures wasn't about to let them down.

Curt Siodmak was commissioned to write a sequel and he turned in a script titled "Wolfman Meets Frankenstein" in early 1942. Universal Studios had realized a profit with *Frankenstein* (1931) based upon the novel by Mary Shelly. Boris Karloff's performance as the monster remains a haunting and brilliant depiction of a tortured soul. This was followed by *The Bride of Frankenstein* (1935) which is now considered one of finest horror films. Karloff's reprisal was equally brilliant. The third installment, *Son of Frankenstein* (1939) teamed Karloff with Basil Rathbone and Bela Lugosi in a brilliant performance as Ygor, Doctor Frankenstein's demented assistant.

These three Frankenstein films, with Boris Karloff as the monster, helped create a culture of monster mania that persists to this day. Frankenstein's monster became the embodiment of evil. The creature looms large over a culture where the name "Frankenstein" is now synonymous with evil. No matter that the creature had no name; the monster himself became Frankenstein himself by default.

Naturally, Universal wanted to keep the series alive, but Karloff wasn't open to the long, grueling hours in Jack Pierce's make-up chair. A successor needed to be found, and quickly. Lugosi, who originally turned down the monster's role in the 1931 film because he wasn't interested in masking his features with make-up, was again briefly considered. But there was really only one actor that could effectively replace such a skilled thespian as Boris Karloff. So it was that Lon Chaney followed in Karloff's footsteps for *Ghost of Frankenstein*.

Released in 1942, *The Ghost of Frankenstein* was an instant smash. Chaney was re-teamed with his co-stars from the *Wolf Man*, Ralph Bellamy and Evelyn Ankers. Bela Lugosi reprised the pivotal role of Igor, Doctor Frankenstein's demented assistant from *The Son of Frankenstein*.

At the conclusion of *Son of Frankenstein* the monster is destroyed when he's pushed into a boiling sulphur pit. Screenwriter W. Scott Darling, working from a story by Eric Taylor, continued the storyline and revived the monster. But by now the creature was half blind and seriously injured; his movements slow and cumbersome. Karloff had introduced these traits in *Son Frankenstein* and Chaney's responsibility was to play the creature with less animation than Karloff. The result was an ominous depiction. Chaney perfected the creature's slow gait, and with his arms outstretched he created the image of Frankenstein's monster that persists to this day. Chaney's performance is underrated. *The Ghost of Frankenstein* benefits from his brooding interpretation of a psychotic creature. A chilling scene featuring the monster chained to a chair becomes all the more frightening when the camera locks onto Chaney's brooding countenance. Chaney's monster is just as frightening as Karloff's and certainly equally as murderous.

The Ghost of Frankenstein solidified Chaney's reputation and paved the way for another sequel. But with Chaney reprising his role as Larry Talbot the producers needed yet another actor to play Frankenstein's monster. Initially, Universal opted to have Chaney play both roles. That fact was reported by *Variety* on October 14, 1942 and Universal intended on using doubles and stunt men to complete the illusion. But at the last minute cooler minds prevailed and the role was offered to Bela Lugosi.

Much has been made of Bela Lugosi's casting as the tortured creature, Ygor, with many biographers claiming he took the part because he was finding it difficult to land roles. This is true: in fact, in 1942 Lugosi wasn't being offered the best scripts. He took the role because he recognized the popularity of Universal's monster films would only add to his reputation and hopefully lead to better roles. And he needed the money.

The ongoing success of the four Frankenstein films was enough to convince Universal Studios executives that a fifth installment would also prove financially successful. Curt Siodmak's screenplay pitting two monsters against each other was given the green light for production. It was only logical that Chaney would reprise his role as Larry Talbot, but yet another replacement for the role of Frankenstein's monster may have been problematic. Bela Lugosi's name was enough to send shivers down an audience's spine because of his reputation from Dracula twelve years earlier. With quality roles difficult to find he was no longer averse to donning Jack Pierce's monster make-up. Universal executives felt that the marquee names of Lon Chaney, Jr. and Bela Lugosi would ensure a profit.

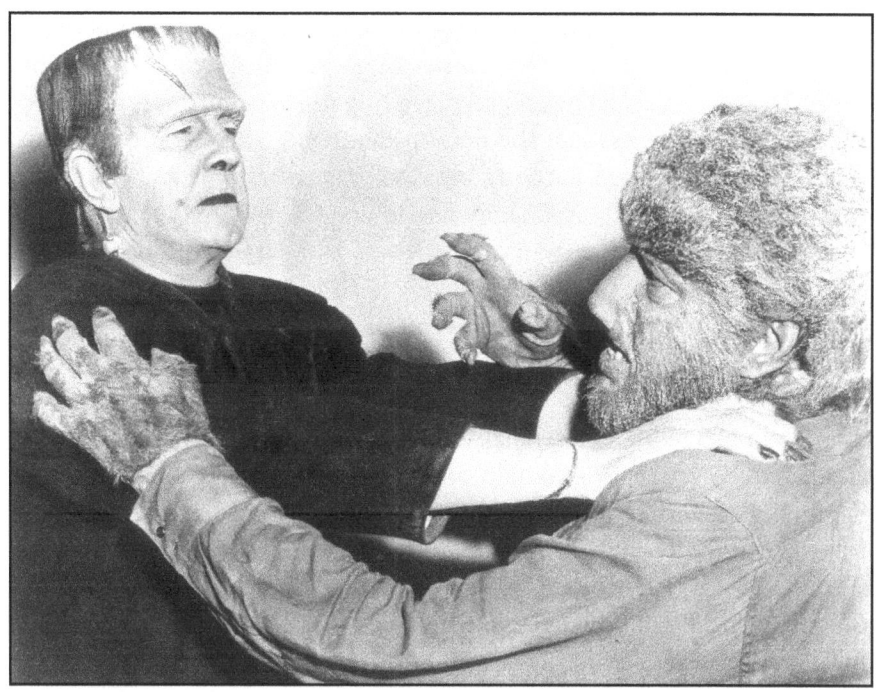

Frankenstein Meets the Wolf-Man (1943) featured Bela Lugosi as the monster with Lon Chaney, Jr. reprising his role as Larry Talbot, the tortured lycanthrope.

Universal Studios had become the horror film capital. With *Dracula, Frankenstein, The Bride of Frankenstein, Son of Frankenstein* and *Ghost of Frankenstein* proving lucrative in re-releases, Universal was now primed for *Frankenstein Meets the Wolf Man,* the fifth in the Frankenstein series and a direct sequel to *The Wolf Man.* This landmark film would be the first teaming of monsters onscreen and would set a much emulated trend that persists all these decades later.

Screenwriter Curt Siodmak had jokingly said to producer George Waggoner over dinner one evening "Why don't we make a picture Frankenstein Wolfs the Meat Man—I mean, Frankenstein Meets the Wolf Man."[76] Waggoner wasn't amused but sometime later he told Siodmak that *Frankenstein Meets the Wolf Man* was his next assignment. Siodmak created the plot device of freezing the Frankenstein monster in ice thus enabling him to be revived by Larry Talbot. The ice would explain how the monster survived his alleged death at the conclusion of *The Ghost of Frankenstein.* Siodmak recognized that such plot devices need not be entirely logical. They only needed to work at a minimal level given the audiences willingness to suspend their disbelief in the first place.

The Frankenstein films all follow a continuity, albeit sometimes rather loosely. In *The Ghost of Frankenstein* Ygor's brain is transplanted into the monster's skull. As Lugosi had played Ygor it was only natural that he should play the monster in the next installment. With the monster now freed from the ice and partially blinded, Lugosi was instructed to portray the monster stiffly, as Chaney had in *The Ghost of Frankenstein*. This continuity involving the monster's physical ailments would be misinterpreted by critics years later who had failed to follow the continuity. Both Chaney's and Lugosi's characterization makes sense, but Lugosi would suffer the most at the hands of critics who dismissed his performance as mere caricature.

Siodmak's revised screenplay (still titled *Wolfman Meets Frankenstein*) and dated March 31, 1942, would commence production in October 1942. Siodmak had written a fascinating story. Awakened in his tomb by grave robbers, Lawrence Talbot once again finds himself free to roam the fog-shrouded fields. After being injured he awakes in Queens Hospital under the care of Dr. Frank Mannering (Patric Knowles). Talbot insists that he's a murderer but Dr. Mannering is convinced Talbot is suffering only from a mental trauma. Seeking a cure for his lycanthropy, Talbot escapes from the hospital and reunites with the old gypsy Maleva, once again played by Maria Ouspenskya. Maleva believes that Talbot might be cured by Dr. Frankenstein and the two of them journey far by wagon until they reach Vasaria where Frankenstein had made his home. Here they learn that Dr. Frankenstein had perished with his monster some years earlier and an anguished Talbot transforms into a werewolf that very night as the full moon breaks free of the clouds. Soon, the body of a young woman is found with her jugular slashed and the villagers take to the woods searching for the wolf they believe is responsible. Talbot, still in werewolf form, is pursued into the mountains and takes refuge in the ruins of Frankenstein's castle. Crashing through the rotting floorboards he plunges into an ice cavern beneath the castle. When he awakens much later, Talbot, again in human form, explores his surroundings and discovers a block of ice containing a human figure. Chipping away at the ice he discovers it's Frankenstein's monster, still alive in a state of suspended animation. Talbot frees the monster from the ice and asks the creature to lead him to Frankenstein's medical journals. Talbot believes the secret to his cure might lie in Frankenstein's notes. A search of the ruins fails to uncover the journals but Talbot finds a photograph of Baroness Elsa Frankenstein (Ilona Massey). Seeing that the inscription reads, "To my dear father-," Talbot muses "She's the one that can tell me!" Intent on learning Dr. Frankenstein's secrets of life and death, Talbot arranges a meeting with Elsa pretending to be a prospective buyer of the crumbling ruins. Upon meeting Elsa, Talbot readily admits that he wants Dr. Frankenstein's records on creating the monster but Elsa claims she doesn't have the papers. That night, during Vasaria's "Festival of the New Wine" Talbot becomes enraged by a singer's reference to eternal life. At this point Dr. Mannering emerges from the crowd and confronts Talbot. Mannering wants Talbot committed to an asylum and believes he suffers from bouts of insanity which lead him to murder. Talbot confides in Mannering and reveals that he only wants to die. He explains that Dr. Frankenstein's diary might hold the secret that could permanently end his life, and with it the werewolf's curse. Shortly, the monster emerges, arms outstretched, and the crowd panics. Horrified by the change of events, Talbot escapes with the monster on a wagon. Later, accompanying Dr. Mannering and Maleva to the castle ruins, Elsa offers to reveal her father's diary to Talbot in a bid to end the madness. At the castle they confront the monster and Dr. Mannering can't but help to examine the creature. When Elsa reveal the hidden location of her father's diary both Talbot and Dr. Mannering find themselves fascinated by the wealth of secret knowledge. While Mannering is focused on Frankenstein's secrets of life over death, Talbot still wants only knowledge that will destroy him and end the werewolf's curse. They decide their best course of action is to restore Frankenstein's equipment and the townspeople immediately become suspicious. With the machinery operation, Mannering decides to use the equipment to "draw off the monster's energy." With Talbot and the monster strapped to gurneys, Mannering quickly discovers that he can't destroy Frankenstein's monster. Mannering intentionally infuses the monster with electricity which restores him to nearly full strength. Panicked, Elsa attempts to thwart the experiment and throws a switch which causes an electrical discharge. The laboratory is enveloped in smoke as the outraged villagers approach the castle. Talbot, still strapped to a gurney, transforms into the Wolf Man as the monster pursues a frightened Elsa. The Wolf Man and the monster engage in a furious battle as the villagers blow up the nearby dam. As the two monsters fight Elsa and Mannering escape but Frankenstein's castle and the two monsters are swept away by an onslaught of water and crumbling brick.

This at least was the version that audiences flocked to in 1943. Siodmak's script offered a talking monster which was consistent with previous films. Executives at Universal viewed the completed footage and decided that a monster speaking with a Hungarian accent was too much to bear.

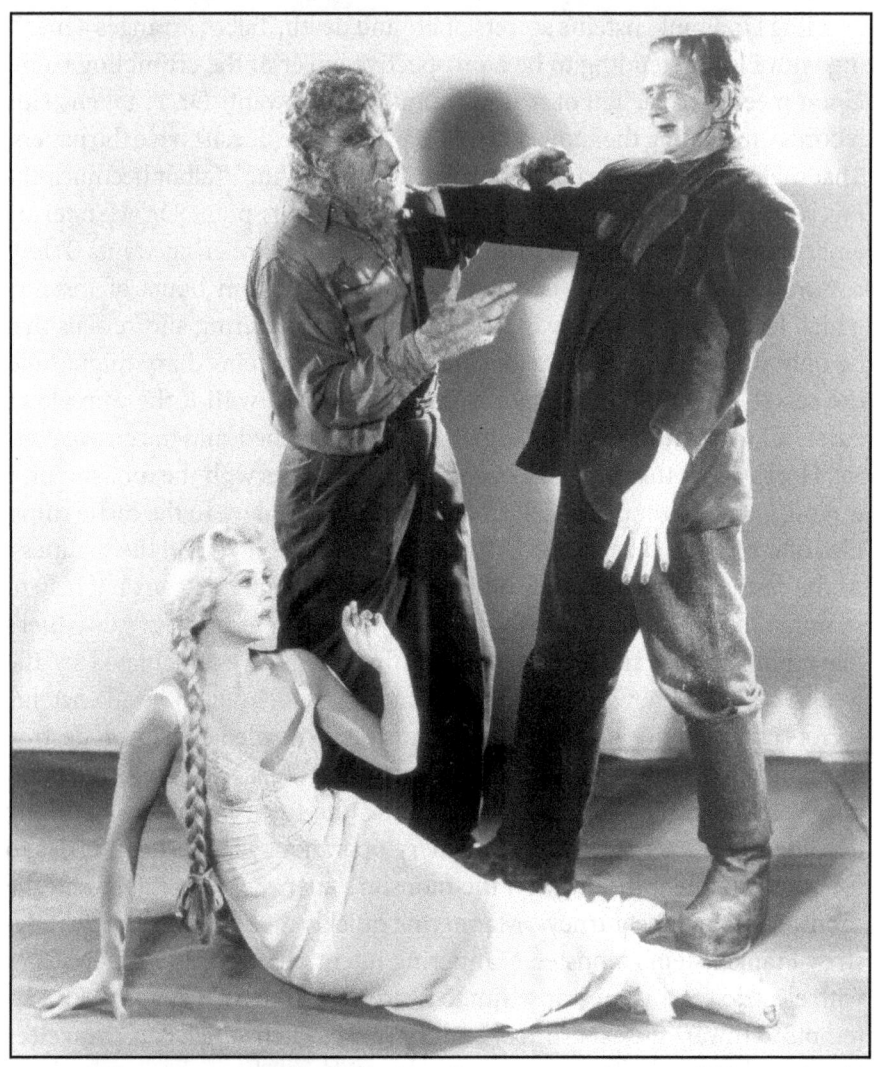

Lon Chaney, Jr. and Bela Lugosi ham it up over a seductive Ilona Massey in this publicity still from *Frankenstein Meets the Wolf-Man*.

Lugosi's dialogue was all cut. Although the film was still successful and now commands a cult following, film fans and scholars have long wondered if the editing was premature. Over the years searches for the lost footage have failed to uncover Lugosi's lost scenes.

A study of Siodmak's shooting script published by MagicaImage Books, compiled and edited by Philip Riley, suggest the film may indeed have worked with Lugosi's dialogue intact. Siodmak wrote an excellent script and Lugosi was, after all, a professional. His brilliant characterization of Ygor in *Son of Frankenstein* and *The Ghost of Frankenstein* should silence those misinformed critics who have long disparaged his talent.

Lugosi's first major scene occurs on page 60 of a 127 page script. His dialogue is terse: "Once I had the strength of a hundred men…It's gone…I'm sick." The shorter dialogue appears to work well even with a Hungarian accent. Undoubtedly the longer passages were problematic for Universal executives fearing audiences would howl with laughter. And sections of Siodmak's dialogue for the monster were hyperbolic: "Dr. Frankenstein created this body to be immortal! His son gave me a new brain. I shall use it for the benefit of the miserable people who inhabit the world, cheating each other, killing each other, without a thought but their own petty gains. I will rule the world! I will live to witness the fruits of my wisdom for all eternity!"[77]

There are echoes of Mary Shelley's modern Prometheus here and a continuity linkage with the previous Frankenstein films, but an articulate monster with a Hungarian accent would soon find itself on the cutting room floor.

Although Bela Lugosi's dialogue was cut *Frankenstein Meets the Wolf-Man* was an effective and popular sequel and offered Lon Chaney some of his best scenes as the tormented Larry Talbot.

Remarkably, the film still works but with the editing it really becomes a Wolf Man picture. Frankenstein's monster has become a minor supporting character. Lugosi's stiff-armed monster, like Chaney's before him, would become a template for imitators. Still, the film is appropriately gloomy and the sets were dark, fog-shrouded, wet with autumn mist, cold as a graveyard. Chaney is superb as the long suffering Larry Talbot. Siodmak, writing in his autobiography years later, remembered Chaney as a man similar to the character he portrayed: "Lon played the part of Larry Talbot with a sincerity that gave the film a value of fear and pity… He *was* Larry Talbot in *Frankenstein Meets the Wolf Man*, who wanted to die. In that picture Lon played himself, which made his part frighteningly believable."[78]

The final battle in the laboratory with Frankenstein's monster was unlike anything seen in films at the time. It offered a memorable visual of two horrific characters pitted against each other as a castle crumbles around them. The Wolf Man snarls and bares his fangs and leaps across machinery as a snarling monster, now restored to full strength, flings machinery about as if it were paper. Lugosi was doubled in some long shots by a stuntman named Eddie Parker. The aging actor was simply unable to endure the long hours in a heavy costume and under such strenuous conditions.

Ilona Massey added a touch of beauty and class as the lovely Elsa Frankenstein, Patric Knowles proved himself yet again a capable leading man and Lionel Atwill as the Burgomaster (mayor) rounds out a cast of stalwart professionals.

Jack Pierce's make-up was an improvement over the previous film. As Universal film collector Steve Campbell noted: "The make-up was close to the original but not exactly the same. But this worked because it explained that Larry Talbot (even though he came back from the dead) was getting older and so was the Wolf Man."[79]

Frankenstein Meets the Wolf Man premiered on March 5, 1943. The publicity blurbs got right to the point: FIEND OF FURY VS. THE NIGHT BORN KILLER! *The Titans of Terror Unleashed…In the Shock Battle of the Century!* The film was an instant smash hit. Audiences, having endured three long years of a war that still had no end in sight, responded with enthusiasm to the splendid moody visuals and solid acting in *Frankenstein Meets the Wolf Man*. British and American forces had hounded Major-General Erwin Rommel across North Africa. Fierce fighting in the Pacific had sent the Japanese reeling, but the war was far from over. *Frankenstein*

Meets the Wolf Man offered date-night chills that could easily be shrugged off, and so the film was equally popular with adults as with children.

The next film in the series, *House of Frankenstein,* would make its debut on December 15, 1944, a full 21 months after *Frankenstein Meets the Wolf Man.* It was not a particularly pleasant time. The war was in its fourth year. On the day that *House of Frankenstein* premiered U.S. forces landed on Mindoro to begin building airfields. The following day the Battle of the Bulge began. Moscow's Red Army was advancing on Budapest. Within days the U.S. 101st Airborne Division would be under siege at Bastogne. The UK civilian casualties for December 1944 would reach 367 killed and over 800 wounded as Britain's Bernard Montgomery fought in the Ardennes. Here was "horror" in its primal form, and it was far more devastating than anything Hollywood could dream up. Like so many films of the period, Universal's famed monster movies were a diversion from harsh reality of a world consumed by madness.

House of Frankenstein starred Boris Karloff who had recently returned to Los Angeles after a successful year on a Broadway stage in *Arsenic and Old Lace* which he followed with a successful two month national tour. Karloff was immensely popular and his name was instantly recognized as a brand name for thrillers and horror films. Universal executives wanted Karloff to help them resurrect Frankenstein's monster yet again.

Curt Siodmak was given the assignment to write a story that reunited the monster and the Wolf Man while including Dracula and the Mummy (which were also profitable horror films starring Lon Chaney, Jr.). Siodmak knew that his assignment was unenviable. At the conclusion of *Frankenstein Meets the Wolf Man* he had drowned both creatures in a watery grave beneath the rubble of Frankenstein's castle. Creating a plausible way to re-unite the creatures, while including additional monsters, was problematic. Universal publicity staff let it leak to the press that a massive horror film was in the works titled *Chamber of Horrors* and would feature the monster, the Wolf Man, the Mummy, and the Invisible Man. Siodmak's task was daunting indeed.

Siodmak developed the concept that screenwriter Edward T. Lowe would use to great effect. He created a traveling "Chamber of Horrors" led by a mad doctor named Gustav Niemann. The Mummy, the Mad Ghoul and the Invisible Man were dropped and the story then focused on Dracula, the Wolf Man and the monster. A hunchbacked character was created to add a further tone of creepiness. Lon Chaney was quickly cast again as Larry Talbot. Karloff refused to don the heavy monster make-up again and so the role of the mad doctor was created to showcase his malevolent persona.

The task of playing the monster now fell to a character actor named Glenn Strange. As the story goes, Strange had reported to Jack Pierce's make-up studio on the Universal lot to receive a facial scar for a bit in a film. Strange, at 44 years old, was a former boxer, rodeo performer and regular character actor. At six feet, four inches tall Strange was an imposing man. Pierce, impressed by Strange's bulk and features, excused himself and called producer Paul Malvern to inform him that he had found the next Frankenstein monster. Originally titled *The Devil's Brood*, shooting commenced on April 4, 1944. The shooting script published by MagicImage Books in 1991 is titled *Destiny* but the name was permanently changed to *House of Frankenstein* before filming was completed.

Bela Lugosi wanted to play Dracula again but indifference by studio executives in addition to their lingering unhappiness by the scenes cut from *Frankenstein Meets the Wolf Man* was enough to dissuade any such casting discussion. The coveted role went instead to a highly respected character actor named John Carradine. Born in New York in 1906, Carradine began his long career in silent films and became a protégé, friend and ultimately drinking companion of John Barrymore. His famous stage roles included Shakespeare's Hamlet. Carradine was enamored of Shakespeare and was known to recite soliloquies and dialogue from the various plays at the drop of a hat. His off-screen activities included membership in the now infamous group "The Olympiads" which included Barrymore, Errol Flynn, W.C. Fields, the artist John Decker, writers Gene Fowler and Sadakichi Hartmann, actors Thomas Mitchell, Roland Young and Anthony Quinn. The exploits of the Olympiads remains legendary, and no less than Errol Flynn would recall late in his life carousing with Barrymore and Carradine in the late 30s and early 40s: "He (Barrymore), John Carradine and I used to go three or four days without sleeping. We'd start out in some bistro at noon, and a week later find ourselves in Mexico or on a yacht off Catalina with a dozen empty bottles on the floor and a gaggle of whores puking their guts up all over the place. That's how we'd go, drinking ourselves to a standstill."[80]

Lon Chaney was also no stranger to the hard drinking Flynn and his companions. While much as been made of their drinking habits the truth is all of these men were dedicated professionals who worked hard to turn in a believable performance. Carradine would create a Dracula that remains unique in film history. Thin, and with wildly expressive eyes along with a stentorian voice, Carradine's Dracula would embody a sophistication and malevolent intelligence that would not be seen again until Christopher Lee tackled the role in the late 1950s.

Anne Gwynne and Peter Coe were cast as Rita and Carl Hussman, J. Carrol Naish as the hunchback Daniel, and Elena Verdugo as the gypsy girl Ilonka. Both Gwynne, Coe and Verdugo had been working steadily in films for several years. It is Verdugo, however, who would be best remembered from *House of Frankenstein* as Larry Talbot's love interest. Born in 1925, Verdugo made her screen debut in 1931 in *Cavalier of the West*. A decade later she began working in films earnestly. Her gypsy Ilonka would remain her best-remembered screen character until she took the role of Consuelo Lopez opposite Robert Young in the late 60s television series *Marcus Welby, M.D.*

By the time he was cast in *House of Frankenstein* J. Carrol Naish was well known to film audiences as a stalwart character actor. Born in New York in 1896, Naish had over seven years of stage experience in Paris and New York before appearing in his first film. Naish was the perfect choice to play the tormented hunchback. His performance remains one of the many highlights from this extraordinary film.

House of Frankenstein pushed the series in a new direction and set the standard for the all-star horror shows that followed.

With Lionel Atwill and George Zucco added in character roles, shooting commenced in April and was completed by May 6 — and history was again about to be made by Universal Studios. The completed film is a gem. Edward T. Lowe's literate script came to life under Erle C. Kenton's stalwart direction. Universal's top-notch production, now a hallmark for horror films, adds the requisite gloom. Karloff and Chaney are superb, as one would expect. Karloff, here playing the mad Dr. Gustav Niemann, has a field day playing the seemingly articulate doctor whose madness simmers just below the surface of his distinguished façade. Chaney, in his third outing as Larry Talbot, is tortured and angst ridden, but his scenes with Elena Verdugo demonstrate a softness to his character that he wasn't always able to convey in other roles. John Carradine's Dracula would prove popular as well, and his take on the sepulchral vampire is both aristocratic and chilling. Dracula, Frankenstein's monster, The Wolf Man, a hunchback and a mad doctor cavorted across the screen in what was billed as "The Greatest Shock Show the World Has Ever Seen!" It wasn't exactly, but for a little less than sixty minutes, it was ok to pretend that it was.

The plot unfolds with Dr, Gustav Niemann escaping from prison with his hunchbacked assistant and soon thereafter killing professor Bruno Lampini. Niemann takes Lampini's identity and control of his "chamber of horrors." Lampini's carnival attraction includes the skeleton of Count Dracula. Accidentally reviving the vampire, Niemann takes advantage of the situation and makes a pact with Dracula. At Niemann's behest Dracula kills the Burgomaster and Dracula, fixated upon the beautiful Rita Hussman, escapes by coach only to have Niemann betray him. With his coffin flung from a wagon, Dracula scrambles for its sanctuary as the sun rises and turns him again into a skeleton. This extended sequence showcases first Karloff and then Carradine. Rita Hussman (Anne Gwynne), upon seeing Dracula's ring, utters the chilling line: "When I look at it I see glimpses of a strange world—a world of people who are dead, and yet alive." In fact, the script gives all of the players wonderfully sepulchral lines, made all the more eerie by Hans Salter's brooding score.

After Dracula's demise Niemann continues on his journey, intent now on uncovering Dr. Frankenstein's records. Arriving in the town of (appropriately named) Frankenstein, the hunchback Daniel is smitten by the beautiful gypsy Ilonka. The town of Frankenstein is an anomaly in the continuity. In *Frankenstein Meets the Wolf Man* the monster and the Wolf Man were swept away by the flood after the dam broke, but the castle was situated on the outskirts of Visaria. Here the castle ru-

Lon Chaney, Jr. and Elena Verdugo in *House of Frankenstein* (1944).

ins are now within view of Frankenstein. The local constabulary asks Niemann to leave as his traveling chamber of horrors isn't welcome in Frankenstein. Reluctantly, they leave the village but not before Daniel convinces Niemann to bring along Ilonka who was injured in an argument with another gypsy. Daniel tells Ilonka they are traveling to Visaria, but that night Niemann and Daniel search the ruins for Dr. Frankenstein's records. Having discovered that the force of the dam's explosion had washed everything into a glacier ice cavern beneath the castle, they locate the frozen bodies of the Wolf Man and the monster. Hoping the two creatures might lead them to Frankenstein's records, Niemann thaws them from their icy tomb.

Larry Talbot's awakening from the death he had so eagerly sought is once again met by anger. "Why have you freed me from the ice that imprisoned a beast that lived within me!" he asks Niemann. Convincing Talbot that he can lift the lycanthropes curse forever, Talbot helps Niemann locate Dr. Frankenstein's journal. Later, with the ailing monster also revived, Talbot laments: "He wanted life and strength; I wanted only death."

Traveling to Visaria where Niemann's laboratory is still intact, Talbot and Niemann work to restore his equipment. Meanwhile, Niemann exacts a vendetta against those that had imprisoned him and the anguished Talbot transforms into a werewolf that very night. The next day a villager is discovered butchered in the woods and fears immediately mount that a werewolf is loose. Later that morning Talbot tells Ilonka that he can only die if he's killed by a silver bullet fired by the hand of one who loves him. Dutifully, Ilonka prepares the cartridges.

That night Talbot transforms into the Wolf Man again and struggles with Ilonka who manages to shoot him with a silver bullet. Fatally injured, Ilonka crawls toward the dying Talbot who has transformed back into a human and she dies clutching his body. Infuriated by her death, the hunchback Daniel blames Niemann and attempts to strangle him. Meanwhile, the enraged townspeople descend upon the laboratory as Frankenstein's monster awakens. The monster kills Daniel by tossing him through a window. Niemann, injured but alive, is lifted by the monster and they make their way outside where they are cornered by the townspeople who set the marsh grass on fire and drive them into a bog where they sink in quicksand. The film's final image of Frankenstein's monster and Dr. Niemann sinking into the black depths of quicksand brought to a close an implausible plot.

Chaney's brief scenes as the Wolf Man and Glenn Strange's scenes as the monster simply aren't fully realized. In fact, the film comes across as a series of vignettes that might have worked better as a longer film. All the same, *House of Frankenstein* is an entertaining film. Today *House of Frankenstein* is highly regarded due to its appropriately gloomy mood, superb make-up, excellent musical score and stylish acting by the principals.

House of Dracula would appear precisely one year later and the albeit loose continuity that had strung so many of the films together was abandoned. *House of Dracula* would premier on December 21, 1945. The war

Lon Chaney, Jr. as the quintessential werewolf in *House of Dracula* (1945).

had been over a few scant months and troops were only beginning the slow process of returning home. The film turned out to be something other than originally envisioned. Intending to capitalize on the success of *Frankenstein Meets the Wolf Man*, a script was commissioned titled "The Wolf Man versus Dracula" and the intention was to cast Bela Lugosi and Lon Chaney. Although the script by Bernard Schubert was quite good, the film was never made. The 2010 publication by Bear Manor Media of the final draft shows great promise. But Lugosi was out of favor with executives and the success of *House of Frankenstein* led to *House of Dracula*.

Again, the title "Destiny" was resurrected, perhaps as a joke, and Edward T. Lowe wrote several versions of the screenplay that would become *House of Dracula*. Budget cuts and contract negotiations bogged down the production. By the summer production was given a green light and Chaney was hired to play Larry Talbot for the fourth time. Glenn Strange was an easy choice to play the monster and John Carradine would reprise his role as Count Dracula. For this film the hunchback would be a female and the role went to Jane Adams, a former model. Her grace and beauty would add the right touch to a story that would give Chaney some fine moments as a leading man. The role of the mad scientist went to Onslow Stevens, a respected alumnus of the Pasadena Playhouse. His film roles since the 30s were well received and executives deemed him the perfect substitute for the ever-popular Karloff who was unavailable due to prior commitments. Stevens had worked alongside John Barrymore in *Counsellor at Law* (1933) and the serial *The Vanishing Shadow* (1934) among many other titles. He brought the same dedication to his craft as Chaney and Carradine.

Lionel Atwill would make his fifth appearance in a Frankenstein film, having previously appeared in *Son of Frankenstein, The Ghost of Frankenstein, Frankenstein Meets the Wolf Man* and *House of Frankenstein*. Jack Pierce would once again prepare his famous make-up for the monster and the Wolf Man. Shooting commenced in September, 1945 and wrapped by late October. Such a quick turn-around is virtually unheard of in Hollywood today. Chaney's scenes as the werewolf were limited and in fact, Jack Pierce had only a modest supply of the yak hair needed to create the Wolf Man's grisly countenance. Yak hair had been imported from Central Asia but was scare during the war.

House of Dracula would become Universal's final serious film featuring Frankenstein's monster, the Wolf Man and Dracula, and the result was a mildly entertaining film. Arriving at the seaside home of Dr. Franz Edelmann in Visaria, Dracula introduces himself as Baron Latos and requests Edelmann's assistance in curing his vampirism. Intrigued, Edelmann accepts the challenge on behalf of medical science. With Nina, his devoted hunchbacked nurse and the nurse Miliza (Martha O'Driscoll), Edelmann begins the research that he hopes will solve the curse of vampirism. Edelmann discovers that Dracula's blood contains a "peculiar parasite" and he schedules a series of transfusions of an anti-toxin. During the first treatment Larry Talbot, now sporting a dashing pencil-thin mustache, arrives at Edelmann's laboratory seeking a cure for his lycanthropy. There is no

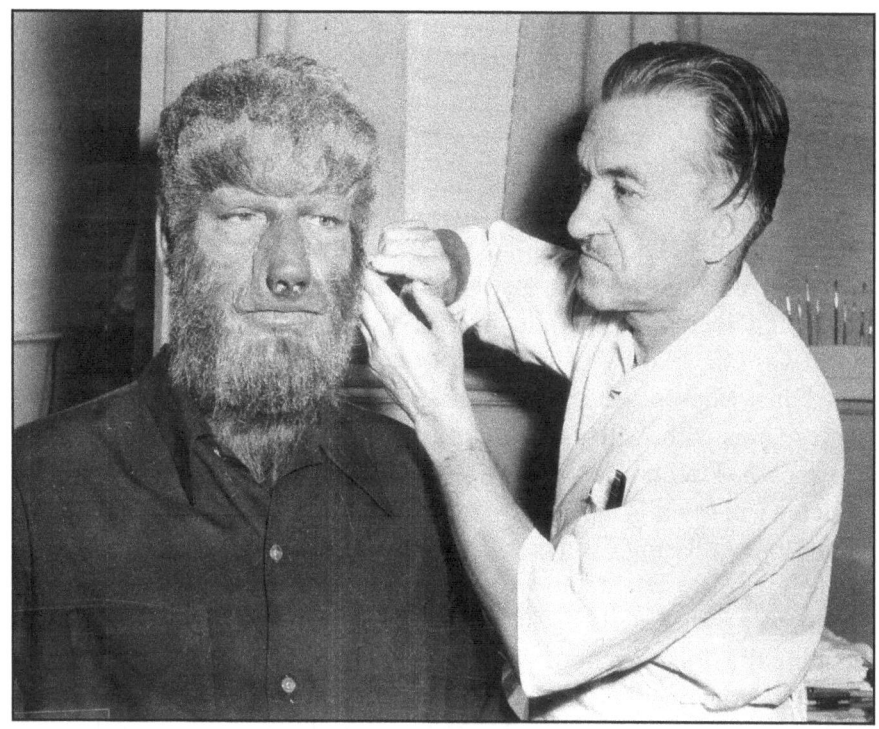

Legendary makeup artist Jack Pierce prepares Lon Chaney, Jr. for his role as the Wolf-Man in *House of Dracula*.

explanation as to how Talbot survived the silver bullet that killed him in the previous film, just as there is no explanation as to how Dracula survived his exposure to the sun.

Immediately *House of Dracula* became an anomaly, connected to the other films only by the characters. It exists in its own fog-shrouded world; an eerie place of dark passages, moody landscapes, and dank passageways. This is the creepy mood that will carry the film.

Later, Edelmann meets with Talbot who has been locked up in jail where he explains his desire to be cured of lycanthropy. Talbot transforms into the Wolf Man before Edelmann and the doctor then takes it upon himself to cure Talbot as well as Dracula. Edelmann strikes upon a laborious process that might cure Talbot but Talbot cannot wait any longer. Distraught, he attempts suicide by flinging himself from a cliff and into the sea.

Believing that Talbot may have been swept into the shoreline caves, Edelmann conducts a search where he locates Talbot as well as Frankenstein's monster lying dormant in the mud. Across the monster's body is the skeleton of Dr. Niemann. This connection to the previous film offers the slimmest plot continuity. Edelmann, having heard the story, recounts how the monster had been driven onto the swamp with Dr. Niemann where they were presumed to have perished in the quicksand. "Frankenstein's creation is man's challenge to the laws of life and death." Edelmann says. Taking the monster to his laboratory, Edelmann seeks to revive the creature against Talbot's protest. After Nina also protests he halts his experiment, and agrees that the monster should not be brought back to full strength. Dracula, meanwhile, works his charm on Miliza who becomes restless as Dracula's influence becomes apparent.

Nina, who doesn't know that Baron Latos is Dracula, discovers observes Latos with Miliza and notices that he doesn't cast a reflection in the mirror. Edelmann confides that Latos is Dracula. Concerned that Dracula will cause Miliza harm, Edelmann performs another transfusion with Dracula. Using his hypnotic powers, Dracula reverses the transfusion and infuses Edelmann with vampire blood. A short time later Edelmann destroys Dracula by sliding his coffin into a patch of sunlight and opening the lid. Once more Dracula is turned into a skeleton.

But with Dracula's blood in his veins Edelmann goes insane. Although he operates on Talbot, he murders a villager and is chased back to his cliffside mansion. With the villagers outraged, suspicion falls on Talbot. Now cured of his lycanthropy, Talbot attempts to stop Edelmann from reviving Frankenstein's monster. Enraged, Edelmann kills Nina and Talbot shoots Edelmann with a Luger he pulls off the body of a constable that had come after Edelmann. Talbot knocks over a shelving unit of toxic chemicals and the laboratory goes up in flames with the monster trapped inside as Talbot escapes with Miliza. Stock footage from *Ghost of Frankenstein* of the monster trapped in a burning building was used for the final scene.

House of Dracula is ponderous at times, but Chaney as the tormented Larry Talbot is a highlight. Glenn Strange's monster is given little attention and the film is really a showcase for Carradine, Chaney and Stevens.

During the 1940s Chaney was immensely popular and he worked steadily in a variety of roles. In addition to portraying the Wolf Man he also played the Mummy in three films: *The Mummy's Tomb* (1942), *The Mummy's Ghost* (1944), and *The Mummy's Curse* (1944). The Mummy make-up was also created by Jack Pierce and Chaney solidified both his reputation and popularity as a feature actor in horror films. His 1943 vampire film, *Son of Dracula*, made Chaney the only actor to play all of Universal's famous monsters.

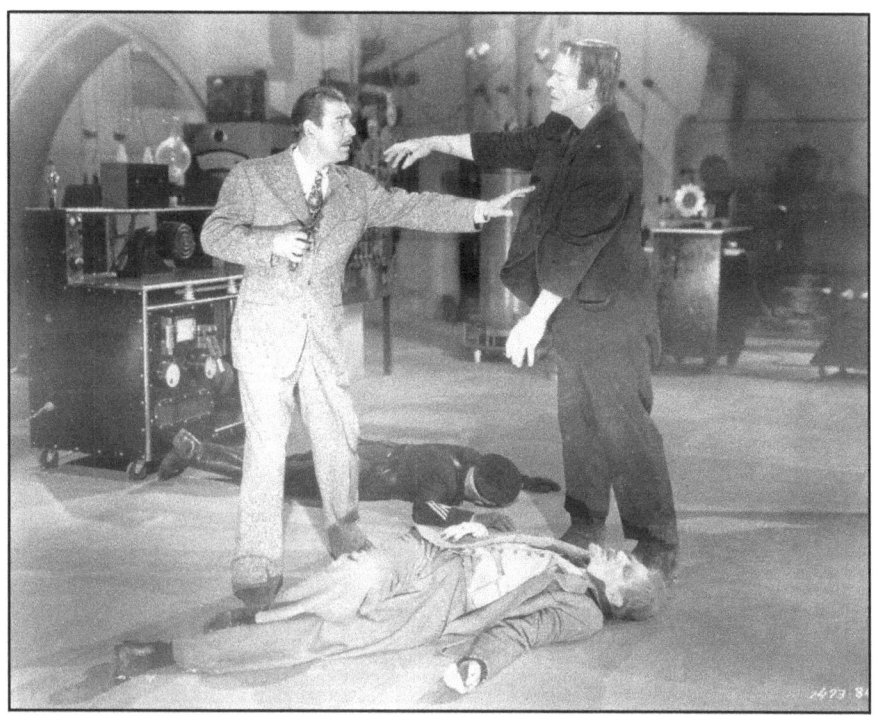

Lon Chaney, Jr. played a mustached Larry Talbot in *House of Dracula*, seen here facing off against Glenn Strange as Frankenstein's monster.

House of Dracula would mark the final time that Jack Pierce would create the Wolf Man make-up. He parted ways with Universal Studios in 1947 and free-lanced in the film industry for many years. He died in 1968.

After *House of Dracula* Chaney took on a supporting role opposite Bob Hope in *My Favorite Brunette* (1947) and *Albuquerque* (1948) starring Randolph Scott. He may have longed for more roles as a leading man, but he demonstrated a willingness to work in supporting roles.

Universal Studios underwent a change in management and in 1947 the studio was now Universal-International. There was dissention in the executive offices as to how best handle the comedy duo of Bud Abbott and Lou Costello. The pair was still popular but production chief William Goetz apparently found them decidedly unfunny. All the same, in January a script was commissioned titled "The Brain of Frankenstein" with Bud and Lou slated to meet the studio's money-making monster. Numerous script revisions occurred but the film went into production and began filming in February. With Karloff again refusing to don the heavy monster make-up,

Lobby card for *Abbott and Costello Meet Frankenstein* (1948).

and also feeling that a comedy film demeaned the character that he had helped create all those years ago, Universal quickly signed Glenn Strange to play Mary Shelley's brainchild.

Lon Chaney, Jr. was the only logical choice to play the Wolf Man, and Chaney was happy to take the role for a fifth time. Chaney loved the character and often referred to the Wolf Man as "my baby." The story opens with Bud and Lou working in a baggage room for an express service in Florida. Receiving a call from Larry Talbot they are warned not to deliver any crates to Mr. McDougal as they contain the bodies of Count Dracula and Frankenstein's monster. McDougal had acquired the bodies for display in his House of Horrors but before he can retrieve them Lou unwittingly frees the slumbering monsters. The film then resorts to a series of mishaps, chases, and contrived coincidences where they become pawns in Dracula's scheme to bring the monster back to his full strength by giving him a new brain.

Abbott and Costello Meet Frankenstein breaks from the continuity established in the previous films and exists as an anomaly, albeit a charming one. With Jack Pierce no longer working at the studio the make-up chores fell to Bud Westmore who recreated the Pirece's lycanthrope make-up for Chaney. Using Pierce's design Westmore created a foam rubber and latex werewolf visage that only took an hour to apply to Chaney. With his assistants Jack Kevan and Emile LaVigne he also recreated the monster's make-up for Glenn Strange but with notable modifications. He forehead scar became a prominent wound, the hair was longer and the monster's bolts were raised on the neck. These changes accentuated the gruesomeness of Frankenstein's monster and this image has become the definitive publicity shot for Universal. For Lugosi's Dracula they powdered his face and applied lipstick which gave the actor a deathly pallor even though the film was shot in black and white.

Abbott and Costello Meet Frankenstein has many fine points. Chaney's final stint as Larry Talbot is typically poignant and angst-ridden. The Westmore make-up was easier for him to handle and offers a visual requiem *né homage* to the classic Jack Pierce visage. Glenn Strange's monster gets more screen time with credit finally coming to Strange for his

Lon Chaney's final stint as Larry Talbot was a combination of humor and horror in the classic *Abbott and Costello Meet Frankenstein*.

interpretation of the role made famous by Boris Karloff. And the dialogue was memorable:

> Larry Talbot: You don't understand. Every night when the moon is full I turn into a wolf.
> Wilbur: You and twenty thousand other guys.

This was Lugosi's second film appearance as Dracula. Prior to filming he had toured in the stage adaptation of *Dracula* to critical acclaim but he still found it difficult to land quality film roles. He made but six films after *Abbott and Costello Meet Frankenstein* and only *The Black Sleep* (1956) opposite Karloff has merit. In fact, *Bela Lugosi Meets a Brooklyn Gorilla* (1952), *Glen or Glenda* (1953), *Bride of the Monster* (1955) and *Plan 9 from Outer Space* (1958) are considered among the worst films ever made. It was a sad end for one of cinema's charming rogues.

Abbott and Costello Meet Frankenstein would revitalize Abbott and Costello's career leading to *Abbott and Costello Meet the Killer* (1949, with Boris Karloff), *Abbott and Costello Meet the Invisible Man* (1951), *Abbott*

Universal's horrific trio—Frankenstein's monster (Glenn Strange), Count Dracula (Bela Lugosi) and The Wolf-Man (Lon Chaney, Jr.) seen here in a publicity still for *Abbott and Costello Meet Frankenstein*.

and Costello Meet Dr. Jekyll and Mr. Hyde (1953 and again with Karloff), and *Abbott and Costello Meet the Mummy* (1955). But sadly nothing they did after *Abbott and Costello Meet Frankenstein* had the same wit and charm.

For Lon Chaney, Jr., however, his career would continue with both highs and lows. He had created for himself a respected career as a character actor, and although he still longed to play leading men, he prospered in westerns, thrillers, mysteries and horror films. Chaney tackled every type of role imaginable. He played Red Lynch in *Captain China* (1950), Trooper Kebussayan in *Only the Valiant* (1951), Borka Barbarossa in *Flame of Araby* (1951), and an acclaimed bit as the townsman Martin Howe opposite Gary Cooper in *High Noon* (1952). These and other roles solidified his reputation as a solid character player.

Throughout the 1960s Chaney worked steadily although by now the solid character roles were less appealing. There would be one final film stint as a werewolf, a strange film shot in Mexico in 1960 and titled *La Casa del terror*. The film is poorly conceived with a nearly incomprehensible plot. Chaney, as a mummy, is extricated from a tomb and taken to a lab where a scientist works to revive the dead. Unable to resurrect the

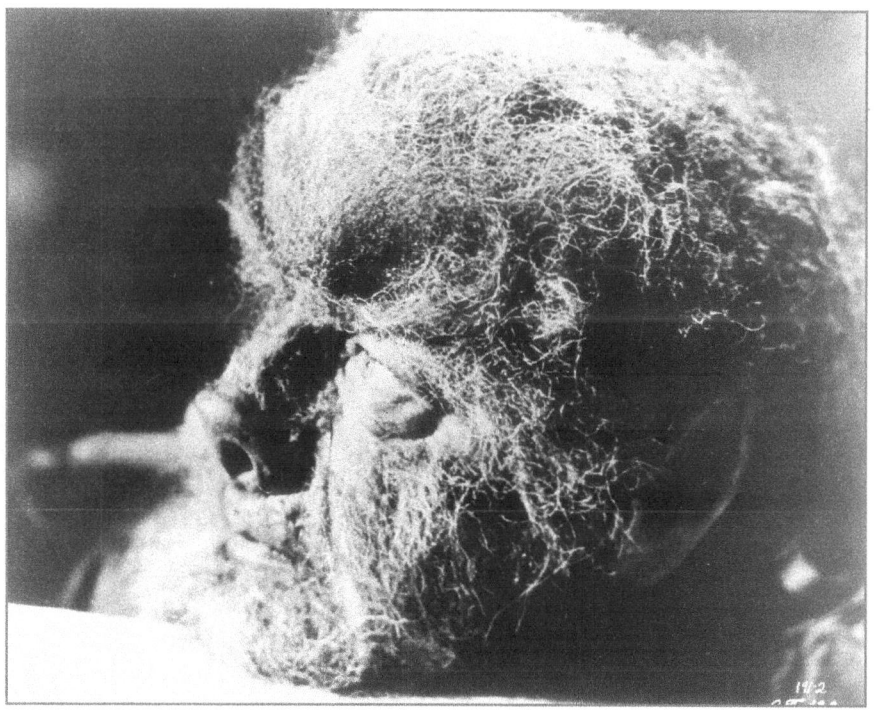

Rare publicity still of Lon Chaney, Jr. as the werewolf in the Mexican feature *Face of the Screaming Werewolf* (1964).

mummy, they are astonished as the full moon turns the mummy into a werewolf who escapes to terrorize the city.

La Casa del terror was edited in the United States and re-released in 1964 under the title *Face of the Screaming Werewolf* which is the title it's best known by today. *La Casa del terror* remains available only in Spanish and is difficult to obtain. The revised version, *Face of the Screaming Werewolf*, is available on DVD. Chaney's make-up as the werewolf echoes the Pierce creation but the film is hardly worth viewing.

Chaney also appeared in dozens of television shows and on one memorable occasion he reprised his Wolf Man role in a cameo appearance. The October 26, 1962 episode of *Route 66* titled "Wizard's Leg and Owlet's Wing" would feature Chaney alongside Boris Karloff and Peter Lorre. *Route 66* starred Martin Milner as Tod Stiles and George Maharis as Buz Murdock. The premise was to have the two characters travel America via Route 66 in a Corvette and engage in miscellaneous adventures. The show was a popular hit and the appearance of Chaney, Karloff and Lorre was intended to render "Wizard's Leg and Owlet's Wing" a special Halloween episode.

Three actors play themselves meeting in a Chicago hotel to discuss the old make-up they once donned for their famous roles. Naturally, the make-up is recreated although it's a far cry from the classic Pierce make-

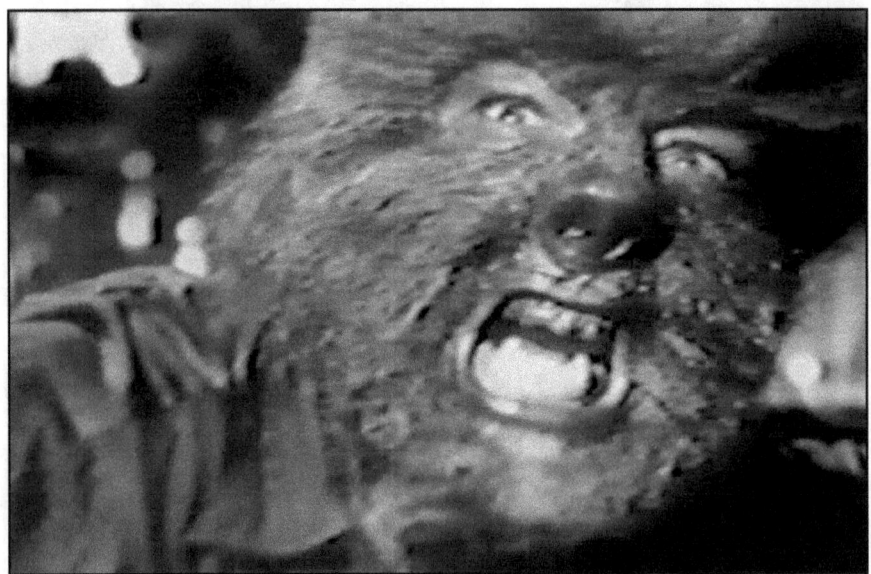

Digital frame enlargement of Lon Chaney, Jr. in *Face of the Screaming Werewolf* (1964).

The October 26th 1962 episode of *Route 66* titled "Wizard's Leg and Owlet's Wing" would feature Lon Chaney, Jr. alongside Boris Karloff made up as Frankenstein's monster, Peter Lorre, Martin Milner and George Maharis. This was Chaney's last appearance in werewolf makeup.

up. Seen today the episode has a nostalgic charm, but of course *Route 66* itself (both the television program and the legendary stretch of highway) have also become objects of nostalgia.

By the late 1960s Chaney had become something of a cult figure among horror film fans but solid roles were lacking. In 1967 he took a role in the lamentable *Hillbillies in a Haunted House*. In 1969 he took roles in *The Female Bunch, Stranger in Town* and *Fireball Jungle*, but all were imminently forgettable. He is last role was in the exploitation film *Dracula Vs. Frankenstein*, a farce without the slightest redeeming value save for his appearance and that of *Famous Monsters of Filmland* editor Forrest J. Ackerman.

In fact, Ackerman was something of a cult figure by that time as well and in a 1999 interview he recalled an evening spent with Chaney: "I sat across from Lon Chaney, Jr., at a banquet with the Count Dracula Society, and I regret to say that he drank his banquet (laughs). Then he got up and said, "Well, I don't know what I can do for you folks. I can growl or would you like me to do Lennie?" Of course he almost got an Academy Award® for his role as Lennie in *Of Mice and Men*. So he ended up doing Lennie that night. And I've got to tell you, within about sixty seconds there was hardly a dry eye in the group. There was a little lump in our throats because he really demonstrated what an excellent actor he could be, but he rarely had the opportunity to display his full talent."[81]

By the time of his death in 1973, Lon Chaney, Jr., had appeared in over two hundred films or television episodes. His signature role will always be that of the tortured Larry Talbot, endlessly seeking salvation from the lycanthrope's horrible curse.

1941's *The Wolf Man* remains the iconic werewolf story, image and performance. In the decades to follow there would be numerous efforts to replicate the film's charm, angst, moody sets and bravura acting, and while some films were quite good, none have come close the Larry Talbot's riveting tale. The creative triumvirate of Curt Siodmak, Jack Pierce and Lon Chaney, Jr. had combined to tell the greatest werewolf story of all.

Paul Naschy and the Werewolf

JACINTO MOLINA WAS BORN IN MADRID, Spain in 1934. Among his earliest memories were of the bombings during the Spanish Civil War. After the war his family settled in Burgos and it was here, while taking walks along the *Paseo del Espolón*, that Molina encountered something that he would later say became a constant fixture in his life—the gothic. In his autobiography Molina wrote: "For me gothic came to be synonymous with ancient mysteries, cryptic messages, witchcraft, obscure necromancers, living gargoyles and enigmatic searching for the Philosopher's Stone."[82]

While Spanish history and culture would have a profound influence on the young Molina, he was also soon being influenced by American culture. As a young man he was exposed to the comic strips of Alex Raymond and Milton Caniff but his literary influences would also include the works of Jules Verne, Mark Twain, Robert Louis Stevenson, the Spanish poet Espronceda and the writer Gustavo Adolfo Bécquer. In short, Molina acquired a multicultural background long before such things became fashionable.

In 1945 his uncle gave him a book of paintings by Jose Gutierréz Solana and a short time later Molina met the famed painter in person. Solana's paintings were often grotesque and depicted garroting, beggars, a bloody Christ figure, and other images that appeared to Molina to come from a museum of horrors. He was fascinated by these images. Solana was imposing and the impressionable Molina would later take inspiration from these influences when he began writing screenplays and acting in the Spanish film industry.

Spain was a politically turbulent country in the aftermath of the Civil War and following World War II Molina experienced several traumatic episodes that would also leave lasting memories. He witnessed a bicycle accident where a friend of his was killed instantaneously when he crashed his bike into a tree; and he encountered the corpses of murdered government guards. But it was during this period in the late 1940s that Molina also watched an imported American film titled *Frankenstein Meets the Wolf Man*. The film was part of a double bill playing in Madrid and Molina instantly became a fan of the Universal monster series. So enchanted was Molina that when his mother asked him what he wanted to be when he grew up he replied much to her astonishment "A werewolf!" Molina began sketching images he recalled from the film and decades later he reproduced his first sketch of Frankenstein's monster and the Wolf Man in his autobiography. His exposure to the American film industry would have a lasting, positive effect on him. He soon became enamored with *Captain Blood*, *Dodge City* and *They Died with Their Boots On* starring Errol Flynn, *Ivanhoe* starring Robert Taylor, and *Winchester '73* and *Broken Arrow* starring James Stewart. His favorite actors as villains were Jack Palance, Richard Widmark and Dan Duryea.

By now, Molina had become acquainted with the paintings of Romero de Torres who often painted nudes in weird settings and surrounded by severed heads or reclining in gloomy places. In the Spanish art world Torres was often dismissed as a "kitsch" painter and Molina thought this was unfair. As his films were later sometimes also dismissed as kitsch products, Molina felt that the kitsch sensitivities of camp and popular images offered both an intellectual and entertaining value of their own. Kitsch, by definition, is something deemed to be in poor taste, but later Molina would remain focused on using those gothic elements he so enjoyed to tell a compelling story.

Molina became a lifelong fan of comic book artists as well and listed drawing and painting as his greatest hobbies. By 1951 he knew that he wanted to become a film director. The visual possibilities of film along with a good story were intriguing to him. With a talent for art and an extensive exposure to Spanish and American literature, Molina was poised for a fascinating career by the mid-1950s. In later years he would cite three American films as having a profound influence—*The Third Man*, *Gilda* and *Duel in the Sun*. All the same, Molina was preparing himself for a career as a surveyor which appeared far more reasonable than a job in the Spanish film industry. This idea was quickly altered to include coursework in architecture. Molina had yet to find his place but as he went through his youthful experiences he was aided by his keen intellect, compassion for humanity, and undying creative impetus.

Molina witnessed numerous tragedies and heartbreaks during his formative years. His romance with a beautiful girl named Mariuca when her obsessive father accidentally killed her brother before killing himself. Mariuca moved away and Molina kept in contact with her by telephone but eventually they drifted apart. He last saw her on a roadside in 1962, the year Marilyn Monroe died, and Molina drove past without stopping. He claimed that he always regretted not stopping to speak with her again.

Molina's reading habits now included Bram Stoker, Edgar Allen Poe, and H. P. Lovecraft. He was indulging himself more and more into the gothic world of tragedy and horror. He enlisted in the army and learned boxing and involved himself in other sports. He was a natural athlete, strong and robust. He became a devotee of weight lifting, a sporting activity that would remain a fixture in his life. He was a Spanish national weightlifting champion and record holder. Molina would retire from professional weightlifting in 1971 holding the title "Supreme Champion of Castille."

By the early 1960s his artistic talents were put to use illustrating the record covers for the Spanish release of songs by Elvis Presley and Bill Haley. He also illustrated the record cover for Frankie Lane's song from *High Noon* in addition to recordings of classical music stars.

In 1960 Molina worked as an extra in the American film *King of Kings* starring Jeffrey Hunter and again as an extra in the Spanish film *El principe encadenado*. But he longed to perform at a higher level than as an extra for American films being shot on location. But tragedy intervened again when his girlfriend at the time, Conchita, was killed in an automobile accident.

By the mid 1960s Molina began taking bit parts in films. He had a role in an Italian western, *La furía de Johnny kid*, and in February 1966 he landed a small role in the American television program *I Spy* starring Robert Culp and Bill Cosby. This landmark program was noted for its location filming, strong scripts and charisma of the stars. Best of all, Molina met Boris Karloff who was co-starring in the episode ("Mainly on the Plains"). Meeting Karloff was a positive experience for Molina who found the aging actor to be a truly kind-hearted gentleman.

In 1967 Molina wrote a screenplay titled *La marca del hombre-lobo* (*Mark of the Wolfman*) but is known today to English speaking audiences as *Frankenstein's Bloody Terror*. The screenplay was an homage to the classic monster films that had starred Lon Chaney, Jr., Bela Lugosi and Boris Karloff. Using his connections in the Spanish film industry Molina began

Paul Naschy introduced the world to the werewolf Waldemar Daninsky in *Frankenstein's Bloody Terror* (1968).

to solicit backing and soon found a production company that was interested in financing the film. The film would be co-funded by a Spanish company and a German company. Molina's script was bold for its time and Spanish film censors objected to the strong erotic elements, violence and the fact that the werewolf was a Spaniard. To appease the censors Molina altered the script, toned down the eroticism and violence, and created a character named Waldemar Daninsky, a Polish nobleman, who became a werewolf. Molina would play Daninsky himself.

The resulting film would usher in what is known today as the golden age of Spanish horror films. *Frankenstein's Bloody Terror* was filmed in both 3D and 70 mm. Immediately, the foreign distributors objected to the name Jacinto Molina stating that it didn't have marquee value. This was actually due to racism among the foreign distributors who felt that a Spanish leading man would hurt ticket sales. Molina created the alias Paul Naschy and thereby unknowingly added to his historic and long-lasting contribution to the film industry. Thus the Paul Naschy-Waldemar Daninsky legend was born.

The film was a box office success and several years later the American release, sometimes double-billed with Lon Chaney, Jr.'s *Dracula vs. Frankenstein,* introduced Paul Naschy and Waldemar Daninsky to a new generation of horror fans. *Frankenstein's Bloody Terror* is a misleading title. Allegedly, the American distribution company wanted "Frankenstein" in the title because of its box-office appeal. No such character appears in the film and the werewolf is billed as a "Wolfstein" in the animated and narrated prelude. As would be the case with all of Naschy's imported horror films, heavy editing would appease American censors but this editing invariably affected the film's narrative. All the same, even with sloppy editing the best of Naschy's films are worth seeing in their English language editions.

Frankenstein's Bloody Terror would ultimately achieve cult status among aficionados of Spanish horror movies but it is far from the best of Naschy's films. Its historic value to both the history of lycanthropes and to the Spanish film industry is far more important than the film's storyline. But as a first effort it's not bad. Waldemar Daninsky, investigating a series of strange events near "Wolfstein Castle," eventually encounters the beast after it becomes revived by two traveling gypsy lovers. After a brief fight, Daninsky is bitten and the Wolfstein creature is killed. Thus inflicted, Daninsky becomes a ferocious werewolf. Seeking the assistance of friends, Daninsky seeks a cure for his lycanthropic affliction. The film establishes several motifs that Naschy would return to in subsequent films: the werewolf in chains, creepy dungeons, beautiful women (one of whom will personify pure evil), and vampires and the resurrection of the dead.

Molina's immersion into his alter-ego of Paul Naschy would begin quickly but not without struggle. Immediately after completing *Frankenstein's Bloody Terror* he wrote the screenplay for *Las noches del hombre lobo* (*Nights of the Werewolf*) and filming was completed in 1968. However, the film was plagued by difficulty, the exact nature of which has not been fully revealed. Prints of the film have never surfaced in the United States and only a few people claim to have seen the film. Molina makes only passing reference to the film in his autobiography. *Las noches del hombre lobo* is one of several rarely seen and elusive films in Molina's filmography. It is by all accounts the second Paul Naschy-Waldemar Daninsky werewolf film and future scholars will be challenged to locate any existing prints.

By 1970 Molina had learned the art of both filmmaking and screenwriting. His background in literature, art and music added a depth of knowledge to everything he attempted. He was quite clearly a Spanish renaissance man and although he never realized it at the time he was having a profound influence on the Spanish film industry. With several successful films completed he had learned that his ideas were profitable, and film executives began paying closer attention.

His 1970 feature, *Los monstruos de terror*, would also suffer from production delays, differences of opinion and a sometimes erratic shooting schedule. When American actor Robert Taylor visited Spain to film a movie he expressed an interest in starring in the film but the film's financial backers vetoed that possibility and instead hired Michael Rennie. The script included a werewolf, Waldemar Daninsky in his second appearance, Frankenstein's monster, a mummy and a vampire. Part gothic monster movie and part science fiction film, the plot has a visitor from the planet Ummo (Rennie) attempting to take over the earth. The battle between the werewolf and Frankenstein's monster was Molina's homage to the classic *Frankenstein Meets the Wolf Man*.

Los monstruos de terror was Molina's first big budget film and while the story doesn't quite work he was justifiably proud of certain scenes that he felt were of high quality. Notably a "really superb materialization of Count Dracula"[83] and the climactic battle of the monsters.

Molina had been thus far billed as Paul Naschy although he allowed his screenwriting credit to be listed as Jacinto Molina. In the span of a few years he had become "horror actor Paul Naschy" for his Spanish audience. The name would become as well known as that of Boris Karloff and Lon Chaney, Jr., and perhaps realizing this, Molina allowed the name to stick. He would remain Paul Naschy for the remainder of his career.

La noche de walpurgis (*Werewolf's Shadow*) would be released in 1971 and the film would go far in making Paul Naschy a popular star in horror films. The third collaboration of Paul Naschy and Waldemar Daninsky would be the charm. Based upon his screenplay and starring Paul Naschy as the werewolf, *La noche de walpurgis* would become Naschy's first international box-office hit. Quick to cite his influences for the film— German expressionism, the paintings of Solana and Goya, medieval folk tales and epic poetry, the Universal Studios horror films, and Victorian ghost stories—he had successfully fused these elements to create a new style of filmmaking that fans referred to as "The Mark of Naschy."

La noche de walpurgis would begin a tremendous cycle of quality Spanish horror films and is largely responsible for revitalizing the Spanish film industry. Spanish films now had international appeal, a fact that was not lost on executives with an eye on box-office receipts. Although Molina was certainly not the sole perpetrator of this cinematic resurgence, he was clearly a leading force in the industry at that time. There was, in fact,

Paul Naschy as Waldemar Daninsky in *The Werewolf Versus the Vampire Woman* with a bare-breasted victim. The film is also known as *Werewolf's Shadow*.

nothing comparable occurring in American horror films during the same period. Lugosi was long dead, Karloff died in 1968, and Lon Chaney, Jr. was suffering from poor health. By comparison, the British horror film industry was also thriving with films that starred Christopher Lee and Peter Cushing. So the rise of Paul Naschy as a film star would resonate for decades to come.

La noche de walpurgis would be released in the United States as either *Werewolf's Shadow* or *The Werewolf Versus the Vampire Woman*. It is among the classics of the Spanish horror films and remains available on DVD today. The opening sequence encapsulates those prurient elements so popular with fans of the horror genre. Two morticians about to autopsy a man's body are murdered when the full moon revives the man (Naschy). Fleeing the morgue, the werewolf takes to the countryside where he encounters a young girl out for a walk. He savagely murders her and the camera lingers on her blood splashed breasts. This leads to the opening credits.

The film then moves to modern Paris and the plot involves two college students (Gaby Fuchs and Barbara Capell) who are interested in Satan-worshipping. At the recommendation of a friend, they visit the French countryside seeking the grave of Countess Wandessa d'Arville de Nadasdy (Patty Shepard). However, their automobile runs out of gasoline and they seek assistance from a man in a nearby manor named Waldemar Daninsky (Nashy, of course). Quite naturally Daninsky is a man with secrets. The two girls soon discover the grave of Countess Wandessa d'Arville de Nadasdy with Daninsky's assistance. The corpse is found with a crucifix styled dagger in its chest which they remove.

From this point the plot unfolds quickly. That night, under a full moon, the re-animated countess crawls from her grave. One of the girls is soon visited by a ghostly female vampire and becomes infected. Daninsky kills one of the vampires by driving a stake through her hear and beheading her. Soon, Daninsky transforms into a werewolf and audiences were treated to snarling, tremors, and spittle flowing from his mouth. Naschy plays the scene very much in the style of Lon Chaney, Jr. although the profusion of drool is a novel touch. Intent on saving himself and the surviving college student, Daninsky is pressed to destroy the countess and her vampire minions.

Werewolf's Shadow has a leisurely pace compared to modern horror films which rely on fast edits. The film's leisurely pace is an asset as it highlights the appealing cast, location shooting, and colorful landscapes.

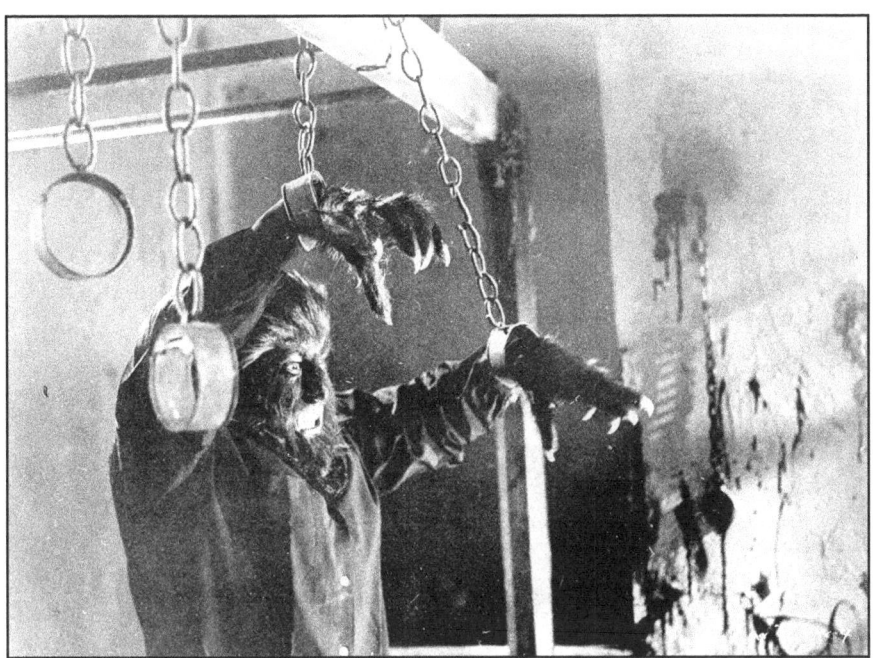

Rare publicity still from *The Werewolf Versus the Vampire Woman* AKA *Werewolf's Shadow*. Paul Naschy again in chains leaving no doubt as to the carnage that will follow once he escapes.

The female nudity is often brief and far less exploitative than would be accepted in just a few short years. The scenes with the werewolf are often gory but the make-up is traditional and owes a great deal to the visionary work of Jack Pierce. The climactic albeit brief battle between the werewolf and the countess is well-staged, and the final shot of the maggot infested body of Countess Wandessa d'Arville de Nadasdy is truly chilling.

The character of Countess Wandessa d'Arville de Nadasdy was inspired by the legend of Countess Elizabeth Bathory, a fifteenth century Hungarian noblewoman who is alleged to have been a prolific serial killer. She was reputed to have bathed in her victims blood in order to retain her youthful beauty. Known by some as "Countess Dracula" or "The Blood Countess," Bathory was said to engage in preserve sexual mutilations and acts of degradation. Molina, having read extensively of Bathory's legend, would return to her several times for inspiration over the course of his career.

Stylistically, *Werewolf's Shadow* is a fusion of the blood splattered films made popular by Hammer Studios in England, with the requisite moodiness that had elevated the best Universal Studios films above the mundane. Naschy was now proven a popular and effective box-office star.

Spanish poster for *The Fury of the Wolfman* (1972).

Waldemar Daninsky returned in *La furia de hombre Lobo* (1972) known as *The Fury of the Wolfman* in the United States. To date, all of the appearances of Waldemar Daninsky were stand-alone stories. There was no viable attempt at continuity as one would expect from a series. Molina was creating his career in stages as financial backing became available. By all accounts, Molina reacted swiftly to his sudden popularity and indulged himself writing screenplays quickly, but effectively. His stories were always good, and the werewolf films would be linked by his greatest creation.

For this film Waldemar Daninsky is bitten by a strange creature in Tibet and becomes marked by the sign of the pentagram. Returning home, he discovers his wife has been unfaithful and he kills her before fleeing into a storm where he is killed by lightning. Resurrected by a mad scientist who is conducting experiments on people chained in a dungeon, the werewolf is subjected to cruelty. Some footage of the werewolf from *Frankenstein's Bloody Terror* was inserted presumably to save on production costs.

The Fury of the Wolfman was another immensely successful film although American audiences have never seen the uncut version. The American version, widely distributed years later on video and DVD, is a bowdlerized print, with a great deal of the gore and nudity excised by the prurient distributors. This is odd given that gore and nudity were strong selling points for films of this nature. *The Fury of the Wolfman* is the least interesting of the Waldemar Daninsky films although it does have its chilling moments. The film lacks the gothic mood and fluidity that added such a tactile quality to *Werewolf's Shadow*.

The script for *Dr. Jekyll y el hombre lobo* (*Dr. Jekyll and the Wolfman*, 1972) was commissioned by a producer who then failed to follow-up with Naschy. The film was later produced after Naschy had become well known in the Spanish film industry. The film was another rousing success and remains among the better Waldemar Daninsky werewolf films. Using Robert Louis Stevenson's famed novella as a starting point, Daninsky travels from Transylvania to London intent on using Dr. Jekyll's transformation formulae to cure his lycanthropy. After the formulae are secured from Dr. Jekyll's grandson, Daninsky takes the formulae and transforms into Mr. Hyde. As one would expect, events spiral out of control with the brutal murder of Dr. Jekyll's assistant. Naschy's bravura performance is the film's highlight. He plays both Mr. Hyde and the werewolf with the necessary angst unseen in a werewolf film since Lon Chaney, Jr.

This fusion of *Dr. Jekyll and Mr. Hyde* and the lycanthrope's legend is a landmark moment in werewolf films. Stevenson's story is a quintes-

German poster art for Paul Naschy's *Dr. Jekyll and the Wolfman* (1972), an underrated thriller.

The artwork for the Spanish lobby card for *Dr. Jekyll and the Wolfman* relied on an image of Lon Chaney, Jr. as the Wolf-Man in addition to the obligatory barebreasted victim. The influence of Jack Pierce's makeup on Chaney is evident throughout Paul Naschy's career.

sential transformation allegory of man into beast and Naschy handled it superbly. The tortured lycanthrope, longing for peace, and the sinister Mr. Hyde, the beast within each of us, meld here into one conflicted personality as envisioned by Naschy.

El retorno de walpurgis (*Curse of the Devil*, 1973) is one of Paul Naschy's better films. The seventh screen appearance of Waldemar Daninsky provided copious gore and nudity, but more importantly, *Curse of the Devil's* storyline accentuates the growing legend of Waldemar Daninsky. Taking plot elements from Curt Siodmak's Wolf Man scripts, Daninsky finds himself cursed with lycanthropy by descendants of an evil witch and his salvation can only come at the hands of a woman who truly loves him.

Having been cursed by a witch, Daninsky is bitten by a wolverine while hunting. Finding himself at odds with a coven of witches, he later unknowingly makes love to one of the witches. The young girl scars Daninsky with a skull that causes a pentagram style wound on his chest.

American poster for *Curse of the Devil* (1973) accentuated the female form.

A subplot involving a serial killer on the loose with an ax elevates the gore factor. The werewolf make-up by Fernando Florido is excellent and strongly resembles the image created by Jack Pierce. Full frontal female nudity, black magic and witchcraft, graphic violence and a tragic love story, all filmed in period settings, add a gothic flavor to *Curse of the Devil*.

Like Larry Talbot before him, Daninsky longs for death in order to end his suffering. As the werewolf Daninsky is a fearsome sight, slavering and growling in a murderous rampage. In all of Naschy's werewolf films the creature's ferocity is elevated far above that of any other screen lycanthrope. The medieval prologue, location setting in a Spanish castle, the gothic mood, beautiful women and sudden violence all contributed to the "Mark of Naschy" that endeared him to millions of fans.

In the span of four years Naschy had created an enduring character and had become Spain's leading horror actor. He was in demand for numerous roles and several of his other films during this period are considered horror classics. He updated the Jack the Ripper legend in *Jack, El destripador de londres* (1971), personified Count Dracula in *El gran amor*

Paul Naschy's werewolf effectively invoked the image created by Jack Pierce and Lon Chaney, Jr.

del conde Dracula (1972), and a hunchback in *El jorobado de la morgue* (1972), and the demented Knight Alaric de Marnic in *El espanto surge de la tumba* (1973). Next to Waldemar Daninsky the character of Alaric de Marnic is Naschy's greatest creation. *El espanto surge de la tumba* is a shocking but fascinating depiction of pure evil. Venerated among gothic film fans, Naschy's *El espanto surge de la tumba* was an *auteur* creation of the highest order.

In 1975 Waldemar Daninsky returned in *La maldicion de la bestia* (*Night of the Howling Beast*). The plot elements draw from several previous Daninsky films. During an expedition in Tibet Daninsky loses his way and encounters two strange women who turn out be cannibal-vampires. Naturally he becomes inflicted and after escaping he rejoins his comrades before they are captured and imprisoned in the fortress of Sekkar Khan. Daninsky is chained in a cell and witnesses the brutalities experienced by his fellow travelers. The graphic nudity and gore are evident throughout, and the werewolf's battle with the Yeti is a *tour de force* action sequence. The pacing is brisk. A solid entry in the ongoing saga of Waldemar Daninsky, *Night of the Howling Beast* is among several Naschy films much in demand by his English speaking fans.

Five years would pass before audiences would see Waldemar Daninsky again, but the wait appears to have been worth it. *El retorno del hombre-lobo* (*Return of the Wolfman*, 1980) remains one of the high points in Naschy's film career. Although the Waldemar Daninsky films are independent of each other, each film offers fresh insight into the mind of the tortured nobleman. Known as *Night of the Werewolf* in the United States, the film would benefit from not only another script by Jacinto Molina and a starring role for Molina's alter ego, Paul Naschy, the directorial reins would be handled by Molina as well. With a decade of quality filmmaking under his belt, Molina knew what he wanted in a Waldemar Daninsky werewolf film. He chose cinematographer Alejandro Ulloa who was highly regarded in European cinema. Ulloa had not only made a name for himself in the Spanish film industry but had worked with Orson Welles on *Chimes at Midnight* (1965) and several popular Italian westerns. As always with Molina, the tactile visuals were as important to the film's success as were the script.

The script would pit Daninsky against Countess Elizabeth Bathory who was portrayed by Julia Saly. Fascinated by Bathory's legend, Molina viewed her as an arch-enemy to mankind, far crueler and evil than even Daninsky himself, who was essentially an unwilling participant in lycan-

The werewolf in chains was a reoccurring motif in Paul Naschy's werewolf films.

thropy. Daninsky was only evil when he transformed into a werewolf, but Bathory was the embodiment of evil, unrelenting in her desire to torture and destroy. The eternal struggle of good versus evil would provide a tangible quality to *The Night of the Werewolf.*

The film was shot over a six week period in the summer of 1980. Castles in Villafranca and Belmonte with additional locations in Navacerrada and Talamanca del jarama provided stunning visuals. Overseeing all aspects of the production, Naschy would prove himself not only a superb actor but director as well. A medieval prologue opens the film and sets the stage for the resurrection of both Daninsky and Bathory. In modern Transylvania Erika, Barbara and Karen (occultists seeking Countess Bathory's grave) are traveling through the Carpathian Mountains when they are attacked by robbers but are saved by a mysterious figure with a crossbow. They escape and make their way to a crumbling castle where they discover the grave of Daninsky. They explore the eerie, cobweb infested castle intent on finding the grave of Countess Bathory. They discover Bathory's grave but keep it a secret as the castle's owner, Mr. Burko, offers them a place to stay. They agree without realizing that Mr. Burko is Waldemar Daninsky, seen here for the first time with a full beard.

However, the girls soon come to realize that Burko is Daninsky. Erika is evil, and plots to release Bathory from her tomb during an astral convergence. Daninsky's deformed assistant, Mircalla, informs Daninsky that Karen is the chosen one capable of freeing him from the lycanthrope's curse. Erika soon kills Barbara, hanging her nude body over Bathory's corpse and slitting her throat. Barbara's blood revives Countess Bathory. Once resurrected, the Countess plans on inducing Daninsky to serve her. Bathory turns Erika into a vampire and induces Karen as well. Daninsky, troubled by the turn of events, transforms into a werewolf and kills Ericka and Bathory.

Paul Naschy's substantial contribution to horror films was epitomized by the werewolf Waldemar Daninsky, his greatest creation.

The Night of the Werewolf is widely regarded as Naschy's masterpiece. The film's many highlights include several werewolf transformation scenes played to the hilt by Naschy; corpse zombies and superb special effects including a levitating coffin. The outstanding cinematography by Alejandro Ulloa offers a visual feast. The fog shrouded hallways, candlelit rooms and dank crypts provide the film its gothic tone. The sets are masterful as are the costumes. Ulloa's camera lingers on the beautiful women whose skin is soft and beautiful and a stark contrast to the werewolf's ferocity or the decaying corpses. Both visually stunning and well-acted, *The Night of the Werewolf* expounds upon those elements from *Werewolf's Shadow* and *Curse of the Devil* to create a modern masterwork of horror.

The 1980s would be a difficult decade for Naschy. Although he was immensely popular, and he worked steadily in both films and television, he suffered financial set-backs and experienced a measure of disdain by elements in the Spanish film industry that disapproved of horror films.

Daninsky would return in a Hispano-Japanese co-production, *La bestía la espada mágica* which is known as *The Werewolf and the Magic Sword* (1983). Naschy had already successfully collaborated in several Japanese productions and was afforded a great deal of respect by producers in the Japanese film industry. In Japan, unlike Spain, film executives recognized Naschy's talent and warmly embraced the idea of a co-production. The werewolf creature, *okami*, also existed in Japanese culture and Naschy wrote a script that combined traditional Japanese ancestral elements but included the character of Waldemar Daninsky. A battle between the werewolf and a tiger were carefully planned and filmed.

The script was based on the legendary Japanese bandit known as "The Beast" who had murdered several people during his exploits in the sixteenth century. The script follows Daninsky from the Inquisition to Japan seeking a wise man named Kian who may possess secrets that can cure his lycanthropy. The story includes strong elements of Japanese black magic. Filming was problematic as one would expect from a production encompassing divergent cultures. Remarkably, Naschy, who also directed the film, persevered. He diligently researched Japanese history and culture and in conjunction with his Japanese team he insured that the sets, costumes, and relevant details were authentic. In later years, Naschy would always credit his Japanese friends—producers and actors alike—for their contribution to *The Werewolf and the Magic Sword*.

Principal photography was completed at Toshiro Mifune's Tokyo studios. When the completed film was screened at a reception legendary Japanese director Akira Kurosawa congratulated Naschy. The film was a

At his best Paul Naschy's werewolf was a fearsome sight, unrelentingly violent and a bestial representation of Satan.

critical and financial success and won the Grand Prix Award at the Brussels International Fantasy Film Festival in 1983. The Spanish film critic Adolfo Camilo Díaz wrote: "This is the Spanish cinema's best ever fantasy adventure film."[84] Naschy considered *The Werewolf and the Magic Sword* among the high points of his filmography. Seldom seen in the United States, fans are quick to secure Spanish video-cassette copies if they become available on e-bay or other Internet merchant sites.

By the time Naschy filmed *El aullido del diablo* (*Howl of the Devil*, 1987) he had appeared in over fifty-five films, many of which he had scripted and directed. And while his reputation as a talented writer and actor were secure, he still experienced animosity in certain quarters of the Spanish film industry. But he had also won many awards and his fans were devoted and enthusiastic by his many roles.

Of course, Waldemar Daninsky was now legendary. But Naschy had gone into a deep depression after the death of his father and this, along with several films that failed to recoup their production costs, undoubtedly contributed to his often tragic outlook on life. Naschy had written the script for *Howl of the Devil* several years earlier. Waldemar Daninsky would only have a cameo in the film. The story involves an actor named

Hector Doriani living in a chalet near Madrid with his nephew and a cruel manservant. The nephew's father, Alex, had been an horror actor similar to the Chaney's, and Hector enjoys tormenting the young boy. Hector, by comparison, had worked in Shakespearian and other classical productions. Hector plays out his fantasies by picking up women and indulging in sadomasochistic sex games before murdering them. Meanwhile, the nephew, Adrian, has created a fantasy about the monsters his late father had once portrayed. The role of he disturbed nephew Adrian was played by Sergio Molina, and thus the son literally followed in his father's footsteps.

Howl of the Devil provides Naschy the opportunity to play various monsters. It is both an homage to his own work while offering a nod to the classic Lon Chaney werewolf that had inspired him all of those years ago. *Howl of the Devil* is a unique entry among the Waldemar Daninsky films. Daninsky is seen but briefly and the story focuses instead on the relationship between Hector and his nephew. The nudity and brutality are all standard fare for a Paul Naschy film. Naschy described *Howl of the Devil* as his own howl of anguish but making the film helped in lifting him from his depression. A very personal film, Naschy appears intent on vanquishing his demons and once again reveling in the creative fire that had made him a household name in the Spanish film industry.

Nearly a decade would pass before audiences would see Waldemar Daninsky again. Although he worked steadily in films and television he seldom worked on a big budget film. The golden age of Spanish horror films had passed and the film industry had changed. Naschy concentrated on solid character roles, often in low budget productions. He began competing again in weight-lifting competitions, once again proving his versatility. There was at this time no actor in Spanish films that embodied such machismo. Naschy was a true original.

In the summer of 1991 Naschy suffered a nearly fatal heart attack. That he survived is due, in part, to his extraordinary willpower and physical strength. Always an introspective man, Naschy would reflect on thirty years in films and wonder if it had all been worth it. In his autobiography, he wondered if he might not have been better off as an architect. However, during his convalescence the Spanish press was considerate of the famed actor.

While recovering he wrote another Waldemar Daninsky script which became *Licantropo: El asesino de la luna llena* or *Lycanthropus: The Moonlight Murders* (1996). But writing the Daninsky script was a way to kill time as Naschy later explained he had no intention of returning to the film business. During this period Naschy also learned that Hollywood director Steven Spielberg was a fan and owned several Paul Naschy titles in his personal collection. During Naschy's recovery his worldwide fan base was organized into several passionate groups who published fanzines and created web sites devoted to Paul Naschy and Waldemar Daninsky. His cycle of legendary films may have ended but his fans were growing in numbers as a new generation discovered Paul Naschy.

When *Lycanthropus: The Moonlight Murders* was announced the Spanish press was in a frenzy. Paul Naschy was back and perhaps no other film at that time was so eagerly awaited. The film suffered from some unfortunate cuts and decisions by director Francisco Gordillo. Still, the film was hailed for its casting of the beautiful Amparo Munozwas. The werewolf Daninsky is given little screen time and the film's impact is lessened by its obvious lack of focus. Clearly, if Naschy had directed himself *Lycanthropus: The Moonlight Murders* would have fared much better. It is, however, not a bad film, but rather it comes across as a film that doesn't reach its full potential. There are intriguing elements and motifs that one would expect from a script by Molina, but with the production controlled by individuals of lesser talent it becomes but a modest entry in the Waldemar Daninsky legend.

In 2004 Naschy made his American debut in the low-budget *Countess Dracula's Orgy of Blood* directed by Don Glut and starring opposite Glori-Anne Gilbert, Arthur Roberts and Danielle Petty (as Kennedy Johnston). *Countess Dracula's Orgy of Blood* is kitch, American style, but lacking the sensuality and gothic mood that made Naschy's films so appealing. The film is pure exploitation, which for many is not a bad thing.

As a man in his late sixties Naschy was aware of the inspiration his films offered not only his fans but other filmmakers. He was determined to bring Daninsky back in yet another high quality film, but his next choice remains controversial among his fans. Naschy agreed to a script penned by Hollywood filmmaker Fred Olen Ray that would provide him another opportunity to advance the legend of Waldemar Daninsky. The film would feature Naschy in a small role and include actresses from both the American exploitation horror market and the pornographic film industry, although there would be no explicit sex.

Tomb of the Werewolf (2004) is much better than most of the small budget, direct to DVD genre films. Director Fed Olen Ray is a veteran filmmaker who understands the elements of visual storytelling, and I think he appreciates his target audience of genre and exploitation film fans. Unlike so many of the independent filmmakers, Fred Olen Ray doesn't condescend to his audience. He provides precisely what the fans want, and in the correct dosages.

Tomb of the Werewolf is a polished low-budget adventure. What minor faults it may possess are understandable given the time constraints and budget limitations that plague all such productions. For example, there is the occasional line of dialogue delivered with an amateurish tone, and the special effects are simple, albeit effective. But *Tomb of the Werewolf* is still far above the mass of exploitation DVDs catering to the horror fan. The casting is effective. The principals are all veterans of independent filmmaking and even some of the minor roles were cast with actors experienced in low budget films. This is advantageous because it means they're professionals and they know what's expected of them.

The set up: Richard Daninsky (Jay Richardson) inherits a castle in Europe and hires a crew from a TV series that explores the supernatural to assist him in searching for a treasure said to be hidden within the castle walls. As it turns out he's related to none other than Waldemar Daninsky, the werewolf. *Tomb of the Werewolf* benefits from the presence of Paul Naschy as Waldemar Daninsky, Michelle Bauer as Elizabeth Bathory and adult film actress Jacy Andrews. Danielle Petty (appearing under the stage name of Kennedy Johnston) is excellent as the television news anchor. Stephanie Bentley shines in a small but crucial role as Eleanore Daninsky, and Beverly Lynne shows off her considerable charms while proving she's also an effective actress.

It's this ensemble of Naschy, Bauer, Andrews, Johnson and Lynne that helps maintain the pacing. The male supporting cast—Jay Richardson, Leland Jay, Frankie C. Cullen, Don Donovan, and Brian Carrillo—perform their perfunctory duties with professional ease. Adult film actress Monique Alexander has small role as one of the werewolf's victims.

Naschy's werewolf make-up is sufficient to evoke memories of his classic roles. His scenes are limited but effective and capitalize on the requisite gore factor, But this film really revolves around Michelle Bauer, a fan favorite who has worked in the horror genre market for years. As Elizabeth Bathory she is sexually appealing and, when the mood suits her, cold and ruthless.

Bauer and the vivacious Jacy Andrews share one of the film's more chilling scenes; a bloodbath of bondage and titillation. Andrews wisely plays the scene shivering with fear. Stripped naked and with her hands tied, she comes to a grisly end when Bauer slits her throat. As her blood gushes across her breasts Bauer suckles at her bosom and eagerly laps up the blood. The scene is emblematic of the lesbian eroticism and gore that have made the horror genre a goldmine for direct to DVD productions.

Tomb of the Werewolf was shot in 24p (progressive frames per second) High Definition with the Sony Cine Alta as opposed to video which is a visually flat medium. The costumes and sets have substance. Fed Olen Ray understands the difference between composing a shot and just shooting video. There is something akin to a color scheme at work and these elements add a sense of visual texture. The musical soundtrack varies between the manipulatively romantic during the sex scenes, to an up-tempo hard rock ferocity during the action scenes.

Creating *Tomb of the Werewolf* was a memorable experience for director Fred Olen Ray. "One of the greatest thrills in my cinematic life was watching the makeup transformation of Paul Naschy into the werewolf, Waldemar Daninsky." Fred told me recently. "When we first decided to produce *Tomb of the Werewolf* the idea was firmly in our heads that we wanted to recreate the classic Naschy werewolf, a financially risky move in this day of digital morphing and Rick Baker level makeup effects. The Paul Naschy style of Wolfman had long fallen out of favor. But I wanted something old fashioned. I felt that was the only way it would work, and in our own impoverished way we tried hard to achieve the 1970s Spanish Horror style for the film with old castles, medieval flashbacks, Elizabeth Bathory. I'd call it the kitchen sink of throwback movies. In retrospect, it was probably too old fashioned for today's modern audiences, but for me it was the chance of a lifetime."[85]

Tomb of the Werewolf is among the best of the direct to DVD features that I reviewed and I suspect its appeal will grow over time. *Tomb of the Werewolf* is not highly regarded among some die-hard Naschy fans. They have failed to note that Fred Olen Ray created a story that was a pure *homage* to the Paul Naschy blockbusters. There are strong elements from *Curse of the Devil* and *The Night of the Werewolf* that add a subtext to the storyline. And providing the aging actor a small role in the film offered Naschy one last outing as Waldemar Daninsky. The casting of Michelle Bauer and Paul Naschy will ensure its occasional reassessment by fans and scholars. Jacy Andrews and Monique Alexander already have a following due to their sexually explicit roles in adult films, while Beverly Lynne and Danielle Petty conduct themselves professionally throughout the mayhem, all of which adds to the future allure of a film destined to become a cult favorite.

Paul Naschy as Waldemar Daninsky in Fred Olen Ray's *Tomb of the Werewolf* (2004), an homage and tribute to Naschy's classic horror films (courtesy of Fred Olen Ray).

The seldom seen *Um Lobisomem na amazonia* (*A Werewolf in the Amazon*, 2005) is a retelling of the H. G. Wells classic *The Island of Dr. Moreau*. Here Naschy play a scientist who turns into a werewolf. The film was never released in the United States. When Paul Naschy died in 2009, he left behind a completed Waldemar Daninsky screenplay titled *Los ojos del lobo* which has yet to be filmed.

In his autobiography Molina compared himself to an alluring broken toy: "Marginal characters have always held an appeal for me," He wrote, "the same kind of appeal you find with broken toys."[86] Although he had changed Spanish genre filmmaking, entranced millions of fans worldwide, and helped make Spanish actors reputable with his sterling performances, Molina felt both snubbed and ridiculed by factions in the Spanish film industry. His was dissatisfied by the elitist snobs in Spain and felt that he was being subjected to unfair animosity. "Characters like Wolfgang Gotho, Waldemar Daninsky, Count Dracula and Alaric de Marnac are creatures with no future who share both my own bitterness and the cinematic ostracism to which they are subjected by the poisoned pens of frustrated and envious individuals."[87]

Although his last years were often difficult there were several tributes including several published by *Fangoria* magazine, and numerous fan sites began to appear on the Internet. In the end, the fans never gave up on Paul Naschy. His contribution to the Spanish film industry, however, was undergoing a positive transformation at the end of his life. The critical acclaim that had eluded him during his heyday in the 1970s was now being heaped upon him in profusion, and by all accounts he was a grateful and humble man. Jacinto Molina better known as Paul Naschy enjoyed a diverse number of roles over a thirty year period ranging from a werewolf, a priest, a roman general, a mummy, a terrorist, a policeman, a newspaperman and dozens of others. As Paul Naschy he became the ultimate matinee idol.

Naschy had a positive influence on modern filmmakers including Los Angeles based film director Steve Latshaw. His 1995 horror thriller, *Jack-O*, is a cult classic and Latshaw recently wrote and directed *Return of the Killer Shrews* (2011). Latshaw is quick to praise Naschy:

> "My first encounter with Paul Naschy was in a tiny screening room at WAND-TV, Ch. 17, in Decatur, Illinois. It was the fall of 1976, a Sunday night, and I was working as a 16mm news photographer/editor for the station, at the tender age

of 17. First Pro Job, should have been more excited about learning my trade. But I was actually more excited about getting to watch the station's monster movie collection in private screenings for myself in this hidden back room, which I did every Sunday night. I was a monster kid at heart. Still am. At the time, our station ran a Friday Night Horror Extravaganza hosted by Dr. Terror. At the time, the station telecine was grinding through a series of low budget drive-in pictures and foreign imports. I liked to think I was previewing the films for the editing staff… in that screening room I got my first looks at Ted Mikel's *Astro Zombies* and Al Adamson's immortal *Dracula Vs. Frankenstein*, courtesy of some beautiful color prints.

"This particular Sunday I wanted to see something a little more traditional, like the old Universals, but with color and some gore… some genuine excitement and action, unlike those slowly paced Hammer flicks. Thumbing through the reels on the film rack, I came across something on three reels, as I recall, yellow plastic reels with red leader. And scrawled on that 16mm leader, courtesy of a sharpie marker, were the words *Frankenstein's Bloody Terror*. Well, I knew a little something about this one… I'd read about Sam Sherman's attempts to get a Frankenstein movie in drive-ins in the summer of 1970… missing the deadline because he hadn't finished his *Dracula Vs. Frankenstein* epic… and subsequently slapping a Frankenstein title on a Spanish werewolf movie. Could this be it?

"I spooled it up and sat back for the ride of my life… action, gore, color and more action, with this musclebound Spanish guy named Naschy chewing the scenery and everything else as believably as he possibly could in a role like this. His Waldemar Daninsky character, that tragic werewolf, was a dangerous, edgy, romantic and ultimately sad character had many more shadings than Chaney's Larry Talbot or Oliver Reed's doomed villager.

"And, wow, that opening, Sam Sherman's attempt to tie it in with the Frankenstein canon with that animated cartoon title monster ('Wolf-Stein! Wolf-Stein!')… great stuff. Of course I later learned that this was the debut of Naschy's Waldemar.

And I became a life-long fan. How would I sum them up? Naschy's films revolved around the amazing concept of werewolf as doomed action hero. Because, in my view, Waldemar was just that. An action hero. The movies had enough visual nods to the old Universal's to wet your nostalgia… and they were mounted on a scale that made them look like Errol Flynn's Technicolor Warner Brothers swashbucklers. Or at least *The Master of Ballantrae*. They moved fast, bit hard and always left you wanting more. What else do you want from a werewolf?"[88]

In all of his films Naschy is the alpha male, born to seduce beautiful women and strong enough to vanquish any foe. He exudes confidence with his body language and his romantic demeanor, exerting his animal magnetism in every scene. Perhaps in some ways he was a throwback to the personality actors from Hollywood's golden age who had such a profound influence on his career. Naschy could be as subtle and angst-ridden as a method actor, but most of the time he was perfectly at ease being Paul Naschy, formerly Jacinto Molina, and proud to be a Spaniard.

Naschy's best werewolf films—*La marca del hombre-lobo, La noche de walpurgis, Dr. Jekyll y el hombre lobo, El retorno de walpurgis, La maldicion de la bestia, El retorno del hombre-lobo* and the American homage directed by Fred Olen Ray, *Tomb of the Werewolf*—all constitute a remarkable contribution to lycanthopic lore and legend.

A Survey of Werewolf Films

THE WEREWOLF MYTH TRANSCENDS generations and touches numerous mediums. The oral history of lycanthropy inspired the ongoing body of werewolf literature and made possible the iconic visualizations by Lon Chaney, Jr. and Paul Naschy. But werewolf stories offer more than simply an image of a man-beast committing atrocious acts. These are tales about the dark places of the human soul. They are often allegories meant to enlighten us and they touch upon those nameless fears that lurk in the labyrinthine recesses of mankind's tortured mind.

Yet there are no werewolf characters in fiction that have achieved the same popularity as Bram Stoker's *Dracula* or Anne Rice's Lestat from *Interview with the Vampire*. The film industry created Larry Talbot and Waldemar Daninsky and while the literature of lycanthropy is populated by memorable characters, none have endured with the same level of cultural recognition as Dracula and Lestat. Werewolves, however, are far more frightening than vampires. Their ferocity and strength make them nearly invincible, and the best werewolf stories offer a combination of violence, sensuality and tragedy.

Hollywood filmmakers embraced lycanthropy from the beginning. *The Werewolf*, filmed in 1913, involves the Indian legends of people transforming into vengeful wolves. A Navajo woman named Kee-On-Ee believes that her dead husband has returned to haunt her. Kee-On-Ee becomes a witch and her daughter, Watuma, is taught to hate all white men and attacks them after transforming into a wolf. Prints of *The Werewolf* were destroyed by a fire in 1924 and reputedly only eighteen minutes of footage remain. Although *The Werewolf* is an inconspicuous beginning for movie werewolves, Hollywood screenwriters would eventually become as prolific as the novelists and folklorists that preceded them.

The first great werewolf film of note, *The Werewolf of London* (1935), would utilize make-up by Jack Pierce and set the tone for all Hollywood werewolves that followed. Henry Hull was cast as Wilfred Glendon in a Universal Studios horror film based upon an original story by Robert Harris and with a screenplay by John Colton. Jack Pierce, who had mad a name for himself with his superb make-up for *Frankenstein*, *The Mummy* and *The Bride of Frankenstein*, was given the choice opportunity of turning Hull into a lycanthrope.

There are several common misconceptions regarding *The Werewolf of London*. The first misconception, widely repeated on the Internet and in a few reference books, is that the film was based upon Guy Endore's *The Werewolf of Paris*. This is not true. The story and screenplay were commissioned by Universal Studios and green-lighted for production to capitalize upon their previous horror films. There is no similarity between *The Werewolf of London* and *The Werewolf of Paris*. The second misconception is that Jack Pierce's make-up was toned down because Hull's vanity prohibited his features from being fully obscured. This is an injustice to both Hull and Pierce. While it's true that the werewolf's final appearance was influenced by Hull's opinion, it had nothing to do with vanity. It was a matter of aesthetics and those personal choices an actor chooses when creating a characterization. Hull strongly believed that too much make-up diminished the character's humanity and so chose a minimalist approach to Pierce's hirsute concept. In fact, the final creation remains an effective and frightening depiction of a werewolf.

Henry Hull in *The Werewolf of London* (1935), the first truly outstanding werewolf film.

The story follows Glendon, a botanist, to Tibet where he is seeking the mariphasa plant. It is here where Glendon is attacked and bitten by a werewolf. Back in London Glendon is warned by fellow botanist, Dr. Yogami (played masterfully by Warner Oland), that he is subject to the werewolf's curse. Eventually, fearing that his lycanthropy will destroy him, Glendon begins experimenting with the mariphasa plant to prevent his transformation into a werewolf. Initially, he is successful. Quite soon, however, Glendon transforms into a werewolf and flees his laboratory in a frenzy. Loping through the fog-drenched streets of London he eventually murders a young woman. The plot then pits Glendon against Yogami who is also a werewolf. The film comes to a brisk conclusion with Glendon eventually being shot by a Scotland Yard Inspector and, in his death throes, apologizing to his wife Lisa (Valerie Hobson).

The Werewolf of London is an excellent film and benefits from the attention-to-detail that would become hallmarks of the Universal horror films. Realistic and moody sets, superb acting, and a truly menacing monster would set the standard for horror films to come. If not for Chaney's depiction of Larry Talbot five years later *The Werewolf of London*

Jack Pierce's make-up for Henry Hull in *The Werewolf of London* (1935) foreshadows his classic makeup on Lon Chaney, Jr. five years later.

Poster art for The *Return of the Vampire* (1944).

might be better remembered. As it stands today, the film is given scant attention. But the images of Hull as the snarling werewolf would have a far-reaching influence. His werewolf is not quite as powerful as the lycanthrope that would soon simmer beneath Larry Talbot's skin, but it is nonetheless memorable.

The Undying Monster (1942) is a minor entry among werewolf films. Based upon the truly wretched novel by Jesse Douglas Kerruish, the film fares better than Kerruish's tepid prose, thanks to an intelligent screenplay by Lillie Hayward. Lacking is the bravura performance of an actor in full-lycanthopic make-up, but the film manages a sinister tone and works best as a thriller.

Cry of the Werewolf (1944) is an interesting film starring Nina Foch. The plot involves a princess who has the ability to change into a wolf. This film hints at a subculture of knowledgeable lycanthropic devotees (family members) who are intent on keeping the lycanthrope's existence a secret. But these elements are far from fully realized and the film really resorts to traditional thriller techniques to tell a rather flat story. *Cry of the Werewolf* is rarely seen and often dismissed in retrospectives on horror films. Still far removed from the quality of the Chaney films, it does possess those horrific characteristics that elevate the action above the mundane.

Return of the Vampire (1944) is far better known and well worth viewing. For only the third time Bela Lugosi was cast as a vampire (Following *Dracula* and *Mark of the Vampire*). As Armand Tesla he is not far removed from Count Dracula. Lugosi never bothers with any intricate characterization, nor is any such method acting expected. As Tesla he is simply playing Dracula with a different name, just as he was in *Mark of the Vampire*. Since Dracula was a role that Lugosi cherished he plays the role with an identical personality.

Return of the Vampire ushers in the era of modern vampire stories on film. The film begins in October 1918 at the end of World War I. The first character to appear on screen is actor Matt Willis as the werewolf, Andreas, in a fog shrouded cemetery. Andreas is dressed as a common businessman in a suit and tie, but when he visits Tesla's coffin he speaks perfect English. The sight of an articulate, non-bestial werewolf is jarring. This moody opening sequence in which Andreas encourages Tesla to rise from his coffin is a virtuoso set-piece of gothic horror.

Andreas informs Tesla that one of his victims has been transported to a clinic where we learn that Lady Jane Ainsley (Frieda Inescort) confers with professor Saunders (Gilbert Emery) who consults an article written by Tesla about vampires and werewolves. Meanwhile, Tesla materializes in the Saunders home and attacks the granddaughter Nikki. Suspicious that Nikki and the patient, who has died, were bitten by a vampire, Saunders and Lady Jane visit the cemetery in search of the vampire's coffin. Andreas arrives just as they drive a stake through Tesla's heart thus ending curse of lycanthropy. Andreas is transformed again to his human form.

Lugosi is seen only in profile or as a shadow until the scene changes to twenty-three years later. During the bombing of London in World War II the cemetery is struck by German bombs which unearth several bodies and coffins. Two gravediggers, sent to re-inter the corpses, discover Tesla's body with the spike in the chest. Believing this to be a "bomb splinter" they remover the spike and thus unwittingly revive Tesla again.

Andreas, now working as an assistant in Lady Jane's clinic, is upset to learn that one of Lady Jane's associates, Sir Frederick Fleet, intends on examining Tesla's body to determine if he was, in fact, a vampire. Wandering in the cemetery alone later, Andreas encounters Tesla who again transforms Andreas into a werewolf.

Tesla takes on the identity of Hugo Bruckner, a scientist recently escaped from a Nazi camp. Seeking revenge against Lady Jane, Tesla targets Nikki, now grown into a beautiful young woman. In the denouement Andreas saves Nikki from certain death and Tesla is killed when his body is exposed to the sunlight. In the final seconds of the film Lady Jane asks Sir Frederick if he believes in vampires now and he claims he doesn't. As the film closes he looks at the camera and asks "Do you people?" The cornball ending notwithstanding, *Return of the Vampire* is a solid horror film. Lugosi is perfectly menacing or erudite as his scenes demand, and the articulate werewolf Andreas is given ample screen time. The makeup, clearly inspired by the famous Jack Pierce creation, offers enough of a carnivorous slant to give the character a dangerous aura. *Return of the Vampire* premiered before World War II ended thus making it the first modern fusion of the vampire-werewolf film.

After World War II, and with Universal Studios unofficially retiring their famed Wolf Man series, werewolf fans helped make *She-Wolf of London* (1946) into a successful film. However, *She-Wolf of London* is a romantic thriller lacking in any true werewolf. The script involves Phyllis Allenby, a beautiful young woman played by June Lockhart who believes she suffers from the "curse of the Allenbys." A "wolf-woman" has been seen prowling a nearby park and Phyllis becomes concerned that she might be a lycanthrope. Although Jack Pierce was on staff for make-

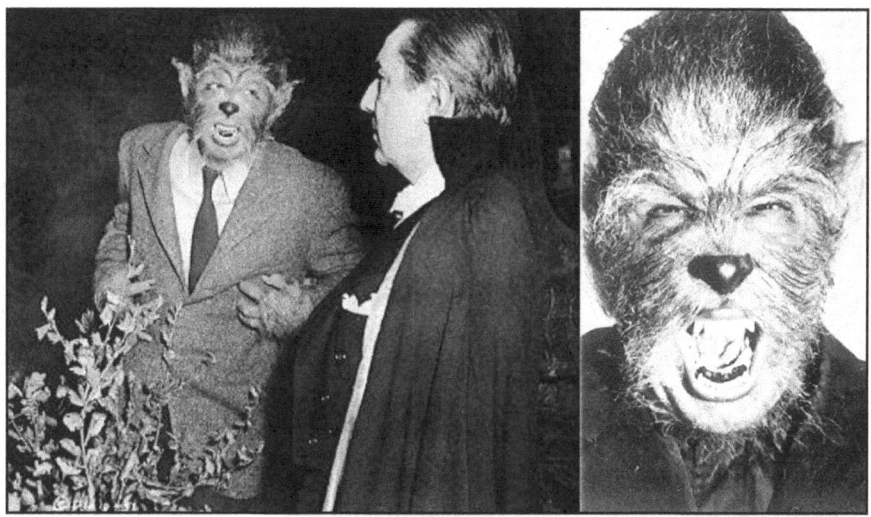

Matt Willis as the werewolf and Bela Lugosi as a vampire in the 1944 classic *Return of the Vampire*.

up chores the lack of any hirsute protagonist is a disappointment. At best, *She-Wolf of London* is an effective 1940s era horror-thriller although bereft of any truly terrifying scenes.

After World War II the film industry changed dramatically. Gone was the studio system that had tailored productions for individual stars. Independent and free-lance talent were widely in use by 1950 and method actors became the rage. The grand personality actors of the 30s and 40s—Errol Flynn, James Cagney, Gary Cooper, Humphrey Bogart, to name a few—were soon eclipsed by method actors like Marlon Brando, Montgomery Clift and Paul Newman. Realistic dramas supplanted the adventure film, and traditional horror films were replaced by the science fiction craze.

Horror films quickly became low-budget productions. This is a stark change from a decade earlier when films like *The Wolf Man* were given an A-list budget. In the mid-1950s horror films were being produced for the popular drive-in movie market. "Date Flicks" as they became known, were often low-budget thrillers or science fiction melodramas. Not all of these films were necessarily bad, but many lacked the polish that would have elevated them above the grind-house circuit.

The Werewolf (1956) is a modest exception to the poor quality films. It is still far from being a great movie, but under producer Sam Katzman's tutelage it had enough flare to make it memorable. Filmed near Bear Lake,

The Werewolf (1956) starred Steve Ritch as a tortured lycanthrope clearly inspired by Larry Talbot.

California, the script by Robert Kent involves around a man (Steve Ritch) who survives an auto accident and become a subject for experiments by two scientists who are attempting to create a vaccine for nuclear-radiation poisoning. Injected with a strange serum containing wolf's blood by the two scientists, the man transforms into a murderous werewolf.

Hailed by many as the first blending of science-fiction and werewolf lore, *The Werewolf* is another in a long line of films where the lycanthrope is visually similar to the iconic vision created by Jack Pierce for Lon Chaney, Jr. As with the werewolf in *Return of the Vampire*, the creature make-up accentuates a fuller mane of hair and tones down the canine look to the nose. These variations were enough to prevent an outcry of visual plagiarism while satisfying the werewolf fans who demanded an authentic hirsute creature.

The opening sequence of *The Werewolf* is *film noir* style sequence in a neon-lit diner with swing music playing from a jukebox. The plot follows a confused stranger in the town of Mountaincrest who kills a thug outside a tavern and is pursued by townspeople into the forested hills. Immediately suspecting either a rampaging wolf or something sinister, the sheriff organizes a search to track down the killer. Evading the police, the conflicted stranger backtracks and seeks medical advice from the local doctor whose daughter Amy (Joyce Holden) offers the requisite blonde attraction. Anguished by his amnesia he confesses to having killed a man and convinced that something terrible has happened to him, he eventually flees the doctor's office. Feeling sympathetic for the tortured stranger, Amy and her father ask the sheriff to take the man alive if possible. Meanwhile, the man's wife and son have been searching for him since his car accident. The two doctors who had injected the victim with the serum also arrive in Mountaincrest seeking their escaped patient. When one of the doctors discovers the man, whose name is Marsh, hiding in a hillside cave and audiences are finally treated to an on-screen transformation. Stylistically, the transformation from man to wolf is created with same frame-by-frame dissolve used in *The Werewolf of London* and *The Wolf Man*. When Marsh is captured the two conniving doctors attempt to kidnap him but Marsh transforms into the werewolf, kills the doctors and once again flees into the hills. Soon thereafter the savage creature is trapped on a bridge and killed. Steve Ritch plays the tortured Marsh as Chaney had played Larry Talbot, an emotionally distraught victim seeking answers to his plight. The theme of a man conflicted by the bestial side of his nature is consistent in all of the better werewolf films from any period. The acting throughout *The Werewolf* is solid and the script is better than average. Over the years the film has been featured in retrospective film conventions to a positive response.

The postwar realism in film would have an effect on the target audience of teenagers and the theme of mankind's inner beast is readily apparent in the cult classic *I Was a Teenage Werewolf* (1957) starring Michael Landon. The film was released by AIP (American International Pictures) and directed by Gene Fowler, Jr. The economic prosperity and cultural changes would have a direct effect on the script which involves a troubled teenager, Tony Rivers (Landon), who soon suffers from lycanthropy. Suffering from a major case of "teen angst" the embattled youth is prone to sudden mood swings and occasional violence. Eventually, he's encouraged to seek the medical advice of Dr. Brandon who subjects the youth to hypnotherapy. Brandon's intention is to regress Rivers back "to the primitive past that lurks within him." But Brandon ultimately triggers the transformation of Tony into a werewolf.

Filmed in under ten days with a reported budget of $82,000, *I Was a Teenage Werewolf* was a box-office sensation and earned over $2 million in its first two weeks of release. Several scenes offered popular cultural references that added a tone heretofore unseen in a werewolf film. In one notable scene at a Halloween party, where the teens are heard to make references to "Squares" while listening to rock and roll music ("Eeny, Meeny,

Michael Landon in *I Was a Teenage Werewolf* (1957).

Miney, Mo" by Jerry Blaine and sung by Ken Miller). Rivers becomes enraged when a friend blows a horn in his ear. The blatant anti-rock and roll motif isn't surprising given that numerous religious organizations during this period vehemently protested a style of music they felt was having a detrimental effect on young people.

One of the film's highlights has River entering a gymnasium where a beautiful girl in form-fitting leotards is exercising on the parallel bars. Rivers, standing next to the school bell, is shocked into a transformation when the bell suddenly goes off. The audiences' first view of the werewolf is seen from the girl's up-side-down point-of-view. The effect is startling.

The werewolf make-up by Philip Scheer is a variant of the creature from *Return of the Vampire* and *The Werewolf*. As in *The Werewolf* (and much later in the Paul Naschy films) the werewolf here drools profusely: this adds a canine ferocity to the werewolf's countenance. The sight of a werewolf in a High School leather jacket is a contrast to the suit and tie werewolf from *The Werewolf of London* and *Return of the Vampire*. The werewolf has become an image of repressed masculinity, unleashed with lycanthropy, but primitive in nature. The themes of teenage alienation and rebellion had seldom been fully realized on film, and by using the science fiction device of a deranged scientist responsible for the lycanthrope's existence, *I Was a Teenage Werewolf* found a responsive audience.

The cast is excellent, including character actor Whit Bissell as Dr. Brandon, Yvonne Lime as Arlene Logan (yet another gorgeous blonde), and Barney Phillips as Detective Sergeant Donovan. The film's popularity spawned several notable imitations. *I Was a Teenage Frankenstein* followed within a few months, *Blood of Dracula* (1957 and featuring a young female vampire with lycanthropic characteristics, *i.e.,* canine-style fangs and *canis lupus* hair), while *Teenagers from Outer Space* and *Teenage Zombies* both premiered in 1959. Equally as popular, *I Was a Teenage Frankenstein* also starred Whit Bissell as a descendant of Dr. Frankenstein. *I Was a Teenage Frankenstein* made possible *How to Make a Monster* (1958) which featured both the teenage werewolf and the teenage Frankenstein monster.

How to Make a Monster offers a clever change from the traditional plot device and focuses on a *faux* insider's look at the motion picture industry. Set on the lot of American International Studios, best known for their horror films, executives decide on eliminating the horror films in favor of rock and roll musicals. The plan is unpopular with make-up artist Pete Drummond (Robert Harris). Currently working on a film titled *Teenage Frankenstein Vs, the Teenage Werewolf,* Drummond initiates a devious

How to Make a Monster (1958) teamed the teenage werewolf (Gary Clarke) with the teenage Frankenstein (Gary Conway).

plot against the executives by using mind control drugs in the make-up used by the actors playing the teenage werewolf and teenage monster. He begins by inducing the werewolf actor (Gary Clarke) into killing one of the studio executives. His murderous spree continues with the teenage monster (Gary Conway, reprising his role from *I Was a Teenage Frankenstein*) until his crimes are revealed by the actors themselves. Drummond perishes in a fire that also destroys his collection of rubber monster masks that he had so lovingly created for the horror film market.

How to Make a Monster was filmed in black and white but the final ten minutes were filmed in color for shock effect. This famous sequence features the props and masks actually used in other AIP films such as *She-Creature* and the Martian from *Invasion of the Saucer-Men*. The trilogy of *I Was a Teenage Werewolf*, *I Was a Teenage Frankenstein* and *How to Make a Monster* are considered the best of the 1950s teen angst horror cycle.

The traditional horror film was nearly non-existent with American filmmakers by 1960, but the ever resourceful British industry was undergoing its own horror renaissance at Hammer Studios. Commencing with *The Curse of Frankenstein* (1957) Hammer horror films introduced

American audiences to Christopher Lee and Peter Cushing with *Dracula* (1958, known in the United States as *Horror of Dracula*), *The Revenge of Frankenstein* (1958), *The Mummy* (1959) and *The Brides of Dracula* (1960). Although the characters of Count Dracula and Dr. Frankenstein and his creation were inspired by the works of Bram Stoker and Mary Shelley, the films were fresh interpretations rather than remakes. Executives at Hammer Studios had no intention of infringing on the characters or plots from the Universal Studios films.

Oliver Reed in the Hammer Films production *Curse of the Werewolf* (1961) which was loosely based upon the novel *The Werewolf of Paris* by Guy Endore.

Curse of the Werewolf (1961) was the only werewolf film made by Hammer Studios and remains among the best. Inspired by Guy Endore's *The Werewolf of Paris*, the script by John Elder (a pseudonym, the writer was actually producer Anthony Hinds) the story is set in 18th Century Spain and begins when a servant girls is raped by a beggar. Her child, Leon (Oliver Reed), is born on Christmas day and cursed with the mark of a lycanthrope. By the time he is a young man Leon has begun showing signs of lycanthropy. His friend Alfredo discovers that Leon is a werewolf and seeks to assist his friend but Leon is unwilling to accept that he's a werewolf. His murderous transformation is enough to later convince him that his death by a silver bullet is the only solution to his condition. Although *Curse of the Werewolf* utilized the Guy Endore novel as its primary source material, there is little resemblance between the two stories.

The make-up by Roy Ashton was not only inspired by Jack Pierce's make-up for Lon Chaney, Jr. but partially modeled on Pierce's classic interpretation. Oliver Reed's expressive features and sophisticated mannerisms evoke the cruelty lurking beneath his daytime persona, and whilst in werewolf guise he is violent and unsympathetic. Yet his depiction of Leon is as sympathetic as Chaney's Larry Talbot, but unlike Talbot Leon is

Lobby card for *Curse of the Werewolf*.

cursed at inception when his mother's body is invaded by a demonic creature. Thus *Curse of the Werewolf* becomes an allegorical Christian tale.

Leon is cursed from the onset, unlike Talbot who became a lycanthrope as an adult. Leon's puberty, involving attempting to kiss a dead squirrel back to life, and his sexual exploration in a brothel where he nips at a prostitute's shoulder and draws blood, might all be viewed as metaphors for adolescence similar to the themes of rebellion and alienation found in *I Was a Teenage Werewolf*. While *Curse of the Werewolf* offers traditional elements from past werewolf films, its follows a less linear path. The werewolf itself is not fully seen until late in the film which some viewers found disappointing.

Werewolf in a Girl's Dormitory (1961) is a disappointing entry in the werewolf filmography. A strange, low-budget affair, with an eye on profit through exploitation, the film recounts a murder near a girl's reformatory and the efforts of one girl, Priscilla, to uncover the mystery. Filmed in Europe and shot in black and white, the film was originally titled *Lycanthropus* but renamed *Werewolf in a Girl's Dormitory* for American audiences. The English dubbing is awful and the film lacks merit. There is no nudity or sensuality although the setting in a girl's dormitory is meant to satisfy audiences with a less than prurient nature. The violence is graphically displayed, albeit in black and white, but often comes across as ludicrous. The sight of a woman's corpse with her neck slashed is meant to be horrifying but with the actress instructed to play dead with her eyes bugging out the scene comes across as ludicrous. The subplot involving blackmail slows the already tepid narrative. The werewolf make-up is minimal, with the accentuated fangs and furry hands being the highlight. As bad as it is, *Werewolf in a Girl's Dormitory* is better than some of the films that would follow.

Werewolves on Wheels (1971) is pure exploitation and cross-genre filmmaking that would also spawn imitators. Essentially a biker rock and roll film with a subplot that involves werewolves, the plot follows The Devil's Advocates, a group of Harley-Davidson bikers, on their drug-induced quest across the American highway in search of kicks. Although it wasn't necessarily intended as a commentary on the then prevalent drug culture of the late 60s and early 70s, seen today the film depicts the drug scene as seedy and ultimately destructive. The motorcycle gang leader Adam (Stephen Oliver) and his girlfriend Helen (D. J. Anderson) inadvertently put the group in contact with a Satanic group who drugs their food and places a curse on Helen who soon infects Adam (by biting his neck like

Werewolf in a Girl's Dormitory (1961) was as bad as the title indicates.

a vampire) with lycanthropy as well. Unlike previous werewolf films, the lycanthrope curse is transmitted through black magic and involves unlikable characters.

The film's visual highlights include a nude dance with a snake by D. J. Anderson. A better film than the title implies, *Werewolves on Wheels* is well-acted and offers a unique perspective on werewolf mythology, but is ultimately analogous of the counter-culture movement whose reliance on fast-living and drugs were deemed immoral. There are no heroic characters in *Werewolves on Wheels*. The graphic violence is minimal but includes slow-motion blood splatters in full color, yet another trend in 1970s filmmaking. The actual scenes with werewolves near the conclusion are minimal and the make-up is simple, derivative as always of the Jack Pierce-Lon Chaney collaboration. Directed by Michel Levesque and written by Levesque with David M. Kaufman, *Werewolves on Wheels* attracted a cult following upon its release.

The counter-culture movement of the 60s and 70s, with its focus on the sexual revolution, political awareness, environmentalist concerns, and *avant garde* experimentation in the arts all contributed to the youth culture distancing themselves from the conservative paradigm. Films like *Werewolves on Wheels* would not have been possible ten years earlier. It is a concentrated effort to break away from the classical cinematic form, and while it fails, relying instead on conservative techniques to enhance suspense, it succeeds on the level of depicting the alienation and moral disintegration of America's disaffected youth.

The Spanish production *Dracula contra Frankenstein* (*Dracula, Prisoner of Frankenstein*, 1972) falls short of the quality established by Paul Naschy. A meandering and often amateurish film, director Jess Franco had proven himself a better director than one would guess from this unfortunate film. In fact, Franco is a cult figure among fans of exploitation films. With over a hundred and fifty films to his credit, he has produced a successful variety of exploitation films, with an emphasis on sex, all of which have enabled him to enjoy a devoted fan base. His first major success was *The Awful Dr. Orloff* in 1961 but outside of this film most of his pre-1975 features suffered from a low-budget. This was the primary shortcoming of *Dracula, Prisoner of Frankenstein*, in addition to an incomprehensible storyline. Franco's cult favorites—*The Erotic Rites of Frankenstein* (1972), *The Bare-Breasted Countess* (1973), *Downtown: The Naked Dolls of the Underworld* (1975) and *Lust for Frankenstein* (1998, and starring Michelle Bauer)—are as bad and as popular as their titles would indicate.

Dracula, Prisoner of Frankenstein defies logic. Scrutinizing the available DVD fails to shed light on a murky plot. Apparently, Count Dracula is back from the dead but quickly gets staked by a local physician. That's when Dr. Frankenstein appears, revives Dracula and chums about with

Werewolves on Wheels (1971) was essentially a biker rock and roll film with a subplot that involved werewolves.

his monster, all while a werewolf roams about intent on killing people. This film is a travesty. If not for the fact that Jess Franco has become an acclaimed celebrity this film would never have been released on DVD. Howard Vernon plays Dracula and Dennis Price plays Dr. Frankenstein, but this muddled affair is another reminder that we are now decades past the golden age of Universal horror films when Lon Chaney, Jr. Boris Karloff and Bela Lugosi crept across a fog-shrouded marsh or damp London alley. *Dracula, Prisoner of Frankenstein* is reported to have been an attempt by Franco to pay homage to the Universal Studios films, and there is a hint of this only in the make-up, which is so poorly conceived that the film is embarrassing to watch.

Moon of the Wolf (1972) is an erstwhile attempt at creating a modern horror film. That it fails in this regard by no means infers that it's as bad as films like *Werewolf in a Girl's Dormitory* or *Dracula, Prisoner of Frankenstein*. Based upon the novel by Leslie H. Whitten and starring David Janssen, Barbara Rush, Geoffrey Lewis and Bradford Dillman, *Moon of the Wolf* was made for ABC television's "Movie of the Week" series and filmed on location in Burnside, Louisiana. It follows the general plot of Whitten's novel, with Janssen taking on the role of Sheriff Aaron Whitaker and Dillman playing Andrew Rodanthe. The film achieves a level of suspense and the principals are convincing in their roles. The werewolf make-up is derivative of the Pierce-Chaney image, which by now is what fans of the horror genre had come to expect. The film's southern gothic overtones add another level to the familiar proceedings. The video-cassette release many years later featured an image cropped from a publicity still of Lon Chaney, Jr. as the Wolf Man from *Abbott and Costello Meet Frankenstein*.

The werewolf film may not have been pronounced officially dead by the early 1970s, but, in effect, the horror genre had indeed nearly vanished in the United States. What meager output of horror films at that time with any merit belonged exclusively to Vincent Price and a few energetic independent productions.

The Werewolf of Washington (1973) was an attempt at a comedy thriller, but comes across as a less than interesting satire on American politics, and the Nixon Administration in specific. A reporter, infected by a werewolf bite while in Europe, returns home to become the press aid to the president of the United States and a werewolf by night. Silly, and decidedly dated, *The Werewolf of Washington* is easily forgotten.

La lupa mannara (*Werewolf Woman*, 1976) was released in the United States with most of the nudity excised from the prints. But over the years

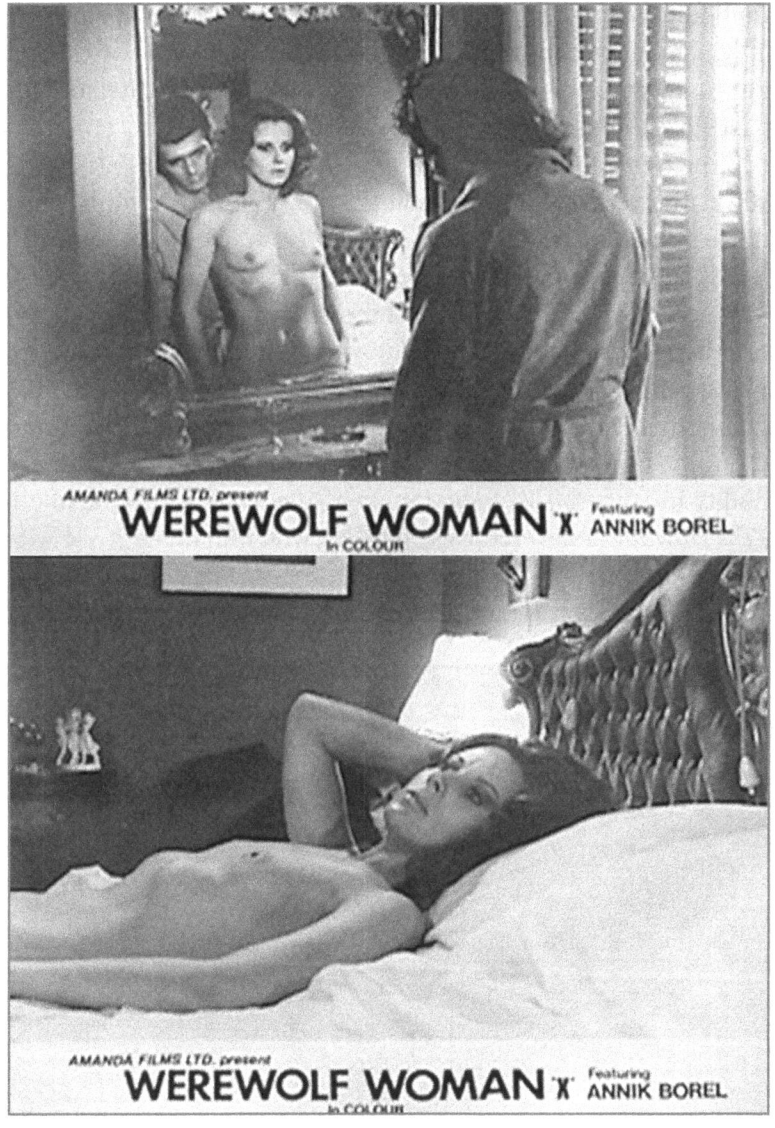

Werewolf Woman (1976) exploited the nudity. The script alludes to a clan of lycanthropes dating back 200 years. Italian Director Rino Di Silvestro managed to fuse these elements into a pro-feminist story with gothic elements.

this film developed a cult following and was highly successful in Europe. *Werewolf Woman* is a feminist rant. Annik Borel plays Daniela, a woman with mental issues who had been raped as a child. After seeing her sister and her sister's husband making love, she becomes deranged and lures the man into the woods where she kills him by biting his neck. Eventually committed to an asylum, the plot deploys a rape and a woman's revenge motif which allows for ample nudity punctuated by violence. The script alludes to a clan of lycanthropes dating back 200 years. Italian Director Rino Di Silvestro manages to fuse these elements into a pro-feminist story with gothic elements.

Over the years the movie's status grew among film buffs who were fortunate enough to see an uncut print. *Werewolf Woman* was rated "X" (for adult audiences) in Europe because of its full frontal female nudity and strong sexual images. In fact, rumors persist that an explicit version exists although this has been denied by the filmmakers. No matter, without being explicit the famous "fellatio scene" leaves little to the imagination. Although Paul Naschy's pivotal werewolf films had already incorporated nudity, from this point on werewolf films would be influenced by the nudity in *Werewolf Woman*, ranging from the erotic to the idiotic.

The Howling (1980) returned the werewolf film to the A-list with this big budget production based upon the novel by Gary Brandner and following Brandner's basic plot. Dee-Wallace Stone plays the role of news

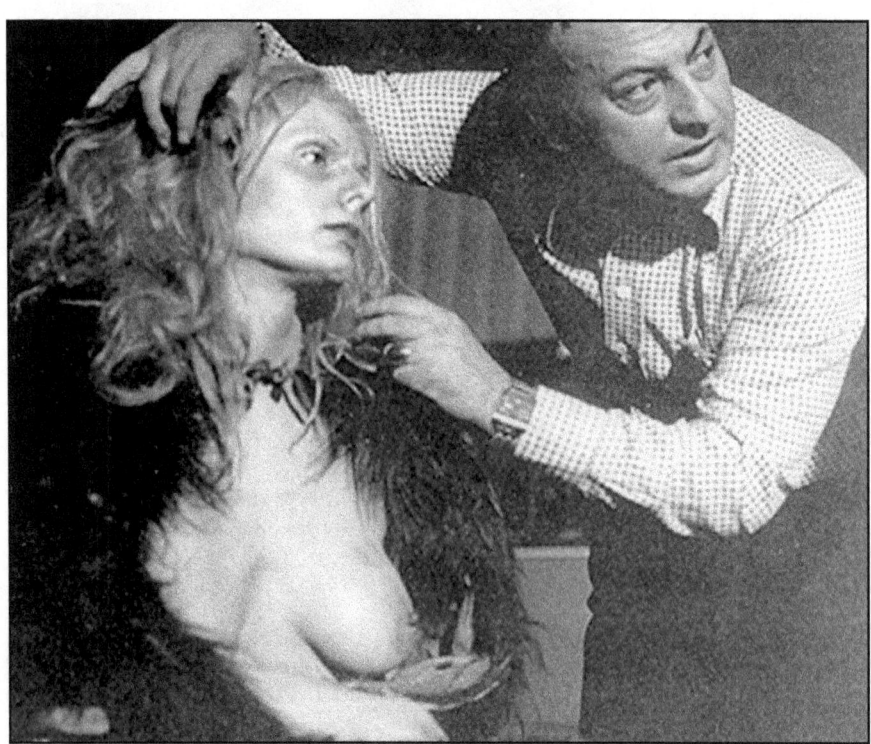

Director Rino Di Silvestro directs Annik Borel in a scene from *Werewolf Woman* (1976).

anchor Karen White and Robert Picardo plays Eddie Quist. The script went through several revisions with the shooting script being credited to John Sayles and Terence H. Winkless. Sayles reportedly re-wrote the Winkless script and his version eliminated many of the scenes that had been included in Brandner's novel. Veteran character actors John Carradine, Kenneth Toby and Slim Pickens all had featured roles. The werewolf transformation was created by Rob Bottin who utilized air-bladders and facial prosthesis to bring the werewolf to life. Some of the differences between the bestselling novel and film are slight—Karen White was Karyn Beatty in the novel and she wasn't a news anchor—while other differences are major such as the inclusion of a werewolf psychiatrist. In the novel Karyn Beatty survives her encounter with the werewolves but her film counterpart dies in the end. All the same, director Joe Dante turned in a polished and immensely popular film.

The Howling was such a box-office success that it inspired six sequels thus becoming the most profitable werewolf series in American films since Universal's Wolf Man films with Lon Chaney, Jr. Unfortunately, outside of a few isolated moments, each subsequent film in *The Howling* series was worse than its predecessor.

The Howling II: Your Sister is a Werewolf (1984) has become a cult favorite, which is possibly an indication of a deeper cultural problem. This film is not bad, although a few scenes are laughable, and whatever potential realized by the first film would be destroyed and buried with subsequent sequels. There are isolated moments in the film that work well. Certainly the actors are all appealing and capable, including Christopher Lee in a small role. After newscaster Karen White's shocking death in the previous film, her brother Ben (Reb Brown) is approached by a stranger named Stefan Crosscoe (Lee) who informs Ben that Karen has become a werewolf. Together they travel to Transylvania to track down and destroy Stirba, Queen of the werewolves, a role handled with seductive aplomb by Sybil Danning. Novelist Gary Brandner co-wrote the screenplay with Robert Sarno. To its credit, *The Howling II: Your Sister is a Werewolf* doesn't come across as serious drama but rather as intentionally campy entertainment. The box-office receipts are an indication that the filmmakers succeeded in creating the kitsch the public demanded.

The Howling III: The Marsupials (1987) is an odd and often ridiculous film with elements borrowed from other popular films, including *Alien* (1980). Set in Australia where a colony of werewolves are intent on destroying the human race, the film borrows the "alien bursting from the stomach" scene from *Alien*, but unlike the latter film this one fails to deliver any suspense. Both *The Howling II: Your Sister is a Werewolf* and *The Howling III: The Marsupials* were directed by Philippe Mora. *The Howling III: The Marsupials* is unrelated to the previous films. Allegedly the story was inspired by a picture of a Thlacine, an extinct Tasmanian wolf.

The Howling IV: The Original Nightmare (1988) takes a fresh approach. Novelist Marie (Romy Windsor), who has been suffering from strange visions, decides to get away with her husband to the picturesque town of Drago. Since Drago was a creation of Gary Brandner, *The Howling IV: The Original Nightmare* returns the series to its source material. Marie soon learns that an evil force has lured her to Drago. Written by Clive Turner and Freddie Rowe, *The Howling IV: The Original Nightmare* never made it to theaters and was released on video-cassette in 1988 and on DVD in 2004.

The Howling V: The Rebirth (1989) was also a direct-to-video feature, directed by Neal Sundstrom and again written by Freddie Rowe and Clive Turner. This time around the story takes place in an Hungarian castle where the proprietors are hoping to attract tourists. Assembling a group together, events turn nasty when the guests start getting murdered. The drawing-room plot should have failed but the production is quite enjoyable, with professional acting by the principal cast—Phil Davis, Victoria Catlin and Ben Cole. Although the Hungarian setting is a cliché in horror films *The Howling V: The Rebirth* orchestrates the suspense and is a much better film than anyone might have anticipated.

The Howling VI: The Freaks (1990) is the real oddball in the series. Combing elements from circus horror films and werewolf lore, *The Howling VI: The Freaks* involves a drifter who becomes part of a traveling carnival. Once he is put on display as a human oddity, the action heats up with the requisite transformation. The plot is convoluted and includes a vampire, which is far from surprising. The cast is fine—Brendan Hughes, Bruce Payne and Michele Matheson—but the implementation of a promising storylines fails to generate any sense of gothic horror. By this point the *Howling* series have become action films with werewolves as the protagonist. *The Howling VI: The Freaks* was quickly released on video-cassette and eventually released on DVD.

The last (to date) in the series, *The Howling VII: New Moon Rising* (1994) was directed by Clive Turner and justifiably considered the worst of the franchise. With characters and inserted footage from *The Howling IV: The Original Nightmare*, *The Howling V: The Rebirth*, and *The Howl-*

ing VI: The Freaks, the meandering plot, poor acting (in some cases local townspeople) qualify the film as one of the worst werewolf films in history. If any lessons can be gleaned from *The Howling* series it's that an excellent novel can sometimes be translated into an excellent film only to have its quality marred by a succession of odd and often truly horrible films at the hands of inept filmmakers.

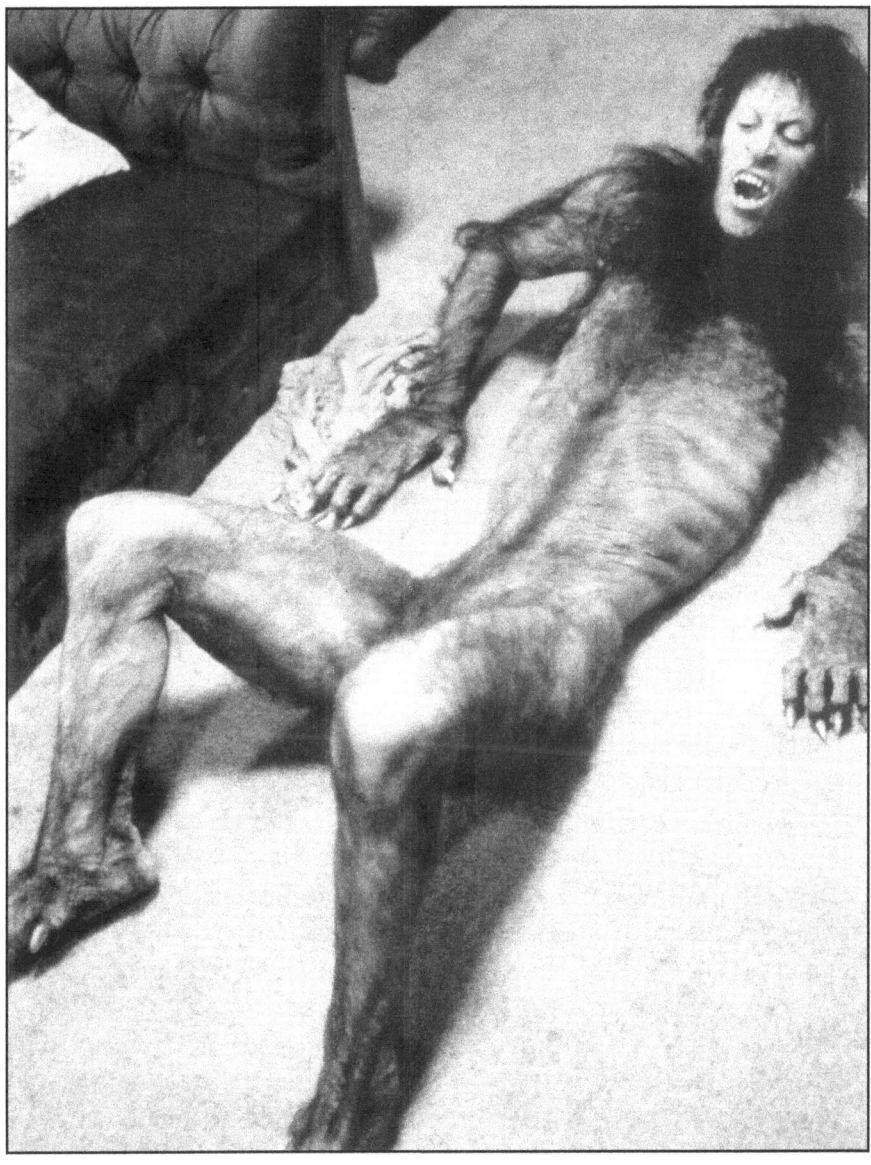

David Naughton in *An American Werewolf in London.* (1981) Rick Baker's superb makeup helped make the film one of the highest grossing werewolf films of all time.

With the success of *The Howling* proving that werewolves were bankable, audiences flocked to *An American Werewolf in London* (1981), the highest grossing werewolf film at that time. Directed and written by John Landis, *An American Werewolf in London* is as unique as it is refreshing. Starring David Naughton, Griffin Dunne and Jenny Agutter, the film follows two backpacking buddies across England where they are attacked by a werewolf on the moors at night. One of the youths, Jack (Dunne), is killed and David (Naughton) is taken to a London hospital to recover. While recuperating his dead friend arrives and informs him that he's now a werewolf. This grisly sequence featuring Dunne as a decomposing talking corpse adds a surrealistic tone to the film. David begins a relationship with a nurse (Agutter) and commences to endure visits by Jack's reanimated corpse. Jack is encouraging David to kill himself to prevent any further mayhem.

The werewolf transformation scene is an original piece of filmmaking. Make-up artist Rick Baker, who has publicly acknowledged a debt of gratitude to Jack Pierce, created the transformation using a body suit, masks, prosthetics, mechanized appliances in conjunction with traditional make-up. This groundbreaking and innovative approach would secure for Baker an Academy Award® for make-up, the first Oscar statuette in a category that had only recently been created. The lycanthrope transformation in *An American Werewolf in London* allows for an on-screen expanding torso, elongated fingers, fangs and claws. Not since Lon Chaney, Jr.'s transformation in *The Wolf Man* had a werewolf been so realistically brought to life.

In 1997 the long awaited sequel, *An American Werewolf in Paris*, would fail to thrill either critics or fans. The plot is loosely connected with the story John Landis had written all of those years before. The film follows Serafine Pigot (Delpy) who is the daughter of David and his nurse lover, Alex (Agutter), from the first film. The film is well acted by Julie Delpy, Anthony Waller and Tom Everett Scott but is lacking in the creative spark that made *An American Werewolf in London* such a sensation. A good film nonetheless, *An American Werewolf in Paris* ranks as one of the better sequels of any werewolf film.

Following in the wake of both *The Howling* and *An American Werewolf in London*, *Wolfen* (1981) was based upon the book by Whitley Streiber. *Wolfen* is an excellent film, but as one might expect in such cases the novel is much better. This was true as well of *The Howling*. Starring Albert Finney, Diane Venora, and Gregory Hines, the plot follows the

Michael J. Fox in *Teen Wolf* (1985)

novel's premise with Finney as the detective. What *Wolfen* is lacking, of course, is the startling transformations audiences were treated to in *The Howling* and *An American Werewolf in London*. No matter, *Wolfen* is a literate, beautifully acted tale of advanced wolf creatures not unlike the traditional lycanthropes.

Silver Bullet (1985) was based upon Stephen King's *Cycle of the Werewolf* and starred Gary Busey, Everett McGill and Corey Haim. King wrote the screenplay himself and the resulting film was quite good. Directed by Dan Attias and produced by the legendary Dino De Laurentis, *Silver Bullet* is a faithful adaptation of the book, thanks in a large part to King's participation. The plot follows the events in Tarker's Mills and incorporates the relationship between the handicapped brother, Marty (Haim) and his sister, Jane (Megan Follows). When his alcoholic uncle (Busey) builds him a new wheelchair its christianed "The silver bullet" and later Marty goes outside where he narrowly escapes being killed by a werewolf. The plot then unfolds along the same general lines as the book. The scenes with the werewolf are fast-paced but the make-up is often nothing more than a wolf's head mask on an actor in a hairy body suit. This is the film's downfall. With Jack Pierce inspired make-up the believability factor might have been elevated. Interestingly enough, in a dream sequence where the werewolf, Pastor Lester Lowe (McGill), envisions his parishioners as lycanthropes the townspeople are seen briefly in just such make-up. *Silver Bullet* offers too many disparate plot elements that don't properly coalesce into the narrative structure, but it works well enough as moderate entertainment.

Teen Wolf (1985) was an outright comedy, a rarity in werewolf films although certain of them were unintentionally humorous. Michael J. Fox stars as high school student Scott Howard who discovers that he's a werewolf. The film plays the scenario for laughs as Scott uses his lycanthropic strength to help win basketball games. Of course there's a love interest (Lorrie Griffin), a school bully, and a concluding basketball sequence where Scott transforms into the werewolf to save his team. Ridiculous though it may be, *Teen Wolf* was effective and popular. A sequel, *Teen Wolf Too* (1987) starring Jason Bateman as Todd Howard, Scott's cousin, was less effective but follows an identical premise, replacing basketball with boxing.

The Monster Squad (1987) was written by Shane Black and Fred Dekker and directed by Dekker. Shane Black is better known today as the scriptwriter of *Lethal Weapon* (1987) starring Mel Gibson and Danny

The Monster Squad (1987) Tom Woodruff, Jr., Tom Noonan, Duncan Regehr, Michael Mackay, Carl Thibault, Michael Fuastino, Brent Chalem, Andre Gower, Robby Kiger and Ryan Lambert.

Glover. An unabashed and affectionate homage to the classic film monsters of the 30s and 40s, the monsters here were created by Stan Winston. The film's opening sequence featuring Dracula, a vampire woman and the attack by angry townspeople (all of which is explained later in the film) is a set-piece of special effects and action. The narrative then switches to present time where a "monster squad"—a group of young teen boys who idolize the classic film monster—and their adventures after receiving a copy of Abraham Van Helsing's diary. They have the diary translated from German and learn that once each century the forces of good and evil clash whereupon an amulet needed to maintain balance becomes vulnerable to destruction. Quite naturally the intrepid youths set out to find the amulet. Their quest coincides with the arrival of Count Dracula (Duncan Regehr) who also seeks the amulet. Using the assistance of Frankenstein's monster, a werewolf, a mummy and an amphibious gill creature, Dracula will let nothing stand in the way of his quest for world domination. If the monster squad can locate the amulet they can open a hole in the universe and cast the monsters into limbo.

The monsters in *The Monster Squad* were inspired by the monsters from the famed Universal Studios movies although the make-up was altered to prevent copyright infringement because the film was distributed through Tri-Star Pictures. The amphibious gill creature was also inspired by Universal's *Creature from the Black Lagoon* series. *The Monster Squad* is an excellent film, widely regarded as a classic in its own right, the perfect *homage* to the classic films starring Chaney, Karloff and Lugosi. Of its many highlights is a truly menacing performance by Duncan Regehr as Dracula even without substantial dialogue. The sets, costuming, make-up, special effects and creatures by Stan Winston are all noteworthy. The teenagers intent on saving the world from Dracula and the monsters are perfectly realized by actors Andre Gower, Robby Kiger, Ryan Lambert, Stephen Macht and Ashley Blank. Tom Noonan's portrayal of Frankenstein's monster is memorable kitsch.

The Monster Squad has been criticized as being a juvenile adventure, which is a fair assessment, but films intended for younger audiences are just as entertaining as those made exclusively for adults. In fact, *The Monster Squad* is a monster movie that falls into the "family film" category which may explain its popularity. It appeals to all age groups and struck a nostalgic chord with its affectionate depiction of the iconic monsters. The 20th anniversary DVD edition included commentary from director Fred Dekker and cast interviews among other tidbits.

My Mom's a Werewolf (1988) is just as silly as the title implies. Intended as a comedy and cast with excellent actors, the film never really achieves any sense of mischievousness, and its certainly lacking in any gothic elements. Susan Blakely stars as a suburban mother who finds herself entangled with her neighborhood lycanthropic pet shop owner. John Saxon is excellent, as is Blakely but the premise fails to offer any surprises. The werewolf here is a perfunctory rehash of previous film werewolves and perhaps less frightening than any werewolf in history.

Full Eclipse (1993) is a solid fusion of science fiction and the werewolf lore. Directed by Anthony Hickox and starring Mario Van Peebles and Bruce Payne, the plot twist here being a Los Angeles police squad comprised of officers with the ability to transform into werewolves. The make-up minimizes the hirsute tendencies of traditional films and retains a semblance of humanity for their appearance which is a unique approach. Lycanthropes have generally been cast as victims in both literature and films but here they are the heroes turned into murderous cops. The plot pits Max Dire (Van Peebles) against a rampaging group of police-werewolves and their gang leader, Garou (Payne). Top-flight action scenes, a unique premise and high production values serve the film well although the film isn't very well known.

Wolf (1994) was a disappointment to fans of the werewolf genre, although there has been a slight critical re-evaluation since its initial release. American novelist Jim Harrison was commissioned to write a screenplay based upon *Wolf*, his 1971 novel. Harrison, who is close friends with Jack Nicholson who reportedly supported Harrison early in the author's career, wrote *Wolf* as a reflection on his bohemian youth. The wolf is a metaphor and has nothing to do with lycanthropes. In the novel, which is subtitled "A False Memoir," the character known as Swanson has abandoned Manhattan to explore the Michigan woods hoping to glimpse the wild wolves roaming the area. As he waits for the wolves he reflects on his adventuresome life. *Wolf* was Harrison's first novel and in the "Author's note" he states that it deals with the years 1956—1960 but written at the age of thirty-three "a juncture when literary souls always turn around and look backward."[89] Harrison went on to write many critically acclaimed novels including *A Good Day to Die, Farmer, Legends of the Fall* and *Dalva*. One of America's pre-eminent literary voices: that his first novel would become a werewolf tale is mind-boggling.

The film starring Jack Nicholson and Michelle Pfeiffer has nothing whatsoever to do with Harrison's novel. The screenplay is credited to Harrison and Wesley Strick. It is widely believed that Elaine May contributed to the script as well. Directed by Mike Nichols, Nicholson plays Will Randall who is bitten by a wolf while driving home from Vermont. Randall works in the publishing industry and finds himself at odds with Stewart Swinton (James Spader). Randall is replaced by Swinton who has been appointed the new editor-in-chief by tycoon Raymond Alden (Christopher Plummer). Simultaneously, Randall becomes involved with Alden's daughter Laura (Pfeiffer). The werewolf transformation on Nicholson is handled in the same fashion as Henry Hull's make up for *The Werewolf of London*; a human resemblance is maintained with only general alterations to evoke a wolf-like countenance. The film's final action scene is a royal battle between Randall and Swinton with Laura revealed to possess lycanthropic tendencies. No matter that *Wolf* deviates from Harrison's novel in every way possible, it remains an effective and chilling film, entertaining and campy enough so that over time its reputation has grown.

Huntress: Spirit of the Night (1995) maintains the proven combination of suspense and nudity, but with superior production values. The focus here is upon a beautiful woman, Tara (portrayed by Jenna Bodner in her screen debut), who returns to the town of Brecon, North Wales for her father's funeral. Here she experiences a sexual awakening which leads her to uncover a family secret. She learns that she is the victim of a curse upon Brecon and, in fact, her primal instincts are awakened along with her sexual desire. The screenplay doesn't allow her a complete transformation into a werewolf; instead, the filmmakers chose to limit her transformation to a reddening of her eyes. However, this effect is realized while she is nude, and as can be expected her nude scenes are prolonged for maximum effect. However, while the nude scenes are manipulative, they are remarkably tasteful. What one might refer to as "the sleaze factor" is missing from these scenes as director Mark Manos chose a stylized choreography for Tara's emotional turbulence. Tara is a lycanthrope as a victim, an element in werewolf lore that dates back to the earliest recorded tales. It is the lycanthropic side of her nature that provides her the stamina required to escape a trap intended to kill her.

Reportedly, *Huntress: Spirit of the Night* was edited, removing a sexually explicit scene which would have resulted in a NC-17 rating. *Huntress: Spirit of the Night* is a step above the usual monster movie. Screenwriter James Sealskin wisely set his story in Wales, which is a refreshing change of pace. The focus is on the characters, their interaction, and Tara's slow realization that she has become a pawn in a darker game. The lovely Jenna Bodner steals the show as Tara, but due credit belongs to director of photography Dan Toader who understands how light can be used to convey emotion. Jenna Bodner is sometimes also billed as Bodnar. The location photography in Bucharest, Hungary (substituting as Wales) adds authenticity to a film that's more an erotic thriller than a werewolf film.

The Werewolf (1996) is another direct-to-video and DVD exploitation film and mildly entertaining. The plot involves archeologists who uncover a werewolf skeleton in Arizona and when one of the crew is scratched by a bone he soon develops lycanthropic tendencies. Starring Jorge Rivero, Richard Lynch, Frederico Cavalli, Adrianna Miles and Joe Estevez, *The Werewolf* incorporates American Indian mythology with lycanthrope mythology. A disjointed effort intended as an action film, the storyline's potential isn't fully realized.

Eyes of the Werewolf (1999) features the appealing Stephanie Beaton in a film that suffers from several shortcomings. Shot on video, the video to DVD transfer is grainy which leaves viewers with the impression that the film is worse than it really is. Still, it is a bad film, primarily due to the uninspired videography, amateurish werewolf make-up, and less than stellar acting. On its plus side all of the participants give it their best effort but the script is meandering. Director Tim Sullivan demonstrates knowledge of pacing in order to elevate the drama, although it's Stephanie Beaton who salvages the film from the dung heap of mediocrity. Her nude scenes, which are plentiful, offer a visual feast for the target audience of males who favor skin over plot. And therein lies the film's problem. It comes across as home video homage to the best of Paul Naschy's films, with emphasis on the nudity. Stephanie Beaton writhes in ecstasy, cups her breasts with her hands, and frolics in a soft core version of sexual frenzy so convincingly that this viewer was profoundly disappointed when the werewolf made his appearance. Given a budget with some potential, a cinematographer instead of a video operator, *Eyes of the Werewolf* might have been interesting. Certainly, Stephanie Beaton has proven herself in some small but diverse roles, but here the focus is on her physical attributes rather than her thespian skills.

The other cast members give the impression of trying hard to make this ridiculous film into an A-list production instead of a cheap home-video knock-off.. Mark Sawyer as Rich, the man who becomes a werewolf, has little to do other than look happy as Stephanie Beaton grinds her naked torso against him. Jason Clark, Tarri Markel, Deborah Hub, Kurt Levee and Lyndon Johnson work overtime to elicit believability. This is no polished group of method actors and there is a strong amateurish tone to the proceedings.

The plot is best summarized by the actual publicity blurb:

> "A laboratory accident leaves Rich blind and at the mercy of an unscrupulous surgeon who performs an accidental eye transplant. Unknown to everyone, including the doctor's band of organ snatching murderers, the eyes were pulled from the sockets of a werewolf. All hell breaks loose when Rich, with the help of a horny nurse, a midget and a lesbian detective, tries to extract revenge during the next full moon."

Eyes of the Werewolf is the cheapest of exploitation films, created and marketed in DVD format in order to realize a profit from an unsuspecting public. Werewolf aficionados might refer to *Eyes of the Werewolf* as a "howler" for reasons that have nothing to do with the full moon.

Rage of the Werewolf (1999) also known as *Planet of the Werewolves* is a direct-to-DVD exploitation film written by Kevin Lindenmuth and Santa Marotta. Better than one might expect, *Rage of the Werewolf* is gory fun. After an asteroid collides with the moon, it changes the moon's orbital rotation which in turn causes thousands of people to become werewolves. Brisk, well-acted and campy, this is the type of film that is clearly fun to make. The action, blood letting and screams are taken in stride by actors Santo Marotta, Tom Nondorf, Joe Zaso, Sasha Graham, Hollis Granville, Mick McCleery and fan favorite Debbie Rochon. The plot is secondary to the action, which is what such films are all about. *Rage of the Werewolf* won second place with audiences at the 1999 Screamfest convention.

The excellent *Ginger Snaps* (2003) was directed by John Fawcett in Canada from a screenplay by Karen Walton and Brett Sullivan. The title takes its name from the ginger snap cookie with lycanthropy in the story as a metaphor for puberty. Two sisters, Ginger and Brigitte, are fascinated with gothic mayhem and death, but their lives become complicated when Ginger is bitten by a wolf and begins transforming into an uncontrollable werewolf. Superbly crafted, with outstanding acting by Emily Perkins, Katherine Isabelle, and Kris Lemche, *Ginger Snaps* is a coming-of-age story that found a responsive audience. The teenage angst theme, a literate script and wonderful casting proved equally successful when the film was released on DVD. High DVD sales encouraged two sequels, *Ginger Snaps 2: Unleashed* (2003) and *Ginger Snaps Back: The Beginning* (2003). Filmed back-to-back, *Ginger Snaps 2: Unleashed* was markedly less successful at the box-office and *Ginger Snaps Back: The Beginning* became a direct to video release. The subsequent films were also well made and entertaining but their less than enthusiastic response may have more to do with the public's distaste with sequels in general than with any lack of effort on the part of the filmmakers.

Blood of the Werewolf (2001) serves up heaping spoonfuls of mediocrity. With its uninspired script and lame actors, it remains a testament to the idea that video has replaced cinematography as the amateur filmmakers preferred venue. It shares the distinction, along with *Eyes of the Werewolf*, of being one of worst werewolf films in history. Sixty years after the release of the Lon Chaney, Jr. classic, *Blood of the Werewolf* represents a regression in the art of filmmaking. Another direct to DVD film and billed as an anthology of three werewolf stories, *Blood of the Werewolf* meanders along an uncertain path with a three-part script by writer-director Bruce Hallenbeck. The first tale involves a writer returning home in search of an ex-love. The make-up for the were-woman (or whatever she is) looks to have been created using Halloween supplies purchased at Wal-Mart. Fortunately, there was no nudity in *Blood of the Werewolf* as the principal cast is so unappealing that even a nude scene couldn't save this lackluster and uninspired video.

Brotherhood of the Wolf (2002) is not precisely a werewolf film but involves a strange wolf creature, albeit briefly. Made in France and directed by Christopher Gans, *Brotherhood of the Wolf* was inspired by actual historical events in the 18th century when a marauding animal believed to be a wolf killed dozens of people near the valley of Auvergne. Known as *La Bete du Gevaudan* ("The Beast of Gevaudan") the creature has become popular in French folklore. Director Gans created a film involving soldiers intent on tracking the beast. Beautifully photographed, *Brotherhood of the Wolf* was an international hit. The beast itself appears to be a combination of computer generated imagery and prosthetics. The film has an epic scope. *Brotherhood of the Wolf* starred Samuel Le Bihan, Vincent Cassel and Monica Bellucci. With its expertly choreographed martial arts sequences, drama and suspense the film earned acclaim in both the American and European marketplace, and it also became a bestseller when it was released on DVD after its successful theatrical run.

Darkwolf (2003) falls somewhere in that murky territory between an A-list film and low-budget knock-off. A reasonable budget allowed the filmmakers some creativity with the werewolf. They chose a combination of animation and animatronics to realize a werewolf that is sometimes an electronically manipulated creature. Finally, there is a small flavoring of full character make-up on actor Rick McCallum. For most of his scenes McCallum wears a modified ape suit with a horrific werewolf visage. This merging of styles isn't quite effective, but it does lend the film a much needed aura of surrealism. The plot is simple: a werewolf on the loose in Los Angeles has picked up Josie's (Samaire Armstrong) scent and now possesses an insatiable urge to mate with her. Another erstwhile effort with professional acting and high production values, *Darkwolf* naturally includes the obligatory nudity and several well-staged action scenes. Written by Geoffrey Holliday and directed by Richard Friedman, *Darkwolf* was shot in 24p (progressive frames per second) High Definition which a growing number of filmmakers believe is the wave of the future. *Darkwolf* is an erotic and entertaining werewolf thriller.

With *Underworld* (2003) the werewolf film once again became a popular and successful franchise. Written by Danny McBride and directed by Len Wiseman, *Underworld* stars Kate Beckinsale as a vampire, Selene,

Kate Beckinsale handled guns and werewolves in the modern classic *Underworld* (2003).

whose career is tracking down and killing a group of werewolves known as Lycans. She becomes involved with a human, Micheal Corvin (Scott Speedman), who gets bitten and begins to suffer from lycanthropy. Selene must decide between love and death. If she kills Corvin then she remains honorable within her own clan, but by saving him she can fulfill her love for him. The device of an underworld of opposing supernatural species isn't unique as we have seen this device in the stories of H. Warner Munn, Jack Williamson, Gary Brander and Whitley Streiber, but *Underworld's* cinematic version with its stylish punk-Gothic visuals and high-tech special effects makes for a rousing entertainment. Len Wiseman's intention was to make an action film that includes vampires and werewolves and with science as the basis for their existence the storyline becomes a feud between two opposing forces, neither of which is less evil or good than the other. The creatures in the film were designed by Patrick Tatopoulos and include animatronics, latex masks, CGI (computer generated imagery) prosthetics, leg extensions and full body suites. Wiseman also chose to limit the werewolf's hair and accentuate their body mass and musculature. The collaboration of the best technology and traditional make-up effects provides *Underworld* a frightening group of monsters.

While most sequels are less than stellar repetitions of the original formulae, *Underworld: Evolution* (2006) defied the odds and became an equally successful extension thanks to a nearly identical crew. Once again

Kate Beckinsale in *Underworld: Evolution* (2006).

under Len Wiseman's direction with a script by Danny McBride, Kate Beckinsale and Scott Speedman return to their forbidden love affair to face off against vampires and werewolves. The plot elaborates on the clan relationships and the efforts to create a hybrid bloodline of the two species. The film left open the possibility for another sequel but with Kate Beckinsale preferring to tackle other roles a prequel was created.

Underworld: Rise of the Lycans (2009) recounts the origins of the vampire and werewolf clans. Rhona Mitra stars as a young woman, Sonja, hiding her relationship with a Lycan. Directing chores this time around fell to former designer Patrick Tatopoulos with a script credited to Danny McBride, Dirk Blackman and Howard McCain. Michael Sheen, Bill Nighy and Rhona Mitra all perform superbly in the final entry of this stylish and riveting series.

Cursed (2003) directed by Wes Craven and starring Christina Ricci was a commercial failure that found a second life after being released on DVD and being sold to television. Ostensibly another teenagers versus a werewolf story, the corny and convoluted plot gets lost in an otherwise well-staged production. The werewolf is a combination of body suit and

Rhona Mitra in *Underworld: Rise of the Lycans* (2009).

make-up, with emphasis on the body suit. The actors themselves can't be faulted as they are all capable and believable, but the film fails to break new ground and comes across as a high budget made-for-television episode for a program that never materialized.

Filmed in Europe, *Werewolf Hunter: The Legend of Romasanta* (2004) stars Julian Sands in a story based upon an 1850s incident in Spain where Manuel Blanco Romasanta murdered thirteen people. Upon his capture Romasanta confessed to being a werewolf. Intelligently written by Elena Serra and Alberto Marini, Sands plays Romasanta as an articulate and charming gentleman. There is no overt werewolf transformation and the film focuses on Romasanta's relationship with Barbara (Elsa Pataky.

The much anticipated big-budget *Van Helsing* (2004) directed and written by Stephen Sommers and released by Universal Studios, was a direct homage to the classic film monsters of the 30s and 40s. The film opens with a black and white sequence that evokes the memory of those classic Universal films. In Transylvania, Doctor Frankenstein (Samuel West) creates a monster (Shuler Hensley) with the assistance of Count Dracula (Richard Roxburgh). But Dracula had deceived Frankenstein and kills him. Dracula has plans of using Frankenstein's experiments to revive the dead for his own purpose. But the monster escapes and is pursued to a windmill which is burned down. Dracula meanwhile, escapes with his *three* undead brides (actresses Silvia Colloca, Elena Anaya and Josie Maran). The film then switches to color photography and the plot picks up a year later. Officials at the Vatican dispatch Gabriel Van Helsing (Hugh Jackman) to kill Dracula while assisting Anna Velarious (Kate Beckinsale) whose brother Velkan (Will Kemp) had recently been killed by a werewolf. Velkan naturally returns as a werewolf and the remainder of the film involves Van Helsing's quest to defeat Dracula.

The film's second major action sequence features Van Helsing and Anna Velarious battling Dracula's brides in a town square in Transylvania. The action sequences are brilliantly choreographed, combing CGI images with live action. It is the only high profile CGI sequence in the film that works effectively. Jackman and Beckinsale are excellent together. Richard Roxburgh's interpretation of Count Dracula is a virtuoso piece of acting that channels Bela Lugosi into a refreshingly menacing version of the iconic vampire. Shuler Hensley as Frankenstein's monster is equally memorable. Will Kemp, the werewolf brother, is excellent in his few scenes but one of *Van Helsing's* flaws is the over-reliance on computer technology for its horrific images. The werewolf is entirely computer generated which

Christina Ricci in Wes Craven's *Cursed* (2003). The cane was a replica of the one used by Lon Chaney, Jr. in *The Wolf-Man*.

is a major disappointment. The technology here fails to provide audiences with a memorable lycanthrope. This is an injustice and particularly unfair is the fact that Will Kemp is never provided an opportunity to roam the fog-shrouded landscape in full creature make-up. The werewolf comes across as a cartoon figure speeding about the set at high speed. Frankenstein's monster is also played for laughs in one unfortunate scene where his hinged skull flaps open and closed. Little flourishes like this went far in detracting from an otherwise excellent production.

Big Bad Wolf (2006) benefits from capable filmmaking and earnest production values. Every effort was made to produce a first-rate lycanthropic thriller and the film nearly succeeds. The plot: A group of college students partying in a cabin are attacked by a monster. A stepfather, Mitchell Toblat (played by Richard Tyson; the name Toblat is an anagram for Talbot, a tribute to Lon Chaney, Jr.), comes under suspicion and a seek-and-kill scenario ensues with Toblat murdering everyone he can get his claws on. The ensemble cast—Trevor Duke, Kimberly J. Brown, Christopher Shyer, Sarah Aldrich and others—exist to be killed, frightened, or both. The werewolf was created using latex masks and a full body suit and the countenance is a variation of all of those werewolves audiences have seen before. *Big Bad Wolf* is a sincere effort to create a wholly original

Kate Beckinsale and Will Kemp in *Van Helsing* (2004). The computer generated werewolf deprived actor Will Kemp (and audiences) of an opportunity for a memorable lycanthrope.

thriller which must count for something. It is neither the best and still far above the worst of the direct to DVD werewolf films.

Werewolf in a Woman's Prison (2006) is equal parts sexploitation and prison drama with a werewolf that resembles a cross between an alien and an insect with glowing red eyes that look like Christmas lights. If it's a bad film then it's a remarkably fun to watch bad film. Nude women splattered in blood and a profusion of lesbian eroticism make *Werewolf in a Woman's Prison* a must-see choice for fans of voyeurism and gore. In one remarkable scene, two women chained topless together in the desert begin licking the sweat off each other in order to survive. What resembles a plot involves a woman's prison where the ladies are exploited for an x-rated website and since one of them, actress Victoria De Mare, happens to be a werewolf, the carnage becomes another cycle of feminist revenge against abusive males. Those prison officials should have known better. Director Jeff Leroy, along with screenwriter Vinnie Bilancio, have created perhaps the ultimate outrageous sexploitation-werewolf film.

Blood and Chocolate (2006) was based on the novel by Annette Curtis Klause and offers an excellent interpretation of the novel. There are noticeable plot differences between the novel and film, which is to be expected, but these variations in no way detract from the film's quality. Similar to the novel, the story follows a teenager, Vivian, who must choose between her love for a young man or her loyalty to her lycanthropic ancestry. True to form, teen angst prevails and the plot thickens with the obligatory betrayals, chases and a reconciliation. *Blood and Chocolate* shares with several other films a quality that comes from its sincerity. There is no exploitation, no unnecessary violence and gore. The film works so well because it focuses on characters and the producers coordinated a set design, costuming and casting that accentuates those merits that come with a reasonable budget and a talented crew. The werewolves here are seen as actual wolves. *Blood and Chocolate* starred Agnes Bruckner, Olivier Martinez and Hugh Dancy and was directed by Katja Von Garnier and Olivier Martinez.

Skinwalkers (2007) found little positive response upon its theatrical release but the uncut DVD release elicited a slightly better impression. Once again using the device of a werewolf culture, this time two opposing werewolf clans, the story involves a thirteen year old boy who will soon begin his transformations as he enters puberty. The boy, Timothy (Matthew Knight), is a half-breed werewolf. Known as the "half-blood" Timothy soon learns that he is prophesied to become the werewolf that

Blood and Chocolate (2006) with Agnes Bruckner and Hugh Dancy was an intelligent well-crafted film based upon the novel by Annette Curtis Klause.

ends the curse. This sets him at odds with an opposing werewolf clan. Also starring Elias Koteas, Sarah Carter, and Rhona Mitra, *Skinwalkers* is essentially another action film hung on a werewolf plot. It entertains as action films are meant to entertain. The creatures here were created by the Stan Winston Studio.

Made for television with an eye on a lucrative mass-market DVD release, *Never Cry Werewolf* (2007) featured Kevin Sorbo and Nina Dobrev in another action-werewolf thriller. *Never Cry Werewolf* has been criticized for being an unauthorized scene-by-scene remake of *Fright Night* (1985) with the vampire replaced by a werewolf. The comparison is not without merit but it matters little. Even the lovely Nina Dobrev can't salvage the pedestrian action. The werewolf is another oversized beast with an elongated snout and remarkably large teeth. Like so many werewolf films before it, *Never Cry Werewolf* is entertaining at a juvenile level and as easily forgotten as the popcorn you ate while watching it.

Hybrid (2008) falls into that identical category of popcorn thriller with a tad more emphasis on gore. Another fusion of science fiction and lycanthropy, the twist here involves cross-species organ transplants. A dash of Native American mysticism fails to provide relief from the often slapstick exploitation. Advertised as "A new breed of terror!" *Hybrid*

Publicity still for *Skinwalkers* (2007).

malfunctions as a blind man receives a wolf's eyes and soon starts seeing people as prey. Actors Justine Bateman, Tinsel Korey and Corey Monteith must certainly have enjoyed the action. Films like this are often more fun to make than they are to watch.

Twilight (2008) and its sequel *New Moon* (2009) capitalized upon the sensational series by author Stephanie Meyer. Although primarily another vampire story, the werewolf's feature prominently in the gothic-romantic plot. Neither film received any positive reviews of note, although audiences responded enthusiastically to both films. Meyer's plot is retained with but slight variations. The poor critical reaction to these films has resulted in an unfortunate negative backlash against the excellent books by Meyers whose original work will undoubtedly stand the test of time whereas the films may become better known as cultural oddities. Poorly conceived, unintentionally campy, with professional high-budget gloss evident in every scene, the *Twilight* series is destined to become a fixture on cable television every Halloween.

The Wolfman (2010) was an eagerly anticipated remake when Universal Studios announced the production as early as 2005. Disagreements over the script and a change in directors delayed the filming for several years. When filming was completed Universal Studio executives determined that some brief scenes and add-ons were needed. Rick Baker cam-

Rick Baker's award winning makeup for Benicio Del Toro in *The Wolfman* (2010) remake. Another in a long line of visual tributes to Jack Pierce and Lon Chaney, Jr.

paigned for and succeeded in landing the coveted job of make-up artist on a film touted as a remake of the 1941 classic. Actor Benicio del Toro was reportedly a driving force in getting the film made. A longtime fan of the Chaney film, del Toro and Rick Baker insisted that the make-up should resemble the iconic image created by Jack Pierce for Chaney. And not unlike the experience Chaney had with Pierce, the make-up application would take several hours. Baker would win another Academy Award® for "Best Achievement in Makeup" for his work on the film. That del Toro was remaking *The Wolfman* with Baker generated excitement among horror film fans. Ultimately, some computer generated imagery was used in the transformation. Director Joe Johnston, who signed on to the film only three weeks before shooting commenced, later explained that he had to accept that some sequences would have to be handled in post-production using computer generated images.

Written by Andrew Kevin Walker and David Self with an on-screen credit stating "Based upon the motion picture screenplay by Curt Siodmak," *The Wolfman* is a gloomy but polished big-budget film that entertains without being great. It belongs with *The Howling, An American Werewolf in London, Underworld* and the Paul Naschy films as among the best modern film versions of the werewolf mythology. Quite naturally it fails to surpass the superior 1941 version, but the attempt is noble. With Siodmak's concept as a starting point, the plot would deviate sharply from the original storyline in the final reel.

Benicio del Toro is superb as Larry Talbot but the primary difference here is that his version of Talbot is emotionally conflicted at the onset, and for reasons that would only become known at the conclusion. Chaney's Talbot was cheerful, literate and charming, only becoming a tortured man *after* he was bitten by a werewolf. This distinction is crucial in appreciating both versions.

The plot: Shakespearean actor Larry Talbot returns home after learning of his brother's death. On the train to the family estate in Blackmoor an elderly man (Max Von Sydow) gives Talbot a silver, wolf's head cane which Talbot is told originated in Gevaudan, France where centuries past "The Beast of Gevaudan" had murdered dozens of people. Once at Blackmoor, Talbot reunites with his father, Sir John (Anthony Hopkins) and Gwen Conliffe (Emily Blunt) and soon thereafter learns that his brother had been mauled to death. His brother's death is upsetting to Talbot whose mother we learn had committed suicide when he was young. Learning that gypsies are in the area, and hearing rumors that his brother's death might be attributed to a werewolf, Talbot visits the gypsy camp and encounters Maleva (Geraldine Chaplin) who warns him that something evil had befallen his brother. When a werewolf then attacks the gypsy camp Talbot is seriously injured. At Talbot Hall on the Blackmoor Estate Talbot is nursed back to health by Gwen. During his convalescence his father's manservant, Singh (Art Malik), reveals that he has silver bullets and intimates that there is a great evil at work in Blackmoor. Meanwhile, Inspector Aberline (Hugo Weaving) arrives from London to investigate the recent murders. Talbot later finds is father in the mansion's catacombs where he has built a shrine to his dead wife. Inside the room there is also a chair fitted with restraining straps. Sir John locks himself in the room and leaves his son to fend for himself. That night Talbot transforms into a werewolf and kills several townspeople. In the morning it is his father who leads the police to the hiding place where the Talbot had hidden. He is incarcerated in the insane asylum where had had been held as a child after his mother's death. Talbot is subjected to ice-water torture by a sadistic physician. During his incarceration his father visits him and explains that, years before, he had been inflicted with lycanthropy while visiting in India. Talbot then remembers having seen his father in werewolf form all those years ago when he killed his wife. Thus the younger Talbot's lifelong melancholy is explained. But Larry Talbot is now a werewolf as well for it was his father's attack that had injured him. Later, Talbot again transforms into a werewolf and escapes the asylum. Here the film takes on the symbolism of Greek tragedy where the conflict between a father and his son ends in death. This element was present in the 1941 version, but there it concluded with the father surviving the son. In Greek mythology the younger generation is seen as overthrowing the older generation as with the conflict of Oedipus and Laius. The elder Talbot has set in motion a chain of events that will ultimately result in his being killed by his son, and his son as well should forfeit his life as a result of these actions. The climactic battle between the two men after each has transformed into a werewolf is reminiscent of the fight in *Frankenstein Meets the Wolf Man*.

The Wolfman is a brooding film lacking the elegiac narrative that could have elevated it into a study of emotion and destiny. Several plot elements and supporting characters are either unfulfilled or discarded too quickly. What does work is its sincerity to tell a good story which is all the better thanks to the outstanding acting of Anthony Hopkins and Benicio del Toro.

House of the Wolfman (2010) starred Ron Chaney. The werewolf was played by actor Billy Bussey for the action scenes.

House of the Wolfman (2010) brings us full circle to the legacy popularized by Curt Siodmak, Jack Pierce and Lon Chaney, Jr. with this direct to DVD homage starring Chaney's grandson, Ron Chaney. *House of the Wolfman* is far removed from the elements of Greek and Biblical tragedy that textured the 1941 and 2010 film versions of the Talbot werewolf curse. Intentionally campy, the plot was advertised as: "Five people lured by a MAD DOCTOR…subjects in the most fiendish experiment of all time!" These unlucky five, believing they have been invited to the castle owned by Bela Reinhardt (Chaney) to learn if they will benefit from an inheritance, are soon subjected to long stretches of dialogue, meaningful glances, and spooky music. There is no action until the final few minutes and the film's seventy-five minutes is excruciatingly long. *House of the Wolfman*'s appeal lies in Ron Chaney's appearance. Written and directed by Eben McGarr, the production, including the sets and black and white photography, are quite good. Particularly intriguing is the performance by Michael R. Thomas as Dracula. With costuming and a Hungarian accent identical to that of Bela Lugosi, Thomas nearly steals the show. In one uncanny scene, a snippet from the 1931 *Dracula* is re-imagined and Michael Thomas could be Lugosi's doppelganger. But he is given little to do while the cast—Dustin Fitzsimmons, Jeremie Loncka, Sara Raftery, Cheryl Rodes, Jim Thalman, Saba Moor-Douchette and John P. McGarr—scramble about. *House of the Wolfman* is dedicated to Michael R. Thomas who passed away shortly after the film was completed. Although Ron Chaney's Bela Reinhardt transforms into a werewolf the creature was actually played by stunt-actor Billy Bussey who effectively conveys the malevolent energy required. Bussey, along with actor Craig Dabbs as the Frankenstein's monster, provides the film its best scenes. The make-up for the film is credited to various crew: make-up by Michelle Chung, key special effect make up Ana Preciado, and special effects make up Ron Karkoska, Mark Villalobos. Not to be taken seriously, *House of the Wolfman* is the type of Halloween treat that will find an audience with the collegiate crowd every October.

Ultimately, it is impossible to ignore the triumphant 1941 film starring Lon Chaney, Jr. It has stood the test of time and its influence has been evident in every werewolf film since.

The elements of lycanthropy accentuated in these films included demonic possession as its focus. But it also involved archetypal fears, social criticism, religious symbolism and an endless fascination with violence. Even the bad films can be seen as commentary on sexual repression which in the context of the filmmaker's screenplay often morphs into sexploitation.

In the past decade the werewolf mythology has nurtured a pop culture of books and films. Quite clearly few filmmakers and writers have been able to resist the lure of the werewolf. A broad spectrum of approaches to the lycanthrope, diverse talent and cultural perceptions, religiosity and large and small budgets have all contributed to a growing mythology where the werewolf, tormented and bestial, roams forever the darkest recesses of man's soul. The current cycle of werewolf films may have exhausted its potential but the lycanthrope has endured for centuries, and undoubtedly the beast said to lurk within us all will experience yet another rebirth in both films and literature. The cycle of the moon is endless.

Selected Werewolf Filmography

The Werewolf (1913)
Director: Henry MacRae. Story credited to Ruth Ann Baldwin.
Cast: Clarence Burton, Marie Walcamp, Phyllis Gordon, Lule Warrington, Sherman Bainbridge, William Clifford.

Note: A complete version does not exist. Most prints were believed lost in a fire in 1924.

The Werewolf of London (1935)
Director: Stuart walker. Story and screenplay: Robert Harris and John Colton.
Cast: Henry Hull, Warner Oland, Valerie Hobson, Lester Matthews, Lawrence Grant, Spring Byington, Clark Williams, J.M. Kerrigan, Charlotte Granville.

The Wolf Man (1941)
Director: Geoge Waggner. Screenplay: Curt Siodmak.
Cast: Lon Chaney, Jr., Claude Rains, Ralph Bellamy, Warren Williams, Patric Knowles, Bela Lugosi, Evelyn Ankers, Maria Ouspenskaya, Fay Helm, J.M. Kerrigan.

The Undying Monster (1942)
Director: John Brahm. Screenplay and story: Lillie Hayward, Michael Jacoby. Based on the novel by Jessie Douglas Kerruish.
Cast: James Ellison, Heather Angel, John Howard, Bramwell Fletcher, Heather Thatcher, Aubrey Mather, Halliwell Hobbes, Matthew Bolton.

Frankenstein Meets the Wolf Man (1943)
Director: Roy William Neill. Screenplay: Curt Siodmak.
Cast: Lon Chaney, Jr., Ilona Massey, Patric Knowles, Lionel Atwill, Bela Lugosi, Maria Ouspenskaya, Dennis Hoey, Don Barclay, Rex Evans, Dwight Frye, Harry Stubbs.

Cry of the Werewolf (1944)
Director: Henry Levin. Story and Screenplay: Griffin Jay and Charles O'Neal.
Cast: Nina Foch, Stephan Crane, Osa Massen, Blanche Yurka, Barton MacLean, Ivan triesault, John Abbott, Fred Graff, John Tyrell, Robert Williams.

House of Frankenstein (1944)
Director: Earle C. Kenton. Story and Screenplay: Curt Siodmak and Edward T. Lowe.
Cast: Boris Karloff, Lon Chaney, Jr., J. Carrol Naish, John Carradine, Anne Gwynne, Peter Coe, Lionel Atwill, George Zucco, Elena Verdugo, Sig Ruman, William Edmunds, Glenn Strange, Charles Miller.

Return of the Vampire (1944)
Director: Lew Landers. Story and Screenplay: Randall Faye, Griffin Jay and Kurt Neumann.
Cast: Bela Lugosi, Frieda Inescort, Nina Foch, Miles Mander, Roland Varno, Matt Willis, William Austin, Jeanne Bates, Billy Bevan.

House of Dracula (1945)
Director: Earle C. Kenton. Screenplay: Edward T. Lowe.
Cast: Lon Chaney, Jr., John Carradine, Martha O'Driscoll, Lionel Atwill, Onslow Stevens, Jane Adams, Ludwig Stossel, Glenn Strange, Skelton Knaggs.

She-Wolf of London (1946)
Director: Jean Yarbrough. Screenplay: George Bricker. Story by Dwight V. Babcock.

Cast: Don Porter, June Lockhart, Sara Haden, Jan Wiley, Lloyd Corrigan, Dennis Hoey, Martin Kosleck, Eily Maylon.

Abbott and Costello Meet Frankenstein (1948)
Director: Charles T. Barton. Screenplay: Robert Lees, Frederic I. Rinaldo, John Grant.
Cast: Bud Abbott, Lou Costello, Lon Chaney, Jr., Bela Lugosi, Glenn Strange, Lenore Aubert, Jane Randolph, Frank Ferguson, Charles Bradsteet.

The Werewolf (1956)
Director: Fred F. Sears. Screenplay: Robert E. Kent and story by James B. Gordon.
Cast: Steve Ritch, Don Megowan, Joyce Holden, Eleanore Tanin, Kim Charney, Harry Lauter, Larry J. Blake.

I Was a Teenage Werewolf (1957)
Director: Gene Fowler, Jr. Screenplay: Herman Cohen, Aben Kandel.
Cast: Michael landon, Yvonne Fedderson, Whit Bissell, Tony Marshall, Dawn Richard, Barney Phillips, Ken Miller.

How to Make a Monster (1958)
Director: Herbert L. Strock. Screenplay: Herman Cohen, Aben Kandel.
Cast: Robert H. Harris, Paul Brinegar, Gary Conway, Gary Clarke, Malcom Atterbury, Dennis Cross, Morris Ankrum, Walter Reed.

Curse of the Werewolf (1961)
Director: Terence Fisher. Screenplay: Anthony Hinds, based upon the novel by Guy Endore.
Cast: Clifford Evans, Oliver Reed, Yvonne Romain, Catherine Feller, Anthony Dawson, Josephine Llewellyn, Richard Wordsworth, Hira Talfrey, Justin Walters, John Gabriel.

Werewolf in a Girl's Dormitory (1961)
Director: Paolo Heusch. Screenplay: Julian Barry.
Cast: Barbara Lass, carl Schell, Curt Lowens, Maurice Marsac, Maureen O'Connor, Mary McNeeran, Grace Neame.

Face of the Screaming Werewolf (1964)
Original title: *La casa del terror*
Directors: Gilberto Martinez Solares, Rafeal Portillo, and Jerry Warren (American sequences).
Cast: Lon Chaney, Jr., Yerye Beirute, George Mitchell, Fred Hoffman, Rosa Arenas, Ramon Gay, Alfredo Wally Barron, Oscar Ortiz de Pinedo.

Frankenstein's Bloody Terror (1968)
Original title: *La marca del hombre-lobo*.
Alternate titles: *Mark of the Wolfman, Hell's Creatures, The Werewolf's Mark*.
Director: Enrique Lopez Eguiluz. Screenplay: Jacinto Molina.
Cast: Paul Naschy, Dianik Zurakowska, Manuel Manzaneque, Rosanna Yanni, Gualberto Galban, Aurora de Alba, Julian Ugarte, Jose Nieto, Carlos Casaravilla.

Assignment Terror (1970)
Original title: *Los monstruos de terror*.
Alternate titles: *Dracula Versus Frankenstein, Operation Terror*.
Director: Tulio Demicheli. Screenplay: Jacinto Molina.
Cast: Michael Rennie, Karin Dor, Craig Hill, Patty Shepard, Angel del Pozo, Manuel de Blas, Peter Damon, Paul Naschy.

The Werewolf's Shadow (1971)
Original title: *La noche de walpurgis*.
Alternate titles: *The Werewolf Versus the Vampire Woman, Blood Moon, Walpurgis Night*.
Director: Leon Klimovsky. Screenplay by Jacinto Molina and Hans Munkel.
Cast: Paul Naschy, Gaby Fuchs, Barbara Capell, Andres Resino, Yelena Samarina, Jose Marco, Betsabe Ruiz, Patty Shepard.

Werewolves on Wheels (1971)
Director: Michel Levesque. Screenplay: David S. Kaufman, Michel Levesque.
Cast: Steve Oliver, D. J. Anderson, Gene Shane, Billy Gray, Gray Johnson, Barry McGuire, Owen Orr, Anna Lynn Brown, Leonard Rogel.

Dracula, Prisoner of Frankenstein (1972)
Original title: *Dracula contra Frankenstein.*
Director: Jesus Franco. Screenplay: Jesus Franco, Paul D'Ales.
Cast: Dennis Price, Howard Vernon, Paca Gabaldon, Alberto Dalbes, Britt Nichols, Genevieve Robert, Anne Libert, Luis Barboo.

The Fury of the Wolfman (1972)
Original titles: *La furia de hombre lobo.*
Alternate titles: *The Wolfman Never Sleeps.*
Director: Jose Maria Zabalza. Screenplay: Jacinto Molina.
Cast: Paul Naschy, Perla Cristal, Veronica Lujan, Miguel de la Riva, Mark Stevens, Pilar Zorrilla, Jose Marco, Francisco Amoros, Javier de Rivera.

Dr. Jekyll and the Wolfman (1972)
Original title: *Dr. Jekyll y el Hombre Lobo.*
Alternate titles: *Dr. Jekyll Versus the Werewolf.*
Director: Leon Klimovsky. Screenplay: Jacinto Molina.
Cast: Paul Naschy, Shirley Corrigan, Jack Taylor, Mirta Miller, Jose Marco, Luis Induni, Barta Barri, Luis Gaspar, Lucy Tiller.

Moon of the Wolf (1972)
Director: Daniel Petrie. Screenplay: Alvin Sapinsley based upon the novel by Leslie H. Whitten.
Cast: David Janssen, Barbara Rush, Bradford Dillman, John Beradino, Royal Dano, John Davis Chandler, Geoffrey Lewis, Claudia McNeil, Dan Priest.

The Werewolf of Washington (1973)
Director: Milton Moses Ginsberg. Screenplay: Milton Moses Ginsberg.
Cast: Dean Stockwell, Katalin Kallay, Henry Ferrentino, Despo Diamantidou, Thayer David, Nancy Andrews, Clifton James, Biff McGuire.

Curse of the Devil (1973)
Original title: *El retorno de walpurgis.*
Alternate Titles: *Return of the Werewolf, The Black Harvest of Countess Dracula, The Return of the Walpurgis.*
Director: Carlos Aured. Screenplay: Jacinto Molina.
Cast: Paul Naschy, Fabiola Falcon, Mariano Vidal Molina, Maritza Olivares, Jose Manuel Martin, Elsa Zabala, Eduardo Calvo, Ana Farra, Fernando Sanchez Polack, Ines Morales.

Night of the Howling Beast (1975)
Original title: *La maldicion de la bestia.*
Alternate titles: *Hall of the mountain King, Horror of the Werewolf, The Curse of the Beast, The Werewolf and the Yeti.*
Director: Miguel Iglesias. Screenplay: Jacinto Molina.
Cast: Paul Naschy, Mercedes Molina, Silvia Solar, Gil Vidal, Luis Induni, Josep Castillo Escalona, Ventura Oller, Veronica Miriel, Juan Velilla, Carmen G. Cervera, Papa Ferrer.

Werewolf Woman (1976)
Original title: *La lupa mannara.*
Alternate titles: *Daughter of a Werewolf, She-Wolf, Terror of the She-Wolf, The Legend of the Wolf Woman.*
Director: Rino Di Silvestro. Screenplay: Rino Di Silvestro and Howard Ross.
Cast: Annik Borel, Howard Ross, Dagmar Lassander, Tino Carraro, Elio Zamuto, Osvaldo Ruggieri, Andrea Scotti, Frederick Stafford, Felicita Fanny, Isabella Rose.

Night of the Werewolf (1980)
Original title: ***El retorno del hombre-lobo.***
Alternate titles: ***Return of the Wolfman, The Craving.***
Director: Paul Naschy. Screenplay: Paul Naschy.
Cast: Paul Naschy, Julia Saly, Silvia Aguilar, Azucena Hernandez, Beatriz Elorrietta, Rafael Hernandez, Pepe Ruiz, Ricardo Palacios, Tito Garcia, David Rocha.

The Howling (1981)
Director: Joe Dante. Screenplay: John Sayles, based upon the novel by Gary Brandner.
Cast: Dee Wallace, Patrick Macnee, Dennis Duggan, Christopher Stone, Belinda Balaski, Kevin McCarthy, John Carradine, Slim Pickens, Elisabeth Brooks, Robert Picardo.

An American Werewolf in London (1981)
Director: John Landis. Screenplay: John Landis.
Cast: David Naughton, Jenny Agutter, Griffin Dunne, John Woodvine, Lila Kaye, Joe Belcher, David Schofield, Brian Glover, Rik Mayall, Sean Baker, Paddy Ryan.

Wolfen (1981)
Director: Michael Wadleigh, Screenplay: David Eyre based upon the novel by Whitley Strieber.
Cast: Albert Finney, Diane Verona, Edward James Olmos, Gregory Hines, Tom Noonan, Dick O'Neill, Dehl Berti, Peter Michael Goetz, Sam Gray.

The Werewolf and the Magic Sword (1983)
Original title: ***La bestia la espada magica.***
Alternate title: ***The Beast and the Magic Sword.***
Director: Paul Naschy. Screenplay: Paul Naschy.
Cast: Paul Naschy, Shigeru Amachi, Beatriz Escudero, Junko Asahina, Violeta cela, Yoko Fuji, Conrado San Martin, Gerad Tichy, Jose Vivo, Yoshiro Kitamachi, Sra Mora.

The Howling II: Your Sister is a Werewolf (1984)
Director: Philippe Mora. Screenplay: Robert Sarno based upon the novel by Gary Brandner.
Cast: Christopher Lee, Annie McEnroe, Reb Brown, Marsha Hunt, Sybil Danning, Judd Omen, Ferdy Mayne, Patrick Field, Jimmy Nail.

Silver Bullet (1985)
Director: Daniel Attias. Screenplay by Stephen King based upon his novel.
Cast: Gary Busey, Everett McGill, Corey Haim, Megan Follows, Robin Groves, Leon Russom, Terry O'Quinn, Bill Smitrovitch.

Teen Wolf (1985)
Director: Rod Daniel. Screenplay: Jeph Loeb, Matthew Weisman.
Cast: Michael J. Fox, James Hampton, Susan Ursitti, Jerry Levine, matt Adler, Lorie Griffin, Jim McKrell, Mark Arnold.

The Monster Squad (1987)
Director: Fred Dekker. Screenplay: Shane Black and Fred Dekker.
Cast: Andre Gower, Robby Kriger, Stephan Macht, Duncan Regehr, Tom Noonan, Brent Chalem, Ryan Lambert, Ashley Bank, Michael Faustino, Mary Ellen Trainor,

The Howling III: The Marsupials (1987)
Director: Philippe Mora. Screenplay: Philippe Mora based upon characters created by Gary Brandner.
Cast: Barry Otto, William Young, Imogen Annesley, Deby Wightman, Lee Biolos, Christopher Pate, Max Fairchild, Jerome Patillo.

Teen Wolf Too (1987)
Director: Christopher Leitch. Screenplay: Timothy Kring. Story by Jeph Loeb and Matthew Weisman.
Cast: Jason Bateman, Kim Darby, John Astin, Paul Sand, James Hampton, Mark Holton, Estee Chandler, Robert Neary.

Howl of the Devil (1987)
Original title: ***El aullido del Diablo.***
Director: Paul Naschy. Screenplay: Paul Naschy.
Cast: Paul Naschy, Caroline Munro, Howard Vernon, Fernando Hilbeck, Joseph garco, Roberta Kuhn, Carmen Plate, Videl Molina, Pascual Marco, Sergio Molina.

The Howling IV: The Original Nightmare (1988)
Director: John Hough. Screenplay: Clive Turner based upon characters created by Gary Brandner.
Cast: Romy Windsor, Michael T. Weiss, Anthony Hamilton, Susanne Severeid, Lamya Derval, Norman Anstey, Kate wedards, Dennis Folbigge.

My Mom's a Werewolf (1988)
Director: Michael Fischa. Screenplay: Mark Pirro.
Cast: Susan Blakely, John Saxon, Tina Caspary, John Schuck, Diana Barrows, Ruth Buzzi, Marilyn McCoo, Marcia Wallace, Geno Silva.

The Howling V: The Rebirth (1989)
Director: Neal Sunderstrom. Screenplay: Freddie Rowe based upon characters created by Gary Brandner.
Cast: Philip Davis, Victoria Catlin, Elizabeth She, Ben Cole, William Shockley, Mark Sivertsen, Stephanie Faulner.

The Howling VI: The Freaks (1990)
Director: Hope Perello. Screenplay: Kevin Rock based upon characters created by Gary Brandner.
Cast: Brendan Hughes, Michele Matheson, Sean Sullivan, Antonio Fargas, Carol Lynley, Jared Barclay, Bruce Payne, Gary Carlos Cervantes.

The Howling VII: New Moon Rising (1994)
Director: Clive Turner. Screenplay: Clive Turner based upon characters created by Gary Brandner.

Cast: John Ramsden, Ernest Kester, Live Turner, Jack Huff, Elizabeth She, Jaqueline Armitage, Jim Lozano.

Wolf (1994)
Director: Mike Nichols. Screenplay: Jim Harrison and Wesley Strick based upon the novel by Jim Harrison.
Cast: Jack Nicholson, Michelle Pfeiffer, James Spader, Kate Nelligan, Richard Jenkins, Christopher Plummer, Eileen Atkins, David Hyde Pierce, Om Puri.

Huntress: Spirit of the Night (1995)
Director: Mark. S. Manos. Screenplay: James Sealskin.
Cast: Jenna Bodnar, George Alexander, Virgil Andriescu, Constantin Cotimanis, Stefan Velniciuc, Charles Cooper, Blair Valk, Diana Marcu, Andrea Nedelcu.

Lycanthropus: The Moonlight Murders (1996)
Original title: Licantropo: *El asesino de la luna llena.*
Director: Francisco Rodriguez Gordillo. Screenplay: Paul Naschy.
Cast: Paul Naschy, Amparo Munoz, Antonio Pica, Jose Maria Caffarel, Eva Isanta, Luis Maluenda, Jesus Calle, Jorge R. Lucas.

The Werewolf (1996)
Alternate title: ***Arizona Werewolf.***
Director: Tony Zarindast. Screenplay: Brad Hornbacher and Tony Zarindast.
Cast; Jorge Rivero, Richard Lynch, Federico Cavalli, Adrianna Miles, Joe Estevez, Jules Desjarlais, R. C. Bates, Tony Zarindast, randall oliver, Heidi Bjorn.

An American Werewolf in Paris (1997)
Director: Anthony Waller. Screenplay: Tim Burns, Tom Stern and Anthony Waller based upon characters created by John Landis.
Cast: Tom Everett Scott, Julie Delpy, Vince Vieluf, Phil Buckman, Julie Bowen, Pierre Cosso, Thierry Lhermitte, Tom Novembre.

Eyes of the Werewolf (1999)
Director: Jeff LeRoy and Tim Sullivan. Screenplay: Tim Sullivan.
Cast: Mark Sawyer, Stephanie Beaton, Jason Clark, Eric Mestressat, Tarri Markell, Tim Sullivan, Kurt Levi, Deborah Huber.

Rage of the Werewolf (1999)
Director: Kevin J. Lindenmuth. Screenplay: Kevin J. Lindenmuth and Santo Marotta.
Cast: Santa Marotta, Joe Zaso, Debbie Rochon, Jay alvino, Joseph Biondi, Ron Ford, Robert V. Galluzzo.

Ginger Snaps (2000)
Director: John Fawcett. Screenplay and story: Karen Walton and John Fawcett.
Cast: Emily Perkins, Katherine Isabelle, Kris Lemche, Mimi Rogers, Jesse Moss, Danielle Hampton, John Bourgeois, Peter Keleghan.

Blood of the Werewolf (2001)
Director: Bruce Hallenback. Screenplay: Stephan C. Seward.
Cast: Joe Bagnardi, Dan Bailey, Helen Black, Mia Borrelli, Bill Chaput, Sasha Graham, Bruce Hallenback.

Brotherhood of the Wolf (2002)
Original title: *Le pacte des loups*.
Director: Christopher Gans. Screenplay: Stephane Cabel, Christopher Gans.
Cast: Samuel Le Bihan, Vincent Cassel, Emilie Dequenne, Monica Bellucci, Jeremie Renier, Mark Dacascos, Jean Yanne, Jean-Francois Stevenin.

Dark Wolf (2003)
Director: Richard Friedman. Screenplay: Geoffrey Alan Holliday. Story by Charles David Scholl.
Cast: Samaire Armstrong, Ryan Alosio, Andrea Bogart, Jamie Bergman, Alexis Cruz, Aaron Van Wagner, Sasha Wlliams, Kane holder, Beau Clark, Steven Williams.

Underworld (2003)
Director: Len Wiseman. Screenplay: Danny McBride. Story by Kevin Grevioux, Len Wiseman, and Danny McBride.
Cast: Kate Beckinsale, Scott Speedman, Michael Sheen, Shane Brolly, Bill Nighy, Erwin Leder, Sophia Myles, Robbie Gee, Wentworth Miller, Kevin Grevioux, Zita Gorog.

Cursed (2003)
Director: Wes Craven. Screenplay: Kevin Williamson.
Cast: Christina Ricci, Shannon Elizabeth, Portia de Rossi, Mya, Kristina Anapau, Daniel Edward Mora, Jesse Eisenberg, Milo Ventimiglia, Johnny Acker, Eric Laden.

Tomb of the Werewolf (2004)
Director: Fred Olen Ray. Screenplay: Fred Olen Ray.
Cast: Paul Naschy, Jay Richardson, Michelle Bauer, Stephanie Bentley, Danielle Petty, Jacy Andrews, Beverly Lynne, Leland Jay, Frankie Cullen, Don Donason, Brian Carrillo, Evan Stone, Monique Alexander, Randy carter.

Werewolf Hunter (2004)
Director: Paco Plaza. Screenplay: Elena Serra.
Cast: Julian sands, Elsa Pataky, John Sharian, Gary Piquer, David Gant, Maru Valdivielso, Luna McGill, Carlos Reig-Plaza.

Van Helsing (2004)
Director: Stephen Sommers. Screenplay: Stephen Sommers.
Cast: Hugh Jackman, Kate Beckinsale, Richard Roxburgh, David Wenham, Shuler Hensley, Elena Anaya, Will Kemp, Kevin J. O'Connor, Alun Armstrong, Silvia Colloca, Josie Moran, Tom Fisher, Samuel West, Robbie Coltrane.

Big Bad Wolf (2006)
Director: Lance W. Dreesen. Screenplay: Lance W. Dreesen.
Cast: Trevor Duke-Moretz, Kimberly J. Brown, Richard Tyson, Sarah Al-

drich, Christopher Shyer, Andrew Bowen, Sarah Christine Smith, Jason Alan Smith.

Werewolf in a Woman's Prison (2006)
Director: Jeff Leroy. Screenplay: Vinnie Bilancio and Jeff Leroy.
Cast: Domiziano Arcangeli, Yurizan Beltran, Vinnie Bilancio, Al Burke, Sean Cain, Victoria de Mare, Eva Derrek, Phoebe Dollar, Magic J. Ellingson, Michelle Fatale, Meredith Giangrande.

Underworld: Evolution (2006)
Director: Len Wiseman. Screenplay: Danny McBride. Story by Kevin Grevioux, Len Wiseman, and Danny McBride.
Cast: Kate Beckinsale, Scott Speedman, Tony Curan, Derek Jacobi, Bill Nighy, Steven Mackintosh, Shane Brolly, Brian Steele, Zita Gorog, Michael Sheen.

Blood and Chocolate (2006)
Director: Katja von Garnier. Screenplay: Ehren Kruger and Christopher B. Landon, based upon the novel by Annette Curtis Klause.
Cast: Agnes Bruckner, Hugh Dancy, Olivier Martinez, Katja Riemann, Bryan Dick, Chris Greere, Tom Harper, John Kerr, Jack Wilson, Vitalie Ursu.

Skinwalkers (2007)
Director: Jim Isaac. Screenplay: James DeMonaco, Todd Harthan, and James Roday.
Cast: Jason Behr, Elias Koteas, Rhona Mitra, Natassia Malthe, Kim Coates, Tom Jackson, Matthew Knight, Rogue Johnston.

Never Cry Werewolf (2007)
Director: Brenton Spencer. Screenplay: John Shepard.
Cast: Nina Dobrev, Kevin Sorbo, Peter Stebbings, Spencer Van Wyck, Melanie Leishman, Kim Bourne, Sean O'Neill, Nahanni Johnstone.

Hybrid (2008)
Director: Yelena Lanskaya. Screenplay: Arne Isen.
Cast: Justine Bateman, Tinsel Korey, William MacDonald, Gordon Tootoosis, Brandon Jay McLaren, Corey Monteith, Robert Borges, Aaron Hughes.

Twilight (2008)
Director: Catherine Hardwicke. Screenplay: Melissa Rosenberg, based upon the novel by Stephenie Meyer.
Cast: Robert Pattinson, Kristen Stewart, Sarah Clarke, Matt Bushell, Gil Birmingham, Taylor Lautner, Gregory Tyree Boyce, Justin Chon, Michael Welch, Anna Kendrick, Christian Serratos, Nikki Reed, Ashley Greene, Jackson Rathbone.

New Moon (2009)
Director: Chris Weitz. Screenplay: Melissa Rosenberg, based upon the novel by Stephenie Meyer.
Cast: Kristen Stewart, Robert Pattinson, Christina Jastrzembska, Billy Burke, Anna Kendrick, Michael Welch, Justin Chon, Christian Serratos, Taylor Lautner, Ashley Greene, Jackson Rathbone.

Underworld: Rise of the Lycans (2009)
Director: Patrick Tatopoulos. Screenplay: Danny McBride, Dirk Blackman, and Howard McCain. Story by Len Wiseman, Robert Orr, Kevin Grevioux, and Danny McBride.
Cast: Michael Sheen, Bill Nighy, Rhona Mitra, Steven Mackintosh, Kevin Grevioux, David Aston, Geraldine Brophy, Leighton Cardno.

The Wolfman (2010)
Director: Joe Johnston. Screenplay: Andrew Kevin Walker and David Self. Based upon the screenplay by Curt Siodmak.
Cast: Benicio Del Toro, Anthony Hopkins, Emily Blunt, Art Malik, David Schofield, Nicholas Day, Cristina Contes, David Sterne.

House of the Wolfman (2010)
Director: Eben McGarr. Screenplay: Eben McGarr.
Cast: Ron Chaney, Dustin Fitzsimons, Jeremie Lioncka, Sara Raftery, Cheryl Rodes, Jim Thalman, John McGarr, Michael R. Thomas, Craig Dobbs, Billy Bussey.

Notes and Sources

ONE: HISTORICAL SURVEY OF THE WEREWOLF LEGEND

1. Adam Douglas, *The Beast Within: A History of the Werewolf*, p. 8.
2. Sabine Baring-Gould, *The Book of Werewolves*, p. 70.
3. Ibid, p. 71.
4. Rossell Hope Robbins, *The Encyclopedia of Witchcraft and Demonology* Robbins, p. 537.
5. Ibid, p. 178.
6. Ibid p. 212.
7. Trial transcript reprinted in *The Wolf Man* (The original 1941 shooting script) edited by Philip Riley, nn.
8. Rossell Hope Robbins, *The Encyclopedia of Witchcraft and Demonology*, p. 324.
9. Ibid, p. 538.
10. Ibid, p 538.
11. Ibid, p. 233.
12. Ibid, p. 234.
13. Ibid.
14. Ibid.
15. Elliott O'Donnell, *Werewolves*, p 149-150.
16. Ibid, p. 151.
17. Ibid, p. 155.
18. Rossell Hope Robbins, *The Encyclopedia of Witchcraft and Demonology*, p. 370.
19. Ibid, p. 346
20. A. Werner, *British Central Africa*, p. 87, 171; and also see Traugott K. Oesterreich, *Possession and Exorcism: Among Primitive Races, In Antiquity, The Middle Ages, and Modern Times*, p. 145.

21. Charlotte Otten, *A Lycanthropy Reader: Werewolves in Western Culture*, p. 34.
22. Godfrey, Linda S.; *The Beast of Bray Road: Tailing Wisconsin's Werewolf*, 42.
23. Denis Dudos; *The Werewolf Complex: America's Fascination with Violence*, p. ix.

Two: The Werewolf in Literature

24. George William MacArthur Reynolds; *Wagner, The Wehr-Wolf*, p. 1.
25. Ibid, p. 23.
26. Clemence Housman, *The Werewolf*, p.5. see also: the Nabu Press edition and *The Literary Werewolf: An Anthology* edited by Charlotte F. Otten which reprints the complete text. The paragraph excised from numerous modern anthologies because of its blatant Christian symbolism reads as follows: "Cold, silence, darkness encompassed the strong man bowed with the dolorous burden; and yet he knew surely that that night he entered hell, and trod hell-fire along the homeward road, and endured through it only because Christian was with him. And he knew surely that to him Christian had been as Christ, and had suffered and died to save him from his sins."
27. Ibid, p.15.
28, Ibid, p.18.
29. Ibid, p. 20.
30. Alden H. Norton, editor; *Masters of Horror* p.61-62, also, *Dracula's Guest and Other Tales of Horror*, p. 70 – 84.
31. Ibid, p.63.
32. Ibid, p. 66-68.
33. Jesse Douglas Kerruish , *The Undying Monster*, p 3.
34. Brian J. Frost *The Essential Guide to Werewolf Literature*, p. 101.
35. Jesse Douglas Kerruish , *The Undying Monster*, p.36.
36. Guy Endore, *The Werewolf of Paris*, p.99.
37. Ibid, p.100.
38. Ibid, p.137.
39. Ibid, p.143.
40. Ibid, p. 215.
41. Ibid, p.214.
42. Ibid, p.223.

43. L. Ron Hubbard, The Great Secret, p.63.
44. Ibid
45. Jack Williamson's *Darker Than You Think*, p. 1.
46. Ibid, p. 69.
47. Ibid, p. 83.
48. Leslie H. Whitten, *Moon of the Wolf*, p.51.
49. Ibid, p. 139.
50. Ibid, p. 187.
51. Ibid, p. 188.
52. Raymond Giles, *Night of the Vampire*, p. 5.
53. Ibid, p.30.
54. Peter Saxon, *Vampire's Moon*, p. 20.
55. Ibid, p.143.
55. Gary Brander, *The Howling*, p. 70.
57. Ibid, p. 108.
58. Whitley Streiber, *The Wolfen*, p. 183.
59. Stephen King, *Cycle of the Werewolf*, p. 14.
60. Stephen King, *IT*, p. 377.
61. Jeffrey Goddin, *Blood of the Wolf*, p. 195.
62. Roger Zelazny, *A Dark Traveling*, p.11.
63. Ibid, p. 77.
64. Cheri Scotch, *The Werewolf's Kiss*, p. 217.
65. Cheri Scotch, *The Werewolf's Touch*, p. 5.
66. Annette Curtis Klause, *Blood and Chocolate*, p. 30.
67. Ibid, p. 30-31.
68. William Gagliani, *Wolf's Trap*, p. 48.
69. Ibid, p. 180.
70. Tony Gardner, *Werewolf Island*, p. 46.

THREE: LON CHANEY, JR. AND THE WOLF MAN

I relied on several vital books for background information on Lon Chaney, Jr. First, the Universal Filmscripts Series edited by Philip Riley and published by MagicImage Filmbooks are the definitive source on Chaney's appearances as Larry Talbot. For biographical information on Chaney I relied on Don G. Smith's biography. Curt Siodmak's autobiography is also a valuable resource for scholars and fans interested in the origin of Larry Talbot.

71. Don G. Smith, *Lon Chaney, Jr.* p. 27.
72. Curt Siodmak, *Wolf Man's Maker*, p. 262.
73. E-mail from Steve Campbell to Thomas McNulty, July 1, 2008.
74. David Zinan, *Saturday Afternoon at the Bijou*, p. 47.
75. Ibid, p. 47.
76. Curt Siodmak, Philip Riley (editor), *Frankenstein Meets the Wolf Man*, p. 8.
77. Ibid, p. 63.
78. Curt Siodmak, *Wolf Man's Maker,* p. 270.
79. E-mail from Steve Campbell to Thomas McNulty, July 1, 2008
80. Charles Hamblett, The Hollywood Cage, pp. 217-218.
81. Author's interview with Forest J. Ackerman, October 10, 1999.

Four: Paul Naschy and the Werewolf

I relied on Paul Naschy's autobiography, *Memoirs of a Wolfman*, translated from the Spanish by Mike Hodges. Additional biographical information was culled from the website "The Mark of Naschy" maintained by Mirek Lipinski.

82. Paul Naschy; *Memoirs of a Wolfman*, p. 23.
83. Ibid, p. 97.
84. Ibid, p.173.
85. E-mail from Fred Olen Ray to Thomas McNulty, February 4, 2011.
86. Paul Naschy; *Memoirs of a Wolfman*, p. 109.
87. Ibid.
88. E-mail from Steve Latshaw to Thomas McNulty, February 3, 2011.

Five: A Survey of Werewolf Films

Plot synopsis of the films are drawn from the author's notes compiled after viewing video-cassette copies or DVD releases when available.

89. Jim Harrison, *Wolf: A False Memoir*, p. 11.

Bibliography

REFERENCE WORKS

Baring-Gould, Sabine; *The Book of Werewolves*, London, England, Senate, an imprint of Studio Editions, Ltd., 1995 (originally published in 1865).

Clarens, Carlos; *An Illustrated History of the Horror Film*, New York, Capricorn Books, 1967.

Douglas, Adam; *The Beast Within: A History of the Werewolf*, New York, Avon Books, 1992.

Douglas, Drake; *Horror!*, Toronto, Canada, Collier Books, 1969.

Dudos, Denis; *The Werewolf Complex: America's Fascination with Violence*, Oxford, England, Berg Publishers, 1998.

Eisler, Robert; *Man into Wolf: An Anthropological Interpretation of Sadism, Masochism and Lycanthropy*, New York, Greenwood Press, 1996 (originally published in 1950).

Flynn, Niki, *Dances with Werewolves: Memoirs of a Spanking Model*, New York, Virgin Books, 2007.

Frost, Brian J.; *The Essential Guide to Werewolf Literature*, Madison, Wisconsin, The University of Wisconsin Press, 2003.

Gifford, Denis; *A Pictorial History of Horror Movies*, New York, The Hamlyn Publishing Group, 1973.

Glut, Donald F.; *True Werewolves of History*, Rockville, Maryland, Sense of Wonder Press, 2004.

Godfrey, Linda S.; *The Beast of Bray Road: Tailing Wisconsin's Werewolf*, Black earth, Wisconsin, Prairie Oak Press, 2003.

Hall, Jamie; *Half Human, Half Animal*, Bloomington, Indiana, 1st books, 2003.

Hamblett, Charles; *The Hollywood Cage*, New York, Hart Publishing Company, 1969.

Jones, Stephen, editor; *The Mammoth Book of Werewolves*, New York, Carrol & Graf, 1994.

Naschy, Paul; *Memoirs of a Wolfman*, Baltimore, Maryland, Luminary Press, 2003.

O'Donnell, Elliott; *Werewolves*, London, Methuen & Company, 1912, (facsimile copy by Kessinger Publishing, no date).

Oesterreich, Traugott K. (Translated by D. Ibberson); *Possession and Exorcism: Among Primitive Races, In Antiquity, The Middle Ages, and Modern Times*, New York, Causeway Books, 1974.

Otten, Charlotte; *A Lycanthropy Reader: Werewolves in Western Culture*, New York, Dorset Press, 1989 (originally published in 1986).

Riley, Philip (editor); *The Wolf Man* (The original 1941 shooting script), Absecon, New Jersey, MagicImage Filmbooks, Universal Filmscripts Series, Classic Horror Films, volume 12, 1993.

Riley, Philip (editor); *Frankenstein Meets the Wolf Man* (The original 1942 shooting script), Absecon, New Jersey, MagicImage Filmbooks, Universal Filmscripts Series, Classic Horror Films, volume 5, 1990.

Riley, Philip (editor); *House of Frankenstein* (The original 1944 shooting script), Absecon, New Jersey, MagicImage Filmbooks, Universal Filmscripts Series, Classic Horror Films, volume 6, 1990.

Riley, Philip (editor); *House of Dracula* (The original 1945 shooting script), Absecon, New Jersey, MagicImage Filmbooks, Universal Filmscripts Series, Classic Horror Films, volume 16, 1990.

Riley, Philip (editor); *Abbott and Costello Meet Frankenstein* (The original 1948 shooting script), Absecon, New Jersey, MagicImage Filmbooks, Universal Filmscripts Series, Classic Horror Films, volume 1, 1990.

Robbins, Rossell Hope; *The Encyclopedia of Witchcraft and Demonology*, London, Bookplan for Paul Hamlyn Ltd., 1959.

Ruck, Carl A. P., Staples, Daniel Blaise, Celdran, Jose Alfredo Gonzalez, and Hoffman, Mark Alwin; *The Hidden World: Survival of Pagan Shamanic Themes in European Fairytales*, Durhan, North Carolina, Carolina Academic Press, 2007.

Sconduto, Leslie A.; *Metamorphoses of the Werewolf: A Literary Study from Antiquity through the Renaissance*, Jefferson, North Carolina, McFarland & Company Publishers, 2008.

Shah, Sirdar Ikbal Ali; *Occultism: Its Theory and Practice*, New York, Castle Books, no copyright date listed.

Siodmak, Curt; *Wolf Man's Maker*, Lanham, Maryland, The Scarecrow Press, 2001.

Smith, Don G.; *Lon Chaney, Jr.: Horror Film Star*, Jefferson, North Carolina, McFarland & Company Publishers, 2003.

Steiger, Brad; *The Werewolf Book: The Encyclopedia of Shape-Shifting Beings*, Canton, Michigan, Visible Ink Press, 1999.

Summers, Montague; *The Werewolf in Lore and Legend*, Mineola, New York, Dover Publications, 2003 (originally published in 1933).

Unknown author, trial transcript: *A True Discourse, Declaring the Damnable Life and Death of One Stubbe Peter* (London 1590, 1940 reprint)

Werner, A.; *British Central Africa*, London, Constable Publishers, 1906.

Zinan, David; *Saturday Afternoon at the Bijou*, New York, Arlington House, 1973.

FICTION

Banks, L.A.; *Bad Blood*, New York, St. Martin's Paperbacks, 2008.

Banks, L.A.; *Bite the Bullet*, New York, St. Martin's Paperbacks, 2008.

Banks, L.A.; *Undead On Arrival*, New York, St. Martin's Paperbacks, 2009.

Banks, L.A.; *Cursed to Death*, New York, St. Martin's Paperbacks, 2009.

Banks, L.A.; *Never Cry Werewolf*, New York, St. Martin's Paperbacks, 2010.

Banks, L.A.; *Left For Undead*, New York, St. Martin's Paperbacks, 2010.

Brandner, Gary; *The Howling*, New York, Fawcett Gold Medal Books, 1977.

Collins, Nancy A.; *Wild Blood*, Atlanta, Georgia, Two Wolf Press, 2005

Collins, Nancy A.; *Right Hand Magic*, New York, Penguin Paperbacks, 2010.

Douglas, Carole Nelson; *Dancing With Werewolves*, Rockville, Maryland, Juno Books, 2007.

Elwood, Roger, editor; *Vampires, Werewolves and Other Monsters*, New York, Curtis Books, 1974.

Endore, Guy; *The Werewolf of Paris*, Secaucus, New Jersey, A Citadel Press Book, 1992 (originally published in 1933).

Gagliani, William D.; *Wolf's Trap*, Alma, Arkansas, Yard Dog Press, 2003.

Gagliani, William D.; *Wolf's Gambit*, New York, Leisure Books, 2009

Gardner, Tony; *Werewolf Island*, Baltimore, Maryland, Publish America, 2007.

Garton, Ray; *Ravenous*, New York, Leisure Books, 2008.

Ghidalia, Vic (editor) with Roger Elwood; *Beware the Beasts*, New York, Macfadden-Bartell Books, 1970.

Giles, Raymond, *Night of the Vampire*, New York, Avon Books, 1969.

Goddin, Jeffrey; *Blood of the Wolf*, New York, Leisure Books, 1987.

Haining, Peter (editor): *Werewolf: Horror Stories of the Man-Beast*, London, Severn House, 1987.

Harrison, Jim; *Wolf: A False Memoir*, New York, Delta Trade Paperback, 1971

Housman, Clemence; *Werewolf*, North Hollywood, California, Fantasy House, 1973 (partial reprint of the 1896 text).

Housman, Clemence; *The Were-Wolf*, Nabu Press, Charleston, South Carolina, 2010 (complete reprint of the 1896 text).

Howard, Lance; *The West Wolf*, London, England, Robert Hale Publishers, 2001.

Howard, Robert E.; *The Horror Stories of Robert E. Howard*, New York, Ballantine Books, 2008.

Hubbard, L. Ron; *Dead Men Kill*, Los Angeles, California, Galaxy Press, 2008.

Hubbard, L. Ron; *The Great Secret* (includes "The Beast" as a bonus story) Los Angeles, California, Galaxy Press, 2008.

Jones, Stephen; *The Mammoth Book of Wolf Men*, Philadelphia, PA, Running Press Book Publishers, 2009.

Kerruish, Jesse Douglas; *The Undying Monster,* Ashcroft, British Columbia, Ash Tree Press, 2006.

Lowder, James (editor); *Curse of the Full Moon*, Berkeley, California, Ulysses Press, 2010

Maberry, Jonathan, *The Wolfman* (novelization of the screenplay by Andrew Kevin Walker and David Self and the works of Curt Siodmak), New York, Tor Books, 2010.

McCammon, Robert; *The Wolf's Hour*, Burton, Michigam, Subterranean Press, 2010.

Meyer, Stephanie; *Twilight*, New York, Little, Brown and Company, 2005.

Meyer, Stephanie; *New Moon,* New York, Little, Brown and Company, 2006.

Mazzeo, Henry (editor); *Hauntings: Tales of the Supernatural*, New York, Doubleday and Company, 1968.

Millar, Martin; *Lonely Werewolf Girl*; Brooklyn, New York, Soft Skull Press, 2007.

Moskowitz, Sam (editor): *Horrors Unknown*, New York, Walker Books, 1971.

Munn, H. Warner; *The Werewolf of Ponkert*, New York, Centaur Books, 1976 (reprints the "The Werewolf of Ponkert" from *Weird Tales*, July 1925 and "The Werewolf's Daughter" from *Weird Tales* October-December 1928).

Munn, H. Warner; *Tales of the Werewolf Clan, Vol. 1, In the Tomb of the Bishop*, Rhode Island, Donald M. Grant Publishers, 1980 (additional reprints from *Weird Tales*).

Munn, H. Warner; *Tales of the Werewolf Clan, Vol. 2, The Master Goes Home*, Rhaod Island, Donald M. Grant Publishers, 1980 (additional reprints from *Weird Tales*).

Norton, Alden H., editor; *Masters of Horror*, New York, Berkley Publishing, 1968.

Otten, Charlotte; *The Literary Werewolf: An Anthology*, Syracuse, New York, Syracuse University Press, 2002.

Partridge, Norman; *The Man with the Barbed-Wire Fists*, San Francisco, Night Shade Books, 2001.

Preiss, Byron, editor; *The Ultimate Werewolf*, New York, Dell paperback, 1991.

Pronzini, Bill, editor; *Werewolf! A Connoisseur's Collection of Werewolfiana*, New York, Perennial, 1979.

Quinn, Seabury, *Demons of the Night: And Other Early Tales*, Normal, Illinois, Black Dog Books, 2009.

Reynolds, George William MacArthur; *Wagner, The Wehr-Wolf*, New York, Dover Publications, 1975 (reprints the story originally published in 1846)

Robeson, Kenneth, *Doc Savage # 13: Brand of the Werewolf and Fear Cay*, Encinitas, California, Sanctum Productions-Nostalgia Ventures, 2008 (reprints two 1934 Doc Savage stories).

Robeson, Kenneth, *Doc Savage: Brand of the Werewolf*, Bantam Books, New York, 1965 (reprints the 1934 story).

Saxon, Peter; *Vampire's Moon*, Manchester, England, Five Star Paperback, 1970.

Scotch, Cheri; *The Werewolf's Kiss*, New York, ibooks, 2003

Scotch, Cheri; *The Werewolf's Touch*, New York, ibooks, 2003

Scotch, Cheri; *The Werewolf's Sin*, New York, ibooks, 2004

Strieber, Whitley; *The Wolfen*, New York, William Morrow and Company, 1978

Stoker, Bram; *Dracula's Guest and Other Tales of Horror*, New York, Fall River Press, 2010.

Stoker, Bram; *Five Novels: Dracula, The Mystery of the Sea, The Jewel of Seven Stars, The Lady of the Shroud, The Lair of the White Worm*, New York, Barnes and Noble Books, 2006.

Swann, S.A.; *Wolfbreed*, New York, Ballantine Books, 2009

Swann, S.A.; *Wolf's Cross*, New York, Ballantine Books, 2010

Widder, William; *Master Storyteller: An illustrated Tour of the Fiction of L. Ron Hubbard*, Los Angeles, California, Galaxy Press, 2003.

Wieck, Stewart; *When Will You Rage?*, Stone Mountain, Georgia, The White Wolf, Inc., 1994 (anthology of fiction relating to the "Werewolf: the Apocalypse" role playing game).

Whitten, Leslie H.; *Moon of the Wolf*, New York, NY, Ace Publishing, 1967.

Williamson, Jack; *Darker Than You Think*, New York, Tom Doherty Associates, 1999 (originally published in 1948).

Willis, Connie (editor); *The New Hugo Winners, Volume III*; Riverdale, New York, Baen Publishing Enterprises, 1994.

Zelazny, Roger, *A Dark Traveling*; New York, Avon Books, 1987.

INTERNET RESOURCES

www.universalsteve.com: The largest Internet fan resource on the classic Universal Studio monsters. The site is operated by Steve Campbell and includes photographs, movie clips, production information and reviews.

www.naschy.com (The Mark of Naschy): Created prior to Naschy's death and now considered the best Internet resource on Naschy's life and career. Maintained by Mirek Lipinski the site includes biographical data, interviews, filmography, reviews and photographs.

www.werewolf-movies.com: an comprehensive on-line database on werewolf films operated by Noel Clay and featuring an extensive filmography, reviews and photographs.

Index

Adventures of Robin Hood, The 65
A Good Day to Die 155
A Werewolf in the Amazon 124
Abbott and Costello Meet Dr. Jekyll and Mr. Hyde 95
Abbott and Costello Meet Frankenstein 91 – 95, 144
Abbott and Costello Meet the Invisible Man 94
Abbott and Costello Meet the Killer 94
Abbott and Costello Meet the Mummy 96
Abbott, Bud 66
Abbott, Bud 91
Ackerman, Forrest J. 98
Adams, Jane 88
Adamson, Al 125
Adrift Just off the Islet of Langerhans: Latitude 38° 54′ N Longitude 77° 00′ 13″ W 56
Aegineta, Paulus 4
Agutter, Jenny 150
Albuquerque 91
Aldrich, Sarah 165
Alexander, Monique 121
Alien 148
Ameche, Don 62
An American Werewolf in London 149, 150
An American Werewolf in Paris 150
Anaya, Elena 163
Anderson, D. J. 141, 142
Anderson, Kevin J. 56
Andrews, Jacy 121
Ankers, Evelyn 64, 66, 73
Anthony Adverse 65

Antieau, Kim 56
Arbiter, Petronius 5, 25
Armstrong, Samaire 159
Arsenic and Old Lace 81
Ashton, Roy 140
Astro Zombies 125
Atalanta 29
Attias, Dan 151
Atwill, Lionel 84, 88
Autry, Gene 62
Awful Dr. Orloff, The 143
Awful Truth, The 66

Bad Blood 57
Baker, Rick 150, 168, 169
Baker, W. Howard 45
Banks, L. A. 57
Banks, Leslie Esdaile 57
Banta, F. 23
Barbee, Will 41
Bare-Breasted Countess, The 143
Barrymore, John 82
Bateman, Jason 152
Bateman, Justine 168
Bathory, Elizabeth 114, 116
Bauer, Michelle 121
Baxter, Warner 62
Beagle, Peter S. 56, 57
Beast of Bray Road, The 23
Beast With Five Fingers, The 63
Beast, The 40
Beaton, Stephanie 156

Beckinsale, Kate 159, 160
Bécquer, Gustavo Adolfo 99
Bela Lugosi Meets a Brooklyn Gorilla 94
Bell, April 41
Bellamy, Ralph 64, 66
Bellucci, Monica 159
Bentley, Stephanie 121
Bidel, Benoit 12
Big Bad Wolf 165
Bihan, Samuel Le 159
Bilancio, Vinnie 166
Bird of Paradise 61
Bissell, Whit 137
Bite the Bullet 57
Black Cat, The 65
Black Honey 45
Black Sleep, The 94
Black, Shane 152
Blackman, Dirk 161
Blaine, Jerry 137
Blake, Michael 54
Blakely, Susan 154
Bloch, Robert 37
Blood and Chocolate 52, 166
Blood of Dracula 137
Blood of the Werewolf 158
Blood of the Wolf 49
Blue, Sonja 51
Blumenberg, Sophie de 36
Blunt, Emily 170
Bodner, Jenna 156
Bogart, Humphrey 133
Boles, John 62
Boobs 56
Borel, Annik 145
Bottin, Bob 147
Bourgot, Pierre 5, 12
Boyle, Robert (Charles) 68, 69
Bradbury, Ray 37
Brain of Frankenstein, The 91
Brand of the Werewolf 38, 39
Brander, Gary 46, 47, 48, 49, 146, 148, 160
Brando, Marlon 133
Brennan, Joseph Payne 56

Brenryk, Wladislaw 38
Bride of Frankenstein, The 73, 75, 128
Bride of the Monster 94
Brides of Dracula, The 139
British Central Africa 21
Broken Arrow 100
Brotherhood of the Wolf 159
Brown Bomber and the Nazi Werewolves of the S.S., The 57
Brown, Kimberly J. 165
Bruckner, Agnes 166
Busey, Gary 151
Bussey, Billy 172, 173

Cabot, Bruce 62
Cade, Skinner 51, 52
Caesar, Julius 65
Cagney, James 133
Caillet, Bertrand 35, 37
Campbell, Steve 71, 80
Caniff, Milton 99
Capell, Barbara 106
Captain Blood 100
Captain China 95
Caradine, John 82, 84, 88, 147
Carrie 48
Carrillo, Brian 121
Carter, Sarah 167
Case of the Curious Bride, The 65
Case of the Howling Dog, The 65
Cassel, Vincent 159
Catlin, Victoria 148
Cavalier of the West 83
Cavalli, Frederico 156
Cena Trimalchionis 25
Chalem, Brent 154
Chamber of Horrors 81
Chaney, Cleva 60
Chaney, Creighton Tull (see Chaney, Lon, Jr.)
Chaney, Jr, Lon 5, 39, 42, 59- 98, 101, 103, 106, 119, 127, 140, 142, 144, 147, 158
Chaney, Ron 172, 173
Chaney, Sr 59, 61, 62
Chaplin, Geraldine 171

Charge of the Light Brigade, The 66
Charles, Roche 13
Charnas, Suzy Mckee 56
Charyn, Jerome 56
Chimes at Midnight 114
Chung, Michelle 173
Clark, Jason 157
Clarke, Gary 138
Cleopatra 65
Clift, Montgomery 133
Coe, Peter 83
Colbert, Claudette 65
Cole, Ben 148
Collins, Nancy A. 51, 52, 56
Colloca, Silvia 163
Colton, John 128
Conan 37
Conway, Gary 138
Cooper, Gary 95
Cooper, Thomas 19
Cosby, Bill 101
Costello, Lou 66, 91
Costner, Kevin 54
Counsellor at Law 88
Countess Dracula's Orgy of Blood 120
Crabbe, Larry "Buster" 62
Cranston, Ginger 40
Craven, Wes 161
Creature From the Black Lagoon 154
Crispin, C. 56
Cry of the Werewolf 131
Cujo 48
Cullen, Frankie C. 121
Culp, Robert 101
Curse of Frankenstein, The 138
Curse of Rathlaw, The 45
Curse of the Devil 111, 113, 177
Curse of the Full Moon 57
Curse of the Werewolf 140, 141
Cursed 161
Cursed to Death 57
Cushing, Peter 106, 139
Cycle of the Werewolf 48, 151

Dabbs, Craig 173
Dalva 155
Dances with Werewolves: Memoirs of a Spanking Model 55
Dances with Wolves 54
Dancing With Werewolves 54
Dancy, Hugh 166
Daninsky, Waldemar 103 - 126
Danning, Sybil 147
Dante, Joe 147
Darker Than You Think 40, 47
Darkest Night, The 45
Darkwolf 159
Darling, W. Scott 74
Davis, Phil 148
de Havilland, Olivia 66
de Lancre, Pierre 15
De Lint, Charles 57
De Mare, Victoria 166
de Torres, Romero 100
Dead Men Kill 39
Decker, John 82
Dekker, Fred 152
del Toro, Benicio 168 – 171
Delpy, Julie 150
DeMille, Ceil B. 65
Dent, Lester 38
Destiny 82, 88
Devil's Brood, The 82
Diary of a Werewolf 56
Díaz, Adolfo Camilo 118
Dickens, Charles 26
Died with Their Boots On, The 100
Dillman, Bradford 144
Dive Bomber 66
Dobrev, Nina 167
Doc Savage Magazine 38
Dodge City 100
Dodsworth 67
Donlevy, Brian 62
Donovan, Don 121
Donovan's Brain 63
Douglas, Adam 4
Douglas, Carole Nelson 54

Downtown: The Naked Dolls of the Underworld 143
Doyle, Arthur Conan 38
Dr. Jekyll and the Wolfman 109
Dr. Jekyll y el hombre lobo 109, 126
Dracula 31, 59, 62, 65, 127, 131, 173
Dracula contra Frankenstein 143
Dracula Vs Frankenstein 98, 103, 125
Dracula, Prisoner of Frankenstein 143, 144
Dracula's Guest 46, 56
Dracula's Guest and Other Weird Stories 32, 33
Drago, Lucien 50
Dudos, Denis 24
Duel in the Sun 100
Duke, Trevor 165
Dunne, Griffin 150
Dunne, Irene 66
Duryea, Dan 100

Earth vs. the Flying Saucers 63
Eeny, Meeny, Miney, Mo 136
El aullido del diablo 118
El espanto surge de la tumba 114
El gran amor del conde Dracula 113, 114
El jorobado de la morgue 114
El principe encadenado 101
El retorno de walpurgis 109, 126
El retorno del hombre-lobo 114, 126
Elder, John 140
Ellison, Harlan 56
Elwood, Roger 56
Emery, Gilbert 131
Employee's Entrance 65
Endore, Guy 35, 43, 128, 140
Epic of Gilgamesh 5
Erotic Rites of Frankenstein, The 143
Espronceda 99
Essential Guide to Werewolf Literature, The 34, 57, 58
Estevez, Joe 156
Eyes of the Werewolf 156

Face of the Screaming Werewolf 96
Famous Monsters of Filmland 98
Fangoria 124

Farmer 155
Farmer, Philip Jose 56
Faulkner, William 42
Fawcett, John 158
Fay, Alice 62
Feast of Trimalchio 25
Female Bunch, The 98
Fields, W.C. 82
Finney, Albert 150, 151
Fireball Jungle 98
Fitzsimmons, Dustin 173
Flame of Araby 95
Fleetwood, Mick 24
Flynn, Errol 65, 66, 82
Flynn, Niki 54, 55
Foch, Nina 131
Fowler, Jr., Gene 82, 135
Fox, Michael J. 152
Franco, Jess 143, 144
Frankenstein 59, 73
Frankenstein Meets the Wolf Man 75 – 80, 82, 84, 88, 100 - 104, 171
Frankenstein's Bloody Terror 101, 103, 104, 109, 125
Freud, Sigmund 22, 23
Friedman, Richard 159
Fright Night 167
Frost, Brian J. 34, 57
Fuastino, Michael 154
Fuchs, Gaby 106
Full Eclipse 154, 155
Full Sun 56
Fury of the Wolfman, The 109

Gaboriant, Jeanne 13
Gagliani, William 53
Gaiman, Neil 57
Gallatin, Michael 50
Galliez, Aymar 36
Gandillion, Vivian 52
Gandillon, Antoinette 12
Gandillon, Perrenette 12
Gans, Christopher 159
Gardner, Craig Shaw 56
Gardner, Erle Stanley 65

Gardner, Tony 53, 54
Garnier, Gilles 7, 12
Garton, Ray 55
Gaverstein, Wilfred 16, 17
Ghost of Frankenstein 73, 74, 75, 76, 79, 88, 90
Gibson, Mel 152
Gilbert, Glori-Anne 120
Gilda 100
Gilden, Mel 56
Giles, Raymond 43
Ginger Snaps 158
Ginger Snaps 2: Unleashed 158
Ginger Snaps Back: The Beginning 158
Glen or Glenda 94
Glover, Danny 152
Glut, Don 120
Goddin, Jeffrey 49
Godfrey, Linda 23
Goetz, William 91
Gordillo, Francisco 120
Gowdie, Isobel 20
Gower, Andre 154
Graham, Sasha 158
Grandin, Jules de 38
Grant, Cary 66
Granville, Hollis 158
Greensboro Daily News 42
Grenier, Jean 13, 14, 15
Grey, Zane 40
Grierson, Isobel 20
Griffin, Lorrie 152
Grimm, Jacob 25
Grimm, Wilhelm 25
Gwynne, Anne 83

Haim, Corey 151
Haley, Bill 101
Hallenbeck, Bruce 158
Hamilton, Laurell K. 58
Hammand, Oliver
Harris, Charlaine 57
Harris, Robert 128, 137
Harrison, Jim 155
Harrison, Kim 58

Hartmann, Sadakichi 82
Hastings, Hazel 61
Haunting of Alan Mais, The 45
Hayward, Lillie 131
Hellen, Herr 16, 17, 19
Hensley, Shuler 163
Herault, Pierre 11
Hickox, Anthony 154
High Noon 101
Hillbillies in a Haunted House 98
Hinds, Anthony 140
Hines, Gregory 150
Hobson, Valerie 129
Hoffman, Nina Kiriki 56
Hogan, Tom 52
Hold that Ghost 66
Holliday, Geoffrey 159
Holmes, Sherlock 38
Hope, Bob 91
Hopkins, Anthony 170
Hopkins, Howard 52
Horror of Dracula 139
Hound, The 56
House of Dracula 86 - 90
House of Frankenstein 81 – 86, 88
House of the Wolfman 172, 173
Houseman, Laurence 29
Housman, Clemence 29, 32, 38
How to Make a Monster 137
Howard, Lance 52
Howard, Robert E. 37, 40
Howl of the Devil 118, 119
Howling II, The 47
Howling II: Your Sister is a Werewolf, The 47
Howling III, The 47
Howling III: The Marsupials, The 147
Howling IV: The Original Nightmare, The 148
Howling V: The Rebirth, The 148
Howling VI: The Freaks, The 148
Howling VII: New Moon Rising, The 148
Howling, The 46, 47, 48, 49, 146
Hub, Deborah 157
Hubbard, L. Ron 39, 40
Hughes, Brendan 148

Hull, Henry 59, 60, 63, 64, 128 – 131
Hunchback of Notre Dame, The 59, 62
Hunter, Jeffrey 101
Huntress: Spirit of the Night 156
Hybrid 167, 168

I Spy 101
I Walked With a Zombie 63
I Was a Teenage Frankenstein 137
I Was a Teenage Werewolf 135
In the Forest of the Villefere 37
Inescort, Frieda 131
Interview with the Vampire 127
Invasion of the Saucer-Men 138
Invisible Man, The 65
Isaac Asimov's Science Fiction Magazine 57
Isabelle, Katherine 158
Island of Dr. Moreau The 124
Island of Lost Souls 65
IT 48, 49
Ivanhoe 100

Jack, El destripador de londres 113
Jackman, Hugh 163
Jack-O 124
Janssen, David 144
Jay, Leland 121
Johnson, Duffy 43
Johnson, Lyndon 157
Johnston, Kennedy 120

Kaminsky, Stuart 56
Karkoska, Ron 173
Karloff, Boris 59, 62, 64, 73, 74, 84, 91, 95, 96, 101, 106, 144,
Katzman, Sam 133
Kaufman, David M. 142
Kemp, Will 163. 164
Kent, Robert 133
Kenton, Erle C. 84
Kenyon, Sherrilyn 58
Kerruish, Jesse Douglas 34
Kevan, Jack 93
Kiger, Robby 154
King of Kings 101

King, Stephen 26, 32, 48, 49
Klause, Annette Curtis 52, 166
Knave of Hearts 10
Knight, Matthew 166
Knowles, Patric 64, 66, 76, 80
Koja, Kathe 56
Koontz, Dean 26
Korey, Tinsel 168
Koteas, Elias 167
Kurosawa, Akira 117
Kuttner, Henry 37

La bestia la espada mágica 117
La Casa del terror 95
La furia de hombre Lobo 109
La furia de Johnny kid 101
La lupa mannara 144
La maldicion de la bestia 114, 126
La marca del hombre-lobo 101, 126
La noche de walpurgis 105, 126
Lambert, Ryan 154
Landis, John 150
Landon, Michael 135
Lane, Frankie 101
Lane, Terry 39
Lansdale, Joe 57
Las noches del hombre lobo 104
Last Frontier, The 61
Latshaw, Steve 124 - 126
Laurentis, Dino De 151
LaVigne, Emile 93
Le Guinn, Ursula K. 57
Lee, Christopher 106, 139, 147
Left for Undead 57
Legends of the Fall 155
Leiber, Fritz 56
Lemche, Kris 158
Leroy, Jeff 166
Lethal Weapon 152
Levee, Kurt 157
Levesque, Michel 142
Lewis, Geoffrey 144
Licantropo: El asesino de la luna llena 119
Lila the Werewolf 56

Lime, Yvonne 137
Linaweaver, Brad 56
Lindenmuth, Kevin 158
Literary Werewolf: An Anthology, The 56
Little Red Riding Hood 25, 26
Live Girls 55
Lockhart, June 132
Loncka, Jeremie 173
London After Midnight 62
London, Jack 40
Lonely Werewolf Girl 55
Lorre, Peter 96
Los monstruos de terror 104
Los ojos del lobo 124
Love Affair 68
Lovecraft, H.P. 37, 48, 101
Lowder, James 57
Lugosi, Bela 59, 60, 62, 64, 65, 70, 76, 78, 94, 101, 106, 131, 132, 144, 173
Lupo, Nick 53
Lust for Frankenstein 143
Lusto, Dom Vincente da 37
Lycanthropus: The Moonlight Murders 119, 120
Lycaon 17
Lynch, Richard 156
Lynne, Beverly 121
Lytton, Edward George Earle 26, 27, 29

Mackay, Michael 154
MacRinnalch, Kalix 55
Magazine of Fantasy and Science Fiction, The 56
Maharis, George 96
Mainly on the Plains 101
Malik, Art 170
Man-Made Monster 62
Mannering, Frank 76
Manos, Mark 156
Maran, Josie 163
Marcus Welby, M.D. 83
Mariuca 101
Mark of the Vampire 131
Mark of the Wolfman 101
Markel, Tarri 157

Marley, Andrew 51
Marley, Sylvie 50
Marotta, Santa 158
Martinez, Olivier 166
Massey, Ilona 76, 80
Master of Ballantrae, The 126
Matheson, Michele 148
May, Elaine 155
McBride, Danny 159 161
McCain, Howard 161
McCallum, Rick 159
McCammon, Robert 50
McCleery, Mick 158
McCrea, Joel 62
McGarr, John P. 173
McGill, Everett 151
McNeilly, Wilfred G. 45
Meredith, Burgess 62
Merman, Ethel 62
Metamorphosis 5
Meyer, Stephanie 57
Mifune, Toshiro 117
Mikel, Ted 125
Miles, Adrianna 156
Millar, Martin 55
Miller, Ken 137
Milner, Martin 96
Mitchell, Thomas 82
Mitra, Rhona 161, 162
Molina, Jacinto (see Naschy, Paul)
Monroe, Marilyn 101
Monster Squad, The 152, 153
Monteith, Corey 168
Montgomery, Bernard 81
Montoya, Ric 54
Moon of the Wolf 42, 43, 144
Moorcock, Michael 57
Moor-Douchette, Saba 173
Mora, Philippe 148
Mr. Smith Goes to Washington 65
Mummy, The (1931) 64
Mummy, The (1959) 139
Mummy's Curse, The 90
Mummy's Ghost, The 90

Munn, H. Warner 38, 160
Murders in the Rue Morgue 65
Murdock, Buz 96
Murphy, Pat 56
My Favorite Brunette 91
My Mom's a Werewolf 154
Mystery of Marie Roget, The 68
Mystery of Witchcraft, The 19

Naish, J. Carrol 83
Naschy, Paul 99 - 127
Naughton, David 150
Never Cry Werewolf 57, 167
New Hugo Winners, Volume III, The 57
New Moon 57, 168
Newman, Paul 133
Nichols, Mike 155
Nicholson, Jack 155
Night of the Howling Beast 114
Night of the Vampire 43
Night of the Werewolf 104, 114
Night of the Werewolf, The 116
Nighy, Bill 161
Niven, Larry 56
Nondorf, Tom 158
Nonesuch Horror, The 52
Noonan, Tom 154

O'Driscoll, Martha 88
O'Malley, Kathleen 56
Odyssey, The 5
Of Mice and Men 62, 98
Oland, Warner 129
Oliver, Stephen 141
Only the Valiant 95
Otten, Charlotte 56
Ouspenskaya, Maria 63, 64, 67

Palance, Jack 100
Pankejeff, Sergei 22, 23
Parker, Eddie 80
Pataky, Elsa 163
Payne, Bruce 148, 154
Peebles, Mario Van 154

Perkins, Emily 158
Petronius 5
Petty, Danielle 120, 121
Pfeiffer, Michelle 155
Phantom Farmhouse. The 38
Phantom of the Opera, The 59, 62
Phillips, Barney 137
Picardo, Robert 147
Pickens, Slim 147
Pierce, Jack 39, 42, 60, 63, 64, 73, 80, 88, 90, 91, 98, 107, 128, 132, 140, 142
Plan 9 from Outer Space 94
Planet of the Werewolves 158
Plummer, Christopher 155
Poe, Edgar Allan 48, 101
Power, Tyrone 62
Preciado, Ana 173
Preiss, Byron 56
Presley, Elvis 101
Price, Dennis 144
Prince and the Pauper, The 65
Pronzini, Bill 56

Quinn, Anthony 82
Quinn, Seabury 38

Raftery, Sara 173
Rage of the Werewolf 158
Rains, Claude 64, 65, 70
Rains, Frederick 65
Randisi, Robert J. 56
Rathbone, Basil 73
Ravenous 55
Ray, Fred Olen 120 -122, 126
Raymond, Alex 99
Reed, Oliver 140
Regehr, Duncan 153, 154
Return of the Killer Shrews 125
Return of the Master 38
Return of the Vampire 131, 132
Return of the Wolfman 114
Revenge of Frankenstein, The 139
Reynold's Magazine of Romance, General Literature, Science and Art 26

Reynolds, G. W. M. 26, 29, 32
Ricci, Christina 161
Rice, Anne 127
Richardson, Jay 121
Right Hand Magic 52
Riley, Philip 76, 78
Ritch, Steve 133 -135
Rivero, Jorge 156
Robeson, Kenneth 38
Rochon, Debbie 158
Rodanthe, Andrew 42, 43
Rodes, Cheryl 173
Rommel, Erwin 80
Rosemary's Baby 66
Roulet, Jacques 1
Route 66 96, 97
Rowe, Freddie 148
Rowlands, Samuel 10
Roxburgh, Richard 163
Rush, Barbara 144

Salem's Lot 48
Saly, Julia 114
Sands, Julian 163
Sarno, Robert 147
Satan's Child 45
Satyricon 5
Sawyer, Mark 157
Saxon, Peter 45
Sayles, John
Scanlan, Jack 24
Scarlett, Will 66
Scheer, Philip 137
Schiller, Herr 16, 17
Schubert, Bernard 87
Schweitzer, Darrell 57
Scotch, Cheri 50, 51
Scott, Randolph 91
Scott, Tom Everett 150
Sealskin, James 156
Self, David 170
Serra, Elena 163
Shannon, Harry 58
She-Creature 138

Sheen, Michael 161
Shelley, Mary 32, 59, 79, 92
Shepard, Patty 106
Sherman, Sam 125
She-Wolf of London 132, 133
Shining, The 48
Shyer, Christopher 165
Sidney, Sylvia 62
Silver Bullet 51
Silverberg, Robert 56
Silvestro, Rino Di 146
Singing Cowboy, The 62
Siodmak, Curt 59, 62, 63, 69, 75, 78, 80, 81, 98, 170
Skinwalkers 166
Skyscraper Souls 65
Solana, Jose Gutierréz 99
Sommers, Stephen 163
Son of Dracula 90
Son of Frankenstein 73, 74, 75, 79, 88
Sorbo, Kevin 167
Spader, James 155
Speedman, Scott 160, 161
Stanwyck, Barbara 62
Steinbeck, John 62
Stevens, Onslow 88, 90
Stevenson, Robert Louis 29, 99
Stewart, James 100
Stiles, Tod 96
Stine, R. L. 58
Stoker, Bram 31, 32, 46, 56, 59, 65, 101, 127,
Stone, Dee-Wallace 146
Strange Case of Dr. Jekyll and Mr. Hyde, The 29
Strange, Glenn 82, 86, 88, 90, 92, 93
Stranger in Town 98
Street, Delilah 54
Streiber, Whitley 47, 49, 60
Strick, Wesley 155
Stub, Peter (see also, Stump, Peter) 8
Stump, Peter (see Stub, Peter) 9, 10
Sullivan, Brett 158
Sullivan, Tim 157
Sundstrom, Neal 148

Surawicz, F. 23
Swan, Bella 57
Swann, S.A. 57
Swiniarski, Steven 57
Sydow, Max Von 170

Tatopoulos, Patrick 160
Taylor, Eric 74
Taylor, Robert 100
Taylor, Robert 62
Teen Wolf 152
Teen Wolf Too 152
Teenage Frankenstein Vs, the Teenage Werewolf 137
Teenage Zombies 137
Teenagers from Outer Space 137
Tesla, Armand 131
Thalman, Jim 173
The Mummy's Tomb 90
Thibault, Carl 154
Thing in the Fog, The 38
Third Man, The 100
Thomas, Martin 45
Thomas, Michael R. 173
Thrilling Detective 39
Toader, Dan 156
Toby, Kenneth 147
Toler, Sidney 62
Tomb of the Werewolf 120 – 122, 126
Torturer, The 45
Trudeau, Sasha 57
True Blood 57
Turner, Clive 148
Twain, Mark 99
Twilight 57, 168
Tyson, Richard 165

Ulloa, Alejandro 114
Ultimate Werewolf, The 56
Um Lobisomem na amazonia 124
Undead on Arrival 57
Underworld 159, 160
Underworld: Evolution 160
Underworld: Rise of the Lycans 161

Undying Monster, The 34, 131
Unknown 40

Valentine, Joseph 68
Vampire's Moon 45
Vampires, Werewolves and Other Monsters 56
Van Helsing 163
Vanishing Shadow, The 88
Variety 74
Venne, Matt 57
Venora, Diane 150
Verdugo, Elena 83
Verdung, Michel 6
Verne, Jules 99
Vernon, Howard 144
Vidor, King 61
Villalobos, Mark 173
Virgil 5

Waggner, George 62, 69
Wagner, the Wehr-Wolf 26, 27, 29
Walker, Andrew Kevin 170
Waller, Anthony 150
Walton, Karen 158
War and Remembrance 66
Waterloo Bridge 68
Wayne, John 62
Weaving, Hugo 170
Weinberg, Robert E. 56
Weird Tales 37, 38
Welles, Orson 114
Wells, H. G. 124
Werewolf and the Magic Sword, The 117, 118
Werewolf Complex: America's Fascination with Violence, The 24
Werewolf Hunter: The Legend of Romasanta 163
Werewolf in a Girl's Dormitory 141, 144
Werewolf in a Woman's Prison 166
Werewolf Island 53, 54
Werewolf of Camelot, The 57
Werewolf of London, The 59, 60, 63, 64, 128 – 131,
Werewolf of Paris, The 35, 43, 128
Werewolf of Washington, The 144

Werewolf Versus the Vampire Woman, The 106
Werewolf Woman 144 - 146
Werewolf! A Connoisseur's Collection of Werewolfiana 56
Were-wolf, The 29, 30, 31
Werewolf, The (1913) 127
Werewolf, The (1956) 133 -15
Werewolf, The (1996) 156
Werewolf's Daughter, The 38
Werewolf's Kiss, The 50, 51
Werewolf's Shadow 105, 106, 109, 117
Werewolf's Sin, The 51
Werewolf's Touch, The 51
Werewolves on Wheels 141, 142
Werner, A. 21
West Wolf, The 52
West, Samuel 163
Westmore, Bud 93
Whitaker, Aaron 42
White Zombie 65
Whitten, Leslie H. 42, 43, 144
Widmark, Richard 100
Wild Blood 51, 52
William, Warren 64, 65
Williamson, Jack 40, 160
Willis, Matt 131
Winchester '73 100
Wings Over Honolulu 68
Winkless, Terence H. 147

Winston, Stan 154
Wiseman, Len 159, 161
Wizard's Leg and Owlet's Wing 96
Wolf 155
Wolf Man Versus Dracula, The 87
Wolf Man, The (1941) 46, 56, 59 – 73
Wolf Man, The (2010) 168 - 171
Wolf, Gene 57
Wolf's Cross 57
Wolf's Hour, The 50
Wolf's Trap 53
Wolfbreed 57
Wolfen 150
Wolfen, The 47, 49
Wolfman Meets Frankenstein 73
Wolfshead 37, 38
Wood Ed 24
Woodruff, Jr., Tom 154
Wray, Fay 62
Wrightson, Bernie 48

Young, Roland 82

Zaso, Joe 158
Zelazny, Roger 50
Zeus 17
Zucco, George 84

www.ingramcontent.com/pod-product-compliance
Lightning Source LLC
Chambersburg PA
CBHW071436150426
43191CB00008B/1145